Epes Sargent

The scientific basis of spiritualism

Epes Sargent

The scientific basis of spiritualism

ISBN/EAN: 9783337334253

Printed in Europe, USA, Canada, Australia, Japan

Cover: Foto ©Lupo / pixelio.de

More available books at **www.hansebooks.com**

THE
SCIENTIFIC BASIS
OF
SPIRITUALISM.

By EPES SARGENT,

AUTHOR OF "PLANCHETTE, OR THE DESPAIR OF SCIENCE," "THE PROOF PALPABLE OF IMMORTALITY," ETC.

Un scepticisme présomptueux qui rejette les faits sans examen
est plus funeste que la crédulité qui les accepte.

ALEXANDER VON HUMBOLDT.

SECOND EDITION.

BOSTON:
COLBY AND RICH, PUBLISHERS,
No. 9 MONTGOMERY PLACE.
1881.

PREFACE.

THE claim that there is a scientific basis for Spiritualism will be an offence to many. Indeed, the mere announcement of this work has called forth adverse pre-judgments because of its title. But constantly recurring facts, which have stood the test of more than thirty-three years of ridicule, denunciation, and antagonism, must be admitted as having within them some stubborn elements of vitality, if not of scientific verification.

What is science but a collection of truths, suggestive of an inference? According to John Stuart Mill, the language of science is, "This is, or This is not; This does, or does not happen. Science takes cognizance of a phenomenon, and endeavors to discover its law." Surely, under this ruling Spiritualism has a scientific basis in its proven facts.

The man claiming to be scientific, who imagines that he knows all the laws of nature so thoroughly that occurrences like clairvoyance and direct writing cannot take place without transcending the boundaries of scientific recognition, is himself under a hallucination more serious than any which he affects to deplore.

The neglect in all ages of the world to treat these and cognate facts with fearless, scientific scrutiny, has been productive of incalculable mischief. In ancient times, the assumption that all that comes from the unseen world, certified by seeming miracle or preter-human power, must be from God or from gods, led to all sorts of theosophic impositions, superstitions, spurious revelations, and wild delusions.

In mediæval times, and during the witchcraft excitement, monstrous cruelties were practised under the sanction of law through the failure to recognize that nothing occurring in the realm of nature can be supernatural, and that all phenomena whatever are subjects for cool scientific investigation and analysis. Certain remarkable psychic phenomena were construed as Satanic and unnatural, and an ancient Hebrew prohibition, founded in ignorance, was made the excuse for punishing with death innocent persons suspected of producing in others, medially affected, any inexplicable manifestation of abnormal power.

In our own day, though belief in spirits has been repudiated extensively, the credulity of unbelief threatens new dangers. By dismissing the phenomena as impossible, unnatural, or supernatural, specialists in science, — who, however eminent in their own departments, are ignorant of the first rudiments of the psycho-physical science, now inchoate, — instead of checking superstition by their scornful attitude, are really giving it its excuse for being. Persons experimentally sure of the phenomena, finding that they can get no guidance or light from men of science, qualified by laborious study and experiment to explain the occurrences, either put premature constructions on what they witness, or yield a too hasty credence to the assurances of some medium or medial pretender claiming a divine or high spiritual inspiration. Even so it was in the old days of oracles, seers, and myths, and so it may be again, with variations, unless a science, at once searching and liberal, reverent and intrepid, shall interpose to prevent such a revival, and protect the unwary from the frauds and delusions to which a little display of medial power may lead.

The attempt made in 1876, in London, by Professor Lankester, a specialist in physical science, wedded to the materialistic monism of Haeckel, to put a stop to the phenomena through Henry Slade, the medium, and to do this by the strong arm of the law, was simply an act of superstition, prompted by the same fanaticism (taking the form of unbelief instead of belief) which actuated the proceedings of " Matthew Hopkins, of Manningtree, Gent.," the famous English " witch-finder " of the year 1645. The first scientists of Germany at once exempted Slade from Lankester's suspicions; and Zöllner says, in reference to Slade: " The physical facts observed by us in his presence negatived on every reasonable ground the supposition that he, in one solitary case, had taken refuge in imposture. In our eyes, therefore, he was innocently condemned, — a victim of his accuser's and judge's limited knowledge." The recent remarkable occurrences in open church at Knockmore, in Ireland, where hands and living figures have mysteriously appeared, show how important it is that these phenomena should no longer be evaded.

Rationally studied and interpreted, unmixed with delusions self-generated or imposed by others, Spiritualism is the one safeguard against all superstitions. It shows that the unseen world is as much within the

sphere of universal nature as our own; it is the sol-
vent of many mysteries that have perplexed philosophers and stultified historians; it shows that not
spirits, but our own misconstructions and unchecked
pas.ions, are what we have most to fear. That bad
persons have entered its ranks, and that flighty persons have brought it into ill-repute,—that it has been
used to deceive or mislead,—should make the obliga-
tion all the more obvious to the generous mind to help
to sift and co-ordinate its facts and arrest its abuses.

It is therefore with regret that I find so liberal a
champion of truth as R. W. Emerson recommending
ignorance as the best policy in regard to a subject
which, in the hands of fanaticism or imposture, has
been the cause of such great disasters and mistakes,
public and private, as far back as history goes. In a
recent article on "Demonology," this distinguished
writer remarks: "There are many things of which a
wise man might wish to be ignorant, *and these spiritual
phenomena are such.* Shun them as you would the
secrets of the undertaker and the butcher." *Et tu,
Brute?*

This is all wrong, ideally, really, and morally. Even
the comparisons by which the sentiment is illustrated
are vitiated by unsoundness; for however our esthetic
sensibilities may recoil, what is it but pusillanimity
to ignore "the secrets of the undertaker and the
butcher"? Have we no care as to how the cast-off
body of the beloved one may be disposed of? Are
we indifferent as to what sufferings may be inflicted
on the poor brute whose life is to minister to our
carnivorous appetite? The sentiment has no saving
grace; it is hollow and spurious. Not by trying to

make us shun the truth as something disagreeable will
the philosopher deter any but the timid or weak from
finding out all that is genuine and demonstrable in
phenomena foreshadowing a continuous life for man.

Contrast the advice with that of Dr. John W. Draper, the well-known professor of chemistry and physiology in the University of New York. Referring to
the mysteries of life, he says: " God has formed our
understandings to grasp all these things. I have no
sympathy with those who say of this or that physiological problem, ' It is above our reason.' " And, as if
anticipating these supersensual phenomena, which our
Concord sage would have us shun, the eminent physiologist tells us, that the application of exact science
to physiology is " bringing into the region of physical
demonstration the existence and immortality of the
soul of man, and furnishing conspicuous illustrations
of the attributes of God."

Mark too the language of the venerable German
philosopher, I. H. Fichte, uttered a few weeks before
his death in 1879 : " Notwithstanding my age and my
exemption from the controversies of the day, I feel it
my duty to bear testimony to the great fact of Spiritualism. No one should keep silent." A worthy utterance from the son of the illustrious contemporary
of Kant, and the inheritor of his sire's splendid endowments !

The progress of modern Spiritualism has been something marvellous. In less than forty years it Las
gained at least twenty millions of adherents in all parts
of the world. Adapting itself, through its eclectic
affinity with all forms of truth, to all nationalities and
classes, and repeating its peculiar manifestations every-

where among persons ignorant of its forms and its antecedents, it presents the features of a universal truth, the developments of a grand, transcendent science, confirming all the traditions and intuitions of the soul's immortality, and heralding a dawn before whose light every other science, relating to the nature and destiny of. man, must seek to orient itself hereafter.

Of the present volume more than four-fifths is now for the first time published. Passages here and there, often much altered, have been adopted, from contributions made by me during the last thirty years to nearly all the periodical publications devoted to the subject, in England and the United States. As parts of the work were written at long intervals, repetitions of the same line of thought may be found; but these, though critically regarded a blemish, may have their uses for the reader in emphasizing the more essential considerations. Objections to the existence of a fact of nature must needs be unscientific; but as they continue to be brought up against Spiritualism by persons otherwise well informed, I have devoted some space to their refutation.

But the time has gone by when the facts of this volume could be dismissed as coincidences, delusions, or frauds. The hour is coming, and now is, when the man claiming to be a philosopher, physical or metaphysical, who shall overlook the constantly recurring phenomena here recorded, will be set down as behind the age, or as evading its most important question. Spiritualism is not now "the despair of science," as I called it on the title-page of my first book on the subject. Among intelligent observers its claims to scientific recognition are no longer a matter of doubt.

CONTENTS.

CHAPTER I.

THE BASIS: — CLAIRVOYANCE; DIRECT WRITING.

CHAPTER II.

FACTS AGAINST THEORIES.

CHAPTER III.

REPLY TO OBJECTIONS OF WUNDT.

CHAPTER IV.

CLAIRVOYANCE A SPIRITUAL FACULTY.

CHAPTER V.

IS SPIRITUAL SCIENCE HOSTILE TO RELIGION?

CHAPTER VI.

PHENOMENAL PROOFS. — THE SPIRIT-BODY.

CHAPTER VII.

PROOFS FROM INDUCED SOMNAMBULISM, ETC.

CHAPTER VIII.

CUMULATIVE TESTIMONY. — SPIRIT COMMUNICATIONS.

CHAPTER IX.

DISCRETE MENTAL STATES.

CHAPTER X.

The Unseen World a Reality.

CHAPTER XI.

The Sentiment of Immortality.

CHAPTER XII.

The Great Generalization.

THE SCIENTIFIC BASIS

OF

SPIRITUALISM.

CHAPTER I.

THE BASIS. — CLAIRVOYANCE AND DIRECT WRITING.

THE great facts of clairvoyance, and direct, independent writing, have been so widely demonstrated, and are so clearly demonstrable, under proper conditions, that no thorough, sincere investigator now disputes their occurrence. The conditions under which they have taken place have been such as to rule out all possibility of fraud. New testimony in respect to them is offered every day, from every quarter of the globe. Representing, as they do, both the physical and the mental sides of many analogous phenomena, they may be fairly selected as typical facts, now placed beyond dispute, and affording a basis of certainty for a psycho-physical science, warranting an implicit belief in immortality.

"It is a question, in the first instance, of evidence; it then follows, to explain, so far as we can, such facts as may have been established." So wrote the eminent English civilian and prime minister, William E. Gladstone, October 16, 1878, in respect to these phenomena.

This is the rational view of the subject. There are certain specialists, however, in sciences quite distinct from that of psycho-physical phenomena, who assert that no amount of human evidence could make credible to them facts like clairvoyance and direct writing. Dr. William B. Carpenter, of England, disregarding the testimony of his brother, the late Philip Pearsall Carpenter, an eminent naturalist, who satisfied himself while in America of the basic truths of Spiritualism,* tells us that our common sense ought to contradict our senses when these testify to such marvels. And there are grave doctors of medicine, such as Richet, Hammond, and Beard, who declare persistently, through the "Popular Science Monthly," one, that "no well-demonstrated fact has ever permitted us to conclude that such a thing as double sight, or clairvoyance, exists;" the other two, that there never was a case of clairvoyance in the world's history. When men start with the declaration that no amount of human testimony shall prove to them the occurrence of a natural phenomenon, the general conclusion will be, that their concurrence in regard to any fact is not important to the interests of science.

Modern Spiritualism has its reason-for-being in well-established facts, not only of the past, as far back as history extends, but of the present. For these, throughout the ages, but one explanation, accounting for them in their aggregate, has yet been found: it is that which refers them to high preterhuman or supra-material powers, exerted either unconsciously and abnormally by a so-called *human* subject, or put forth by invisible beings, manifesting intelligence and the ability to overcome material impediments, not superable by any physical means known to science.

The word *spiritual* is not here employed as a sufficient solution of the mystery, or as intimating a distinction between *thing* and *nothing*. The very etymology of the word

---

* See "Memoirs of P. P. Carpenter, by his brother, Russell Laut Carpenter. London: C. Keagan Paul, 1880."

spirit (*spiritus*, breath) shows that something occupying space, though attenuated perhaps to invisibility, is intended. But there is a confusion still in the use of the word; for it is applied by different thinkers to signify not only the organic spirit-form and its constituents, but its inner essence, — that which knows and thinks and is the synonyme of mind, or what the French call *esprit*.

According to Leibnitz, the essence of all being, whether mind or matter, is force. The whole universe, bodies as well as minds, is made up of monads, or ultimate atoms, homogeneous in essence, but endowed by the Creator with certain powers, and developed in degrees infinitely diverse. Thus the changes which the monad undergoes are only the gradual and successive evolutions of its own internal powers. Every monad having both body and soul, but being in itself a simple, indestructible essence, the whole material world, even in its inorganic parts, is animated throughout. Thus matter is but an expression of force, and force is the mode of action of that which exists and is alone *persistent*. Material forms have no stability. An organism is a temporary form, from which there is a continual efflux of particles. It is like the flame of a lamp, being ceaselessly fed as it ceaselessly wastes away. The *something* underlying all phenomenal existence is persistent. Matter, as we know it, is incapable of acting of itself; it must be acted upon; but this energy underlying and fashioning all forms is the same to-day as yesterday. The *matter* passes indifferently from mould to mould, retaining no character of individuality. Spirit alone can act; matter is but the result of the act.

Thus in the system of Leibnitz the substantial *does not belong to organs, but to their original elements.* Matter, in the vulgar sense, as something conceived to be without mind, does not exist. There is no death. That which is called death is only the soul losing a part of the monads which compose the mechanism of its earthly body, the living elements of which go back to a condition similar to that in which they were before they came upon the theatre of the world. Thus the immortality of the individual is secure. In giving the monad a body, Leibnitz departs from the traditional conception of corporeality. The body of the monad is not body in the ordinary sense of the word, but a force.

Thus nothing really dies; all exists, and is only transformed. God is not the God of the dead, but of the living. He is the Primitive Monad, the Primitive Substance; all other monads are its fulgurations.

Are the souls of the lower animals immortal? Yes; they have sensation and memory. Every soul is a monad, for the power possessed by every soul to act on itself proves its substantiality, and all substances are monads. That which appears to us as a body is in reality and *substantially* an aggregate of many monads. The materiality through which they express themselves being but a transient phenomenon, it is only in consequence of the confusion in our sensuous perceptions that this plurality presents itself to us as a continuous whole. Plants and minerals are, as it were, sleeping monads with unconscious ideas; in plants these ideas are formative vital forces.

"I am filled with astonishment," says Leibnitz, "at the nature of the human mind, of whose powers and capabilities we have no adequate conception." There is much in Spiritualism that is in harmony with his views. The fundamental idea of his philosophical system is, that the spiritual or theologico-teleological conception of the world should not exclude the physico-mechanical conception, but that the two should be united. Thus he seems to have anticipated the attempt of the pseudo-science, represented by Haeckel, Huxley, Clifford, and others, to find in matter and mechanism an explanation of all mental phenomena. He argues that particular phenomena can and must be mechanically explained; but that we should not, at the same time, be unmindful of their designs, which Providence is able to accomplish *by the very use of mechanical means;* that the principles of physics and mechanics themselves depend on the direction of a Supreme Intelligence, and can only be explained *when we take that intelligence into consideration.*

This is one of the strong points in Leibnitz's system. Reason is not individual; it is universal and absolute, and consequently infallible. There are sophists who dispute this, and who say they know only by experience that a whole is greater than a part; and that, in a world of which they have no experience, two and two may make five. Not all are free who scoff at fetters; and the sophists here stultify their own proposition. The human effort to reason may, according to Leibnitz, often be a failure, but the eternal principle of human reason must be nothing less than divine reason. Every serious conviction must cover a concealed faith in thought, in reason, in God. Experience cannot account-for innate principles; on the contrary, innate principles are required to account for the treasures of experience.

The proved phenomena, indicative of the operation of an intelligent force outside of any visible organism, have been discredited, on various pretences, by the many who have not had leisure or inclination to carry out a faithful investigation. The truly marvellous character of some of the phenomena has provoked ·incredulity; the apparent frauds with which mediums, supposed to be genuine, have been frequently charged, have excited a proper distrust; the extraordinary feats sometimes performed by individuals claiming to be "exposers" of Spiritualism, and the audacity of their assertions, have confounded not a few whose knowledge of the subject was limited.

The idea that because of the marvellousness of an occur-

rence the laws of nature have been violated is, when analyzed, a mere superstition. A medium is lifted to the ceiling, but the law of gravitation is no more violated in the
act than it is when we jump a ditch. Admit the theory of
a spirit-force not subject to the law, and the fact becomes
credible. The frauds charged upon approved mediums, like
Florence Cook, Miss Wood, Mr. Williams, and others, raise
questions, the answer to which will be naturally scouted by
those not intimately acquainted with the history of the phenomena. I will here only intimate what intelligent investigators accept as the solution of *some*, at least, of the cases
in which mediums, previously and subsequently known to
be genuine, have been caught in what seemed *primâ facie*
frauds.

The influences affecting the phenomena are extremely
subtile and imperfectly known. But I have repeatedly
learned this from practical study and experience: The unuttered thoughts, the will, the *animus*, of persons promis-
cuously present at a sitting for phenomena, have an effect
upon their character and facility of production, which is
none the less potent because occult and incredible to the
unprepared mind. I have known a medium — whose honesty was never questioned, and in whose presence the
most indubitable phenomena would readily occur under
the severest test conditions — to be medially paralyzed by
the presence of two or three persons, each bringing perhaps
an adverse spiritual environment, all vehemently opposed
to the success of the experiment, and not only intent on
the detection of fraud, but earnestly hoping to find it. Admitting the Spiritual theory, is it unreasonable to suppose
that such persons may have brought influences which, if
the medium had not intuitively resisted them, would have
so affected her as to confirm their own unbelief and suspicions of trick? That this has been often done where the
transfigured body of the medium has been put forward as

a spirit-form, is more than probable.* If we can believe
the testimony of careful investigators both in Europe and
America, the trick is not an uncommon one. The best way,
however, for the novice, when absolute tests are wanted, is
to trust neither spirit nor medium, but to exact conditions,
if he can get them, which will be a guaranty against misconstruction or deception, whether from the supposed spirit-
world or this.

That genuine mediums may sometimes purposely resort
to fraud in cases where the supersensual power producing
the phenomena is not readily available, is highly probable.
There is, first, the temptation of exciting an exaggerated
estimate of one's ready mediumship; and there is, secondly, the temptation of getting money which might be
refused in the event of failure. Most mediums are dependent on the exhibition of their powers for a support;
and if they sometimes supplement real phenomena by devices of their own, it must not be taken always as verify-
ing the maxim, *False in one thing, false in all.*† That the
charge of fraud is often the result of sheer ignorance on the
part of the accuser, has been repeatedly proved. He has
jumped to conclusions, sincere enough, but which a little

* Allan Kardec (the *nom de plume* of L. D. H. Rivail) relates, in his " Book
on Mediums," a case of *transfiguration*, or change of aspect, of a living body.
In the suburbs of St. Etienne (1858–9), a young girl of fifteen had the faculty of
taking on, at certain times, all the appearances of certain persons dead. The
phenomenon was renewed hundreds of times. On several occasions she took
the appearance of her deceased brother, presenting not only his face, but the
height, size, and *weight* of his body.

† An English Spiritualist, well versed in the phenomena, writes (November,
1878): "I go so far as to say that a sensitive medium may, in his normal state,
be impelled to trick through the agency of his surroundings. He is more to be
pitied than condemned. I have sat at public dark seances with Williams, Herne,
Eglinton, Bastian, and Taylor; and I have also *seen* what I consider real manifestations. Hundreds of others have seen the same in their own private resi-
dences, with the same mediums, and under circumstances where trick was impossible. Such being the case, I do not think a person who is a real *susceptible*
would risk his livelihood knowingly by a trick palpable and easy of detection.
The higher the susceptibility, the more room is there for trick. Often, if the
sitting is too long, and the medium exhausted, low influences will rush in."

more knowledge on his part would have shown to be doubtful or fallacious.

With regard to the so-called "exposers" of Spiritualism,
it has occasionally happened that a person with some little
medial power, not being able to get a living by the display
of it, or becoming disaffected towards Spiritualists as neg-
lectful of his claims, has done his best to get the patronage of the opponents of the phenomena. If he has a glib
tongue, a plenty of what the profane call *cheek*, and some
little skill in sleight-of-hand, he may easily persuade the
inexperienced that some of his tricks are real duplicates
of medial phenomena. In regard to those that are inexplicable as *human* tricks, he may, with the aid of a cabinet
or a curtain, do things in which the co-operation of a low
order of spirits may be the real explanation. In such cases
he always has an excuse ready for not exhibiting in the
light to an audience his *modus operandi*. He will say that
he will explain it at some future time ; or that he cannot
afford to disclose his secret, so long as he can make money
by it. Several of these impostors have succeeded in attracting large audiences and getting from the enemies of
Spiritualism the pecuniary aid which they could not get
from the friends.

Any "exposer" who professes to *know* that clairvoyance
and pneumatography are demonstrable tricks, may be safely
set down as either self-deceived or wantonly a deceiver.
IIis pretence that they are accomplished by sleight-of-hand
is a mere assumption, and he generally knows it to be untrue. Repeatedly during the last thirty-three years I have
had letters of caution from friendly persons, who had great
confidence in their own sagacity, informing me that certain
phenomena I had proclaimed as genuine had been proved
by some itinerant "exposer" to be tricks. In every instance the "exposer" turned out to be either an impostor
or a mere "joker" and pretender ; and up to this time no

one of the phenomena generally accredited by careful and experienced investigators all over the world has been shaken from its basis of actual truth.

The fact that many persons calling themselves Spiritualists have prejudiced their cause by seeking medial light on business or domestic matters, properly under the jurisdiction of their own reason and sense of right, has given rise to a great amount of prejudice among those who have not patiently investigated the various phenomena for themselves. If the inquirer really wants the truth, he will soon divest himself of the objections which the eager credulity of novices, or the frauds of mercenary mediums, may have provoked. He will learn that there are genuine phenomena, justifying the belief in a force preterhuman and spiritual. If the great subject has been abused, it is the fault of those who have kept aloof from it.

An eminent jurist, occupying one of the highest judicial positions within the gift of the people of his State, writes as follows, under date of July 10, 1880 :

" My first attempts at investigation ended in a consciousness of having been imposed upon by fraud ; and the dangerous and immoral principles avowed by those seeming to be leaders in the cause, prevented me for years from having anything more to do with it. But within the last six years, the cause having been purified of some of its excrescences, the light has come to me unsought. Having been accustomed for thirty years to deal with, and the last twelve years to weigh evidence, I have given to the subject my best faculties, always under the dominion of an inborn skeptical nature, and have become thoroughly satisfied as to the two great elementary facts, viz. : a continued existence after death, and that those who have gone before may communicate with persons in the flesh. In being brought to that conclusion, I have yielded only to that which, being scanned as evidence, would bear the most rigid and skeptical scrutiny from the solitary standpoint of reason, unswayed by credulity or superstition."

The Spiritualist's theory is, that life is continuous; that the word *immortal* must be taken in its etymological sense as *not-dying*. Continuity of being must then be a natural effect of present causes. Thus the inquiry into the grounds for a belief in the existence of spiritual organs and powers in our human complex, already manifesting their operation in the earth-life, and forming the basis of life common to this state of being and the next, becomes a strictly scientific and experimental process, dealing with the finer and more recondite parts of the science of physiology, or with the psycho-physiological developments of our mixed nature. It is because the fact of a future life has been confounded with speculative theological or religious questions, that it has shared their reputation as something transcending the verification of science.

There are pious persons who declare that but for the authority of the Bible, they should have no ground for belief either in God or in a future life. On this point, John Page Hopps eloquently remarks:

" What can at present be said to people whose conception of a future life is the *rising again* of an exterminated body?—or who, without reflection, and as by a coarse animal instinct, laugh to scorn the assertion that a *spirit* is a greater reality than a *body?*—or who tell us they must give up belief in immortality altogether, if the texts of Scripture they rely upon are in a book that is not infallible. It does not matter how good, or devout, or otherwise cultivated these people are; their ideas concerning spirit and spirit-life show that in relation to this tremendous subject they are only children. . . . The first thing to do is to take the whole subject out of the realm of mystery, unreality, fantasy, and awe, and to make it the object of cool thought, and, if possible, of scientific experiment."

And this is precisely what the intelligence manifesting itself through these so-called spiritual phenomena seems to be trying to make us do.

"Spiritualism," says the late Dr. Hallock, "is no new problem that ought to have taken the disciples of science by surprise: it has rapped at the door of every thinker throughout the ages for a solution. Wanting it, the popular thought, misdirected by a theology that was stone-blind and remains so, has invested the immortality of its own faith with *grave-clothes*, and converted it into a scarecrow, transforming the most beautiful and sublime process whereby humanity is glorified, into a ghastly skeleton, which its ignorance has named death, and converted it into an object of the profoundest horror. It was for *science* to strip these rags from the immôrtal spirit. Why has it not been done?"

The facts which have been conclusively substantiated by the somnambulic, mesmeric, and spiritualistic phenomena, all forming a related group, of the last hundred years, are regarded as accounting for and corroborating the persistent belief among all races of men, in all ages, that, notwithstanding the dissolution of his physical husk, the individual man, with all the faculties pertaining to his mental, moral, and emotional nature, survives, and, under right conditions, can give proofs of this survival to those whom he left behind on earth. All theories of the genesis of the belief in immortality, which do not admit, as the important original factor, a *knowledge*, got by the experimental method, of actual phenomena, objective and subjective, are defective and delusive.

"The immortality of the soul," says Mr. A. M. Fairbairn, "though a primary, can hardly be considered a primitive religious belief. It involves conceptions at once too abstract and positive to be intelligible to primitive man, and what he cannot conceive he cannot believe."

Spiritualism contradicts this assumption. A life hereafter was conceivable to the primitive man because he had objective proofs of the existence of his departed relatives and friends in organisms of new and enlarged power. It required no metaphysical reasoning to convince him of this fact, any more than of any equally mysterious fact in nature, confirmed by the evidence of his senses and by his limited reasoning powers.

Mr. Herbert Spencer, in the *Fortnightly Review*, May 1, 1870, expresses his opinion that the belief in a double personality may have originated among savages from seeing their moving shadows, or the reflection of their faces in the water; and for a corroboration of this fantastic notion, he refers to the reluctance which certain savages have evinced to having their portraits taken. That there are fools among savages as well as among civilized races is not to be doubted; but it is an arbitrary assumption to suppose that savages generally are so unobservant of cause and effect as to entertain false notions in regard to the cause of a shadow, whether moving or stationary. The large collection of portraits of eminent chiefs of Indian tribes, in possession of the United States government, is a proof that their representative men do not object to having their likenesses taken.

All such far-fetched attempts at explanation proceed from an ignorance of the fact that nearly all the savage races have had frequent experience in objective spiritual phenomena, and that this is the reason why so few of them disbelieve in a dual personality. The phenomenon of palpable form-manifestations by supposed spirits is well known to the North American Indians. Of this I am assured by my correspondent, Mr. Granville T. Sproat, a government agent long resident among the Indians of Lake Superior, and who has testified publicly to the fact. Intelligent Indians were fully persuaded that their deceased friends had reappeared palpably, and at times joined in their dances.

As far back as history goes, the power of divination and

clairvoyance has been regarded by faithful investigators either as a faculty of the human soul developed in some of its states, under peculiar conditions, or else an indication of independent spirit action. From Pythagoras to Plato, from Plato to Plutarch, and from Plutarch to tens of thousands of competent witnesses in the nineteenth century, the phenomena have been admitted. "*Si divinatio est dii sunt*" (if there is divination, there are gods, or spirits), is an old Latin proverb. The deduction is legitimate.

But there are physical phenomena supplementing and confirming those indicating transcendent faculties of perception. Consider the one stupendous fact of pneumatography,* or independent writing. I hold out a clean slate, or I put a sheet of blank paper in a drawer, which I lock, and in a few seconds the slate, or the paper, is covered with intelligible writing. Do you say it is a physical impossibility? That may be. But as it takes place, — our senses and our common sense testifying to the fact, — then it may be a spiritual or psycho-physical possibility; that is, it is not to be explained by any purely physical, or mechanical, or material process known to the most advanced science, or conceivable as independent of mind.

"What pretence have I," says John Wesley, "to deny well-attested facts because I cannot comprehend them?" One of the capital objections is this: "Did you ever see an apparition yourself?" "No; nor did I ever see a murder, yet I believe there is such a thing." Wesley lived to see what he believed to be an apparition, on three occasions.

If the fact of independent writing be disputed, those who bear testimony to it must be regarded either as menda-

---

* I use the word as Kardec does, to designate writing supposed to be executed fly spiritual power. The term *psychography* is used to designate both this and writing by the hands of mediums under the supposed influence of some spirit.

cious or under an hallucination. But when the whole character and extent of the testimony to the momentous fact
are fairly estimated, the attempt to get rid of it by charging
falsehood or imbecility on the tens of thousands of witnesses, will be regarded by judicial minds as a presumptuous evasion, in direct conflict with the principles of
experimental science.

"Science," says John Stuart Mill, "is a collection of
truths. The language of science is, This is, or, This is
not; This does, or does not happen. Science takes cognizance of a phenomenon, and endeavors to discover its law."

We lay stress on this proved fact of pneumatography,
for it is one in which there has been, and need be, no
experimental flaw. If it is rejected, it must, I repeat, be
rejected on principles inconsistent with the experimental
methods of science itself. It is so conclusive as a proof in
broad daylight of mind independent of a visible organism, — of the action of an intelligent force outside of the
human body, and often operating twenty feet or more distant from it, under conditions the most simple and satisfactory, — and it is so easily verifiable, — that nothing but
that extreme incredulity, which is the equivalent of a fat-
uous credulity, can cause a person to doubt the occurrence
of the phenomenon after once witnessing it, or, indeed,
after fairly estimating the testimony in its behalf.

"One good experiment," says Sir Humphrey Davy, "is
of more value than the ingenuity of a brain like Newton's."
Let me briefly relate what I have elsewhere recorded in
detail, namely, my own personal experience. I give it not
as being conclusive, absolutely by itself, but as conclusive
relatively to the same experience got by thousands of competent observers, and by many eminent men of science in
all parts of the world. I took an entirely new, unused
slate, which I had bought twenty minutes before, to the
medium, Charles E. Watkins, in Boston, Sept. 18, 1877.

The slate was what is called a book-slate, and was enclosed in stiff pasteboard covers. I went well aware of all the reports unfavorable to mediums in general and to this one in particular.

After manifesting his clairvoyance by telling me what was written on some dozen slips of paper, which I had rolled tightly into pellets — intelligence which he could not have got from my mind, inasmuch as I could not distinguish one pellet from another, — he permitted me to take my own slate and hold it out away from him in my left hand. He had dropped on the upper surface of the book-slate a piece of slate-pencil not so large as half of a grain of rice. He sat three feet from me, and did not once touch the slate. Although there had been no opportunity of his even making a mark on it without my knowledge, I satisfied myself once more, before I held it out, that it was entirely clean. Instantly there was a sound as of the grating of a pencil, and in less than ten seconds there was a rap, apparently on the slate. I uncovered it, and there was the name of a departed friend, Anna Cora Mowatt. This experiment I repeated several times with the same success, getting names and messages from friends, which would have been none the less extraordinary if the medium had *known* them and their names, which he unquestionably did not.

In one instance, at the same sitting, I got a message of fifty-two words, written with preterhuman celerity. The writing was neat and legible. I have it still uneffaced. The medium and myself were the only persons present, and the noonday sun streamed into the room. There was no escape from the knowledge that a great phenomenon, involving both clairvoyance and intelligent motion, without manual, mechanical, or chemical appliance, had taken place in my presence. If true — if I was not under an hallucination — then no more books need be written to prove that the materialism, which would confine all operations of mind to a material brain — material in the human sense of the word — is an error. If I must reject or question the testimony which my senses and my common sense gave me on this occasion, then must I regard myself as disqualified from testifying to any visible occurrence whatever. No hypothesis of jugglery was within the reach of reason. There was no confederate (in the flesh, at least), and the conditions could not have been more rigorously exclusive of possible fraud. Nothing depended on the moral character of the medium ; and if he had been caught cheating the next day, it would not have affected my convictions, unless the *modus operandi* was so explained that I could see, that with the requisite practice and skill, any one could produce the same manifestation.

The phenomenon was not new to me. Many years before I had got proofs of independent writing on paper in the presence of Colchester, an English medium, who died young. But never had I before, while holding my own new, clean slate, untouched by any other person, got audible writing unequivocally independent of any conceivable process, physical, chemical, or mechanical. If there was not corroborative evidence of the most ample kind from thousands of other witnesses, some of high scientific repute, I might still feel a hesitancy in narrating my own experience : the transcendent nature of the fact might awe me into silence. But such is its authentication now, that while skepticism is always excusable, the outright denial of the phenomenon can proceed only from the ignorant or the reckless.

A recent Scotch writer charges against Spiritualists " an incapacity to give due value to the enormously important evidence of general experience." He writes : "A man duly sensible of the enormous improbability that he is a witness of a reversal of otherwise invariable sequences, or of the

intrusion of a force which does not figure in universal ex
perience, can hardly, whatever be his failings, become the
devoted adherent and expositor of a delusion like Spiritualism."

Superficially scanned these seem like words of wisdom;
but they are in truth as destitute of reason as the incredulity of the tropical chief who would not believe in the
hardening of water because he had never seen ice. He
fully appreciated what our critic calls "the enormous improbability" of there being a force which did not figure in
the experience of himself and his tribe.

The whole adverse argument may be summed up thus:
"The negative testimony of the many ought to outweigh
the positive testimony of the few." The negative testimony of a thousand persons, who have never witnessed a
case of somnambulism, or the fall of a meteor, ought to
outweigh the testimony in regard to them of ten careful
observers! Where would science be if this principle were
carried out generally?

Those persons who scout a fact of nature because it is
not known and accepted by the majority, are quite as narrow and irrational as the tropical chief in their incredulity.
"How do we know," asks the late Professor De Morgan,
"that sequences are to be always invariable; that what has
been must always be?" But the argument need not be
pressed. The Spiritualist is not called on to believe in the
reversal of invariable sequences. Our phenomena have
been known to the intelligent few, under whose observation
they happened to fall, and believed in by the many, in all
ages of the world, except, perhaps, our own.

In a posthumous work on Psychology by George Henry
Lewes, he remarks: "A deep longing for some direct proof
of existence after death has made hundreds of people accept
the grossest impostures of Spiritualism; impostures which
contradicted the most massive experiences of the race, and

which had nothing to support them save this emotional credulity acting where direct knowledge was wholly absent."

That there have been "gross impostures," which have deceived even experienced investigators, there can be no doubt. The man who has counterfeit money palmed off upon him is not he who disbelieves in money, and refuses to take it, good or bad, but he who has reason to know that most of the money in use is genuine. But it is directly contrary to the truth to say that "the most massive experiences of the race" have been opposed to a belief in spiritual manifestations. On the contrary, many of the greatest men that have dignified the race have been full believers in them. The fact is so notorious that I will not at present occupy space in recording some of their names.

It is only within the last century and a half, that skepticism and materialism have been so current as to give even a color of truth to the remark of Mr. Lewes. So far is it from being true that "emotional credulity" can be credited with the conversions, the fact is that a great proportion of converts have been from a class so fixed in their incredulity as to things super-sensual, that only objective proofs of the most decisive kind could attract their serious attention.

According to Mr. Lewes's own confessions, he vacillated greatly in his psychological views. Perhaps, had his earth-life been protracted a little longer, his conclusions in regard to our phenomena, — bitterly opposed as he was to a system, which, if true, made rubbish of many of his ingenious speculations, — might have changed.

Let me resume the subject of my own personal experiences in the psycho-physical phenomena, which, beginning for me as far back as the year 1835, have been multiplied up to the time of my present writing. On the evening of Saturday, the 13th of March, 1880, the Rev. Joseph Cook came to my house, bringing with him four of his friends, two gentlemen and two ladies, one his wife. Watkins had promised to come at Mr. Cook's request (not mine), and he was present before Mr. Cook and his party arrived. He brought with him Mr. Henry G. White, a gentleman whose parents were well known to me, and who had only the week before become acquainted with Mr. Watkins, and tested the phenomena in his presence. Finding him deeply interested, the medium had brought him, and Mr. White had stopped at a shop and purchased five or six small slates.

I am thus particular in stating the exact relations of Mr. White to the experiments, because the only important points which struck Mr. Cook as "unsatisfactory," had reference to his presence and the fact that *his* slates were used, and not those which Mr. Cook had brought, and which were encased in thick wooden covers. I can vouch for Mr. White that he was really no more "the medium's friend" than Mr. Cook himself, and was, like the rest of us, merely an earnest seeker after the truth, and as much interested as any of us could be in detecting anything like fraud.

It had been publicly announced that Mr. Cook would, in his lecture the following Monday, give the result of his experiments at my house. The Old South Church in Boston was crowded to repletion on the occasion. The séance had taken place in my library, nine persons, including myself and the medium, being present. Three of the party were ladies. Here are the public statements of Mr. Cook, contained in his lecture of March 15th, 1880.

The following were the satisfactory points:

1. Five strong gas jets, four in a chandelier over the table and one in a central position on the table, were burning all the while in the library where the experiments took place.

2. At no time were the slates on which the abnormal writing was produced taken from the sight of any one of the nine persons who watched them. The writing was not done, as was Slade's in London and at Leipsic, on slates held under a table.

3. The utmost care was taken by all the observers to see that the slates were perfectly clean just before they were closed.

4. During the first experiment, nine persons clasped each one hand or two, over and under the two slates. The psychic's hands were among the others, and he certainly did not remove his hands from this position while the sound of the writing was heard.

5. Each observer had written on a scrap of paper given him by the psychic the name of a deceased friend and a question addressed to the person named. All the scraps were folded into tight, small pellets and placed in a group on the table and then mixed, until I could not tell my pellets from others in the collection. Half a dozen of the names were correctly given by the psychic, while the pellets remained unopened.

No opinion is ventured here as to the method by which he obtained this knowledge. One of the two pellets which I had thrown into the group contained the following words:. "Warner Cook. In what year was my father born?" I put in one question which could be answered by any one who could read my thoughts. I put in another which could not be thus answered, for I did not know the answer to it.

The psychic, who certainly had not seen me fold or write the pellet, for he was not in the room at the time, told me correctly the name it contained, which was that of my grandfather. He told also correctly the name in the second pellet. I thought this perhaps merely a case of mind-reading. The psychic wrote on a slate, "I wish you to know that I can come. I do so long to reach you. W. C." I judged that this perhaps was fraud, although I was told it came from a spirit.

The psychic, however, began to suffer, or assume singular contortions, and said they were the results of the efforts of a spirit to communicate through him. I very much doubted whether he was not acting a part, and watched him, as all the rest of the company did, very closely in every one of his motions. He placed two slates on a table before him, and a hand, palm downward, on each slate.

He seemed to be making a strong effort of will, and said he could not tell whether the experiment would succeed.

Biting a small fragment, not much larger than four or five times the size of the head of a pin, from the top of a slate pencil, he placed the bit on one of the slates, and called on us all to see that both surfaces were clean. This we did in the full light of five gas burners, to our perfect satisfaction. The psychic then shut the slates with the fragment between them, and required us all to grasp the edges of the slates. He drew my hands into a position near his, and made several strokes over the back of one of them. Meanwhile, his face showed strong efforts of will; his whole countenance energized; he seemed to be in an agony of volition; his features changed their expression to one of great vigor and determination: and yet, while this look was kept up he was shedding tears. It was in this mood of the psychic that the audible writing began and continued.

6. While a dozen hands in full light were tightly clasped about the slates, we all distinctly heard the peculiar grating sound of a slate pencil moving between them. I said "Hist!" once or twice; and, in a nearly perfect silence, we every one of us heard writing going on between the surfaces. Afterward we saw the fragment of pencil which was used, and noticed that it was worn by the friction of writing.

7. The writing found on one of the slates when they were opened was in response to my question, and was as follows: "I think in 1812, but am not sure. Warner Cook."

This date was correct. The doubt expressed in the reply did not exist in my own thoughts, for I knew what the date was. During the writing I was not thinking of the date, however, but very cautiously watching the psychic to detect fraud.

8. In a second experiment the psychic closed the slates in our sight, after they had been washed with a wet sponge which I had myself procured from one of Mr. Sargent's chambers, and had also been heavily rubbed by my handkerchief in presence of us all, as they lay on the table. We were determined that no invisible writing should remain on the slates if any had been put there by sleight of hand, or previously to the gathering of the company. After they had been shut upon the pencil, the psychic, at my request, placed on them two strong brass clamps, one at each end. [Mr. Cook here exhibited to the audience the clamps, hold-

3

ing together the slates in question.] Thus arranged, the slates were placed by him in my right hand, which I extended at arm's length over the back of my chair into the open space of the room, while I left my other hand on the table. The psychic, twice or three times, turned the clamped slates over in my hand, and then returned his hands to the table, where, with the rest of the hands of the company, they were kept constantly in sight. In this position I held the slates a few seconds, and watched both them and the psychic. He appeared to be making no particular effort of will. When the slates were opened, these words were found written on one of their surfaces, in a feminine hand: "God bless you all. I am here. Your loving friend, Fanny Conant." I had never heard of this person, but the name was recognized by several in the company as that of a psychic now deceased, and lately well known in Boston.

9. One of the observers who assisted in the experiments at my request was my family physician, Dr. F. E. Bundy, of Boston, a graduate of the Harvard Medical School — a man of great coolness and penetration of judgment, and by no means inclined to adopt any spiritualistic theory. Another of the observers was Mr. Epes Sargent.* . . . . Of the nine observers, a majority were not only not Spiritualists, but thoroughly prejudiced against the claims made in behalf of the psychic who led the experiments. Written notes of the facts, as they occurred, were taken without an instant's delay by Dr. Bundy and myself.

10. Among the names correctly read in the closed pellets was that of an officer in the regular army, shot dead in one of the preliminary skirmishes of the battle of the Wilderness. The editor present knew the officer well, and the circumstances of his death. The instant the psychic pronounced the officer's name, he fell backward with a quick, sudden motion, like that of one shot through the heart. After a few seconds he wrote the word "Shot," in large letters, on the slate.

11. The hands of the company were so placed on the slates in the first experiment, that the theory of fraud by the use of a magnetic pencil is inapplicable to the facts. One of the observers held an open hand tightly against the

* The omission here is merely a personal compliment.

bottom, and another on the top of the slates, which were perhaps six or ten inches above the surface of the table as it was clasped by the hands. Any magnet concealed in the sleeves of the psychic could not have been so used as to move the pencil.

12. At the close of the experiments, the company unanimously indorsed a paper drawn up on the spot, and were agreed that the theory of fraud would not explain the facts. While they differed in opinion as to whether the slate pencil was moved by the will of the psychic, or by that of a spirit or spirits acting through him, the observers could not explain the writing except by the movement of matter without contact.

Report of the Observers of the Sargent Experiment in Psychography in Boston, March 13, 1880.

At the house of Epes Sargent, on the evening of Saturday, March 13, the undersigned saw two clean slates placed face to face, with a bit of slate pencil between them. We all held our hands clasped around the edges of the two slates. The hands of Mr. Watkins, the psychic, also clasped the slates. In this position we all distinctly heard the pencil moving, and on opening the slates found an intelligent message in a strong masculine hand, in answer to a question asked by one of the company.

Afterwards, two slates were clamped together with strong brass fixtures, and held at arm's length by Mr. Cook, while the rest of the company and the psychic had their hands in full view on the table. After a moment of waiting, the slates were opened, and a message in a feminine hand was found on one of the inner surfaces. There were five lighted gas burners in the room at the time.

We cannot apply to these facts any theory of fraud, and we do not see how the writing can be explained unless matter, in the slate pencil, was moved without contact.

F. E. BUNDY, M. D. EPES SARGENT. JOHN C. KINNEY.
HENRY G. WHITE. JOSEPH COOK.
Boston, March 13, 1880.

Notice now the unsatisfactory points in these experiments :
1. My attention was several times diverted from watching the psychic by his requiring me to put my pencil on the pellets and pass it slowly from one to another of them.

It ought to be stated that he required Mr. Sargent to do the same, and if it had been his object to divert the attention of those most opposed to admitting his claims, he would have done better to have selected Dr. Bundy instead of Mr. Sargent, as another gun to spike. Dr. Bundy's attention was not diverted for an instant, nor was mine at any instant that seemed to me important.

2. Two or three times the psychic and a friend whom he had brought to the room,* left the company and went into the hall together, and I did not know what they conferred about. It is supposed that they left in order that the friend might not be regarded as a confederate.

3. The psychic was easily offended by any test conditions suggested by the company, although he finally adopted the brass clamps which he at first refused to use.

4. The psychic's friend brought to the room the slates which were used, and my slates were not employed at all in the experiments.

The alleged objection to the use of my slates was that they had wood on their backs, and were poor conductors of electrical influences. Although clamps on the slates are no greater guard than one's hands may be, still they amount to something in stating the case to the public. If I had suddenly fallen into a trance, or been mesmerized, while holding the slates, the clamps would have held their place, and some one in the company might not have been in a trance, and would have known what happened.

On the whole, the unsatisfactory points did not appear to outweigh the satisfactory ones. In spite of the former, the observers agree in professing inability to explain the writing unless there was here motion without contact.

In these experiments, as I beg you to notice, there is nothing to decide whether the force which moved the pencil was exercised by the will of the psychic, or by a spirit, or by both.

We do not presume to say how the motion was caused, but only that we do not see how the writing can be explained unless matter in the slate pencil was moved without contact.

Of course the latter fact, if established, and even in the

---

* This refers to Mr. White, whose relations to the experiments I have already explained.

absence of knowledge as to whether the force proceeds from the psychic or from spirits, overturns utterly the mechanical theory of matter, explodes all materialistic hypotheses. and lays the basis for transcendental physics, or a new world in philosophy.

Here is the very freshest pamphlet from Germany on psychical phenomena. It is written by Leeser, a medical candidate at Leipzig University, and defends unflinchingly the theory that the psychic force explains all these phenomena, and is under the control of man exclusively. I came out of Mr. Sargent's library fully convinced that the stress of debate is between that theory and the theory adopted by Zöllner and Crookes, that the force is under the control of both men and spirits. Whatever the ultimate result of experiments by experts in the study of psychical phenomena may be, it is pretty nearly certain to-day that research should concentrate itself upon the double lines of investigation indicated by these two rival theories.

As Mr. Cook has been well abused by some of the religious journals for testifying to what he saw, let me add to his a subsequent experience of my own.

On the afternoon of the 8th of June, 1880, Mr. Watkins came to my house, and proposed to give me a sitting. As the day was a little chilly we went into the dining-room, where there was a fire, and sat at the large dining-table covered with a green cloth. The dimensions of the room are 17 by 19. The only parties present besides myself and the medium were Mrs. E. and Miss W., both inmates of the family — Miss W. never having seen Mr. Watkins, and only entering the room when I called her to take part in the sitting. We locked the two doors to avoid interruption. On the table we placed seven slates, two bought by myself and never used, and one more, the same book-slate which I had used at my first interview with the medium in 1877 ; and four small slates brought by the medium, and carefully moistened and wiped by me. Blank paper and pencils were also placed on the table.

We sat on one side of the table during the experiments,
which were all in broad daylight, while the medium stood
either on the opposite side, or at the head, or moving about
the room, so that nearly his whole person could be seen by
us all the time. First, two of the small slates were placed,
one on top of the other, with a crumb of slate-pencil between, and while we all held them by the rims, the scratching of a pencil was instantaneously audible ; and taking
the top slate from the lower we found on the surface of the
latter, in large, legible characters, " I am here. Lizzie."
Previously to the experiment we were all fully satisfied
that the surfaces were entirely clean. I had washed and
rubbed them carefully. There was no possible chance for
a substitution of concealed slates.

Writing was then got while Miss W. held the slates, and
the medium, not touching them, stood aloof more than four
feet. On my own two new and carefully-cleaned slates,
held out before us by the medium, were written two messages — one of ten words, addressed to me and signed with
my father's name, and one to Miss W. of three words,
signed with the name of a young departed friend, of whom
it is not probable the medium had ever heard. In one instance the two ladies held out each a pair of slates, and
got writing on them simultaneously, the medium not touching them, but standing at the opposite side of the table.

It was then proposed that my book-slate should be used.
It already had writing on both sides, which I objected to
having obliterated. On one side was a letter of sixty
words, got some years before through Watkins, and bearing the name of my sister Lizzie ; and on the other side
were the words, " Your aunt Amelia is present," got
through Mr. W. H. Powell, another medium, for direct
writing.* I finally consented to have the latter inscription

* A Rochester (N. Y.) correspondent of the *Banner of Light*, writes in
that paper of July 17, 1880: " On two occasions, while Mr. Powell was in Roch-

obliterated if it could be done by the unknown force apparently at work. Taking the slate on which the writing in large unfaded letters still stood, I shut the leaf, and placed it in the hands of the medium, who instantly held it out before us all. The scratching sound of a pencil was heard, and in less than twelve seconds he handed the book-slate back to me. I lifted the leaf; the surface on which was the old inscription had been thoroughly cleaned, and on it were the words, "My dear brother: I rub this all out. Lizzie, your sister."

I will not enumerate the many satisfactory proofs of independent clairvoyance (not *mind-reading*) which we got during this remarkable sitting. They amounted in number to fifteen. It has been said that mind-reading and clairvoyance are simply the exercise of one and the same faculty; in the one case there being a perception of thoughts, and in the other, of objects. This is not the place to discuss the question. I will merely say that the detection of a thought may come from a look, or from a movement of one brain in sympathetic relations to another, just as the vibration of one musical chord affects that of another of the same kind, though in a different room. But the detection of what is written in a tightly-rolled pellet, the con-

ester, a figure representing a rose was drawn on the under side of a slate, the medium simply passing his finger over its upper surface, not touching it, however, the finger at no time being nearer than an inch to the upper surface of the slate." The conditions were such as "precluded all possibility of deception, fraud, or collusion." Having witnessed the same phenomenon (June 21, 1879) through the same medium, under strict test conditions, and under the blaze of five gas-burners in my own library, with five of my friends watching the experiment, I can readily accept this statement as accurate. I still have the slate on which the rose was drawn, and the word "Winona" was written by some force unknown. I held the slate myself by one of the wooden rims during the experiment. A scientific committee of six persons, among whom were chemists and physicians, tested the phenomena through Powell, in Philadelphia, in 1879, and reported: "It is one of those peculiar psychological manifestations that we cannot account for." The names of the committee were: Dr. Wm. Paine, Dr. Reuben Carter, B. F. Dubois, John P. Hayes, Alfred Lawrence, F. J. Keffer.

tents of which are unknown to the sitter, would seem to be an achievement somewhat more difficult and inexplicable than thought-reading. Bear in mind that all these experiments took place in broad daylight, and that *the slates and the pellets were never out of our sight for a moment.*

The last and crowning incident of the evening was this : I had written on a pellet, as yet untouched by the medium, the name of my mother. Taking two slates, one placed over the other, he first showed us they were clean, and then placed them on a small work-table in one corner of the room. Then, bethinking himself of more satisfactory conditions, he gave the same slates (as I carefully satisfied myself) to Miss W., went off to the opposite corner of the room, a distance of more than twenty-one feet in a diagonal line, *allowed us to see that the slates were clean* (so there could have been no sleight-of-hand substitution), and told Miss W. to place them with her own hands on the work-table. As soon as she had done this, and resumed her seat, he seemed violently convulsed, and reaching across the table from end to end, seized the hand of Miss W. The paroxysm lasted but a moment; the sound of writing was heard on the distant slate, and the medium, still standing twenty feet off, told Miss W. to take the slates and hand them to me. This she did. I took the upper from the lower, and there, written legibly, and forming seven lines on the slate, were these words : "My dear son and daughter, I am here and I must see you again. Can't say more now. Loving mother, M. O. S."

The extraordinary facts in this experiment were : That the slates were not touched by the medium after they had left my hands till they were brought back to me by one of the ladies and I had read the writing ; that I had just previously satisfied myself that the surfaces were clean ; and that while the direct writing was going on, and could be heard, the medium stood at a distance of twenty-two feet from the slates.

Phenomena like these seem to me to knock out of materialism its *raison d'être*. Where and how can it find an explanation? It is impotent to suggest one consistent with its own dogmas. Here are proofs of an intelligent force acting outside of a human brain, outside of any visible organism. In all ages of the world such a force has been compared to the unseen human breath — *spiritus*.

In May, 1880, having learned from Mr. Watkins that Mr. Hiram Sibley of Rochester, N. Y., a gentleman of wealth, had carefully investigated the phenomena, and had offered him a large sum of money to disclose " the secret of his *trick*," I wrote to Mr. Sibley for confirmation of the statement, and got a satisfactory reply, dated May 10th, 1880, in which he tells me that he and Judge Shurat had paid Watkins a hundred dollars for about ten sittings ; and that they got the independent writing in a way to satisfy them that some unknown power moved the pencil. Mr. Sibley writes : " I offered Mr. Watkins a large sum of money, which I proposed to settle on his wife and children, if he would disclose the trick (if trick it were) by which the manifestation was produced ; and furthermore, I offered to give bonds, if he desired it, that I would not divulge his secret. I am ready to repeat the offer now to any person that can expose or explain the trick, if trick it be."

This offer of several thousand dollars, though publicly made, has never been accepted. The public have been told of one " exposer " who went to Mr. Sibley to explain how it was all done ; but the conditions he wanted were so ludicrously unlike the simple, unconditional way in which the phenomena are produced through Watkins, that the pretender was dismissed as either an ignoramus or a charlatan. The solution of all these pretended exposers is

" sleight-of-hand ; " but there is no possibility of any such jugglery under the conditions.

Mr. J. Edwin Hunt, of the City Treasury Office, Boston, who had been an avowed materialist, hearing of Mr. Cook's experiences in my library, sought to test their truth. He writes, under date of July 11th, 1880, in respect to his visit to Mr. Watkins :

" I came, I saw, and I — was conquered ; that is, I witnessed in his presence the fact of the intelligent movement of matter, without any visible human or other contact. I know that I was not deceived. I not only saw the writing after it was written, but heard the pencil moving while it was being done. I know that there was no writing upon the slates when the pencil was placed between them, and the slates were not out of my sight for a second during the time I sat with Mr. W. The signature to the communication was the name of a personal friend of mine, whose funeral I had attended some three weeks before, and the communication was a direct and pertinent answer to a question addressed to him, and folded securely up, and the question was written a week before I had the sitting. I had never seen Mr. W., nor he me, until the day of the sitting, which was the last day of March, 1880. He had no means of knowing anything about it, and as the question was mixed up with eight or ten others, and was not opened until after the writing on the slate, I did not know myself what was in it until the writing was completed and the pellet was opened. In conclusion, I wish to say that as a result of this experience of mine, I am satisfied beyond all doubt of the existence of an intelligent force outside of the medium or the sitter, and believe that the inference is strong and almost irresistible that this intelligent force is that of an individual human spirit, who once lived in the body."

Mr. John L. O'Sullivan, formerly U. S. Chargé to Portugal, and a gentleman long personally known to me, has published an account of his experiences (May, 1880) with Alexander Phillips, a medium aged twenty-three, at his rooms, No. 133 West Thirty-sixth Street, New York. My friend of forty years, Dr. J. R. Buchanan, was present. Under test conditions, and in full gaslight, they repeatedly got the independent writing. Several Latin quotations were given ; among the rest the following translation of a stanza from Jane Taylor's little nursery poem, beginning " Twinkle, twinkle, little star." The writing, small, close, and back-handed, was finally deciphered thus :

> " Mica, mica, parva stella,
>   Miror quonam sis tam bella,
>   Splendens eminens in illo
>   Alto velut gemma cœlo."

To Mr. O'Sullivan's account of repeated experiments, Dr. Buchanan adds his testimony thus : " To the foregoing statement of Mr. O'Sullivan I would add my indorsement of its absolute and minute correctness."

I have had the pleasure of some correspondence with Mr. Alfred Russell Wallace, the eminent English naturalist. He is the same who shares with Mr. Charles Darwin the honor of having originated the theory of natural selection. He testifies to having witnessed (Sept. 21st, 1877), at a private house in Richmond, on the Thames, the phenomenon of independent writing in a room where the light was sufficient to see every object on the table. Dr. Francis W. Monck was the medium. After describing the experiment in a letter to the London " Spectator " of Oct. 6th, 1877, Mr. Wallace remarks : " The essential features of this experiment are : That I myself cleaned and tied up the slates ; that I kept my hand on them all the time ; that they never went out of my sight for a moment ; and that I named the word to be written, and the manner of writing it, *after they were thus secured and held by me.* I ask, How are these facts to be explained, and what interpretation is to be put upon them ?" Mr. Edward T. Bennett indorses Mr. Wallace's statement in the remark: "1 was present on this occasion, and certify that Mr. Wallace's account of what happened is correct."

In reference to his experiences with Henry Slade, Mr. Wallace testifies as follows:

" Writing came upon the upper part of the slate, when I myself held it pressed close up to the under side of the table, both Dr. Slade's hands being upon the table in contact with my other hand. The writing was *audible* while in progress. This one phenomenon is absolutely conclusive. It admits of no explanation or imitation by conjuring.

" Writing also came on the under side of the slate while laid flat upon the table, Dr. Slade's hand being laid flat on it, immediately under my eyes.

" While Dr. Slade was holding the slate in one hand, the other being clasped on mine, a distinct hand rose rapidly up and down between the table and my body; and, finally, while Dr. Slade's hands and mine were both on the centre of the table, the further side rose up till it was nearly vertical, when the whole table rose and turned over on to my head.

" These phenomena occurred in broad daylight, with the sun shining into the room, and with no one present but Dr. Slade and myself. They may be witnessed with slight variations by any of our men of science, and it is to be hoped that those who do not take the trouble to see them will, at all events, cease to speak disparagingly of the intellectual and perceptive powers of those who, having seen, declare them to be realities."

It is true, as Mr. A. R. Wallace has said, that no man of any authority has been known to question the genuineness of the phenomena after being once thoroughly convinced of their occurrence. But novices in the investigation sometimes fall back in their convictions, after being powerfully impressed by the phenomena as they occurred. We must not be surprised should this prove to be the case with some of the German professors, who, knowing little or nothing of the phenomena, were carried away by the manifestations through Dr. Slade. Possibly they may be laughed out or reasoned out of their convictions.

It is not surprising if, when an inexperienced investigator comes to reason on the phenomena, they should seem to him, after a brief conviction of their genuineness, utterly incredible. Hence the half-way converts not unfrequently turn back. It requires a long preparation for a philosopher or a physicist to be able, like Fichte, to be reconciled to all the facts that conflict with his own past teachings.

Zöllner (born 1834), and who has recorded the phenomena through Slade in some elaborate works, has not retrograded. He will perhaps live to find new reasons for the confirmation of his experiences.

Immanuel Herman Fichte (1797–1879), son of the famous John Gottlieb Fichte, was a Spiritualist long before Slade visited Germany. Just before his death he put forth a pamphlet, in which he asseverates the fundamental facts, and earnestly commends the whole great subject to the attention of the scientific and religious world. He ably answers Haeckel, the enthusiastic materialist, who deplored the " simplicity " of the eminent German physicists who " fell into Slade's trap." Fichte asserts the importance of the results arrived at, and claims that Slade's manifestations belong to the domain of physics.

Professor Ulrici, of Halle (born 1806), was not a witness of the Slade phenomena, though he partially accepted them, on testimony, as confirming much in his own philosophical speculations. Wundt's attack, however, seems to have caused him to draw back a little. He evidently lacked that force of conviction which actual personal knowledge of the phenomena, continued through many years, must always inspire.

Fichte, a resident of Stuttgard, was introduced to the phenomenon of independent writing by the late Baron

Louis Guldenstubbé, who departed this life May 27th, 1873, at his residence, 29 Rue de Trevise, Paris, in his fifty-third year. He was chiefly known by his researches and experiments in pneumatology. Of Swedish origin, he belonged to an ancient Scandinavian family of historical renown, two of his ancestors of the same name having been burnt alive in 1309, in company with Jacques de Melay, by order of Pope Clement the Fifth. The baron lived a retired life, with his accomplished sister. He is affectionately remembered for his noble, gentle, and urbane bearing, and for his numerous unassuming charities. His principal work, " La Réalité des Esprits, et le Phénomène merveilleux de leur Écriture Directe," was published in Paris, by D. Franck, in 1857.

The baron passed the winter of 1869–70 at Stuttgard. A man of culture, independent in his circumstances, and of high social position, he was probably himself a medium, though unconscious of the fact. He got the independent writing, but thought it came as an answer to his prayers for a proof of immortality. My friend, the Rev. William Mountford, of Boston, who knew the baron and witnessed remarkable physical phenomena in his presence, tells me he was an excellent Hebrew scholar and a sincere student of psychic evidences; by no means an enthusiast, but a modest, earnest, truth-seeking gentleman. The testimony of such a person to a palpable, objective phenomenon, with no medium present, unless he was one himself, is exceptionally precious.

Guldenstubbé dedicates his volume to the Count de Szapary, Count D'Ourches, and General Baron de Brévern, three well-known gentlemen, who repeatedly witnessed the phenomenon of independent writing in his presence, sometimes in his own house, and sometimes in old churches and by the side of ancient tombs. The writing was on sheets of paper, which, with a view to scientific verification, were properly marked by the witnesses. The phenomena began August 13, 1856, and Guldenstubbé refers to them in his dedicatory preface as " more brutally conclusive than all reasonings — *plus brutalement concluant que tous les raisonnements.*"

" These phenomena," he tells us, are now fixed " upon an immovable basis of facts;" that " henceforth the immortality of the soul can be regarded as a fact of science," and that Spiritualism " throws a bridge from our world to the invisible."

" You know, gentlemen," he says in his dedication, " that my whole life has been devoted to the study of the supernatural,* and of its relations to visible and material nature. I have regarded as the great end and object of my life the irreversible demonstration of the immortality of the soul, of the direct intervention of spirits, of revelation and of miracle, by the experimental method.

" The phenomena of inspiration, of trance, of invisible medial attraction, of mysterious raps, and the movement of inert, inanimate objects, have helped me on in encouraging me to persevere in my arduous and arid researches ; but all these manifestations are far from being conclusive. These phenomena can, at the most, give us only a revelation of forces and of unknown laws. It is only the direct writing which reveals to us the reality of an invisible world, whence emanate religious revelations and miracles. . . . Henceforth hope can spring afresh in the heart of humanity, — its religious needs in respect to the immortality of the soul, the basis of all truths, being fully satisfied. . . . Let us remember that in regard to all great truths, the more sublime and profound they are, the more

---

* The Baron repeatedly uses the word *supernatural* where Spiritualists generally would say *superhuman.* We have no evidence as yet that the so-called spiritual phenomena are not embraced in the sphere of the natural, since everything phenomenal may be properly so regarded.

they encounter a press of obstacles and are repelled by the
many. It is only in the issue of the shocks of discussion,
engaged in by serious and earnest minds which have been
able to verify the marvellous phenomenon of a direct correspondence from spirits, that human intelligence, being
of a progressive nature, can ultimately be influenced to
admit the truth. . . .

"Let us advance, then, boldly on this line. We may
not stay here to witness the cheering day, the dawn of
which appears to us from afar on the horizon, and which
illustrious geniuses, such as Swedenborg, Bengel, Jung-
Stilling, and Count Joseph de Maistre, have had the presentiment of, and have saluted in the name of a third
revelation, according to the prophet Joel (chap. ii. 28, 29) :
'And it shall come to pass afterward, that I will pour out
my spirit upon all flesh ; and your sons and your daughters
shall prophesy, your old men shall dream dreams, your
young men shall see visions : and also upon the servants
and the handmaids in those days will I pour out my spirit.'

" Our obscure names may be lost under the rubbish and
the ruins which the ages are continually heaping up, but
we shall carry with us into another and better phase of
existence the sweet consolation of having chosen the path
which leads to God. since that which we represent is of
the Eternal Essence."

Among the ocular witnesses of independent writing and
other phenomena through Guldenstubbé, besides the three
already mentioned, were M. Delamarre, editor of *La Pa-
trie;* M. Choisselat, editor of the *Univers;* Robert Dale
Owen, of the United States ; M. Lacordaire, brother of the
great preacher; M. de Bonnechose, the well-known historian ; M. Kiorboë, a well-known Swedish painter. resident
in Paris ; Baron Von Rosenberg, German ambassador at
the Court of Würtemberg ; Prince Léonide Galitzin. and
two other representatives of the nobility of Moscow ; Doc-

tor Bowron of Paris; Colonel Kollmann of Paris; and my friend, the Rev. William Mountford of Boston, Mass., whose communication to me in respect to the baron I sent to the *London Spiritualist*, where it appeared Dec. 21, 1877.

On the 4th of October, 1856, the verse, "O death, where is thy sting? O grave, where is thy victory?" was written by an invisible power in Greek, in the presence of Count D'Ourches, Dr. Georgii, and Baron Guldenstubbé. A fac-simile of it is given in the volume, from which I translate.

It is impossible to read this work by Guldenstubbé without being impressed by the intense sincerity, as well as by the intelligence and eloquence, of the writer.

"Here is a book," he says, "which contains the first positive elements of the great science of direct communication with the supernatural world; the unique basis of all historical religions, from the majestic law of Jehovah, engraved," (as Moses thought,) "by the finger of God himself on the two tablets in presence of Moses, to the words, full of a divine unction, of the holy martyr of Calvary; from the Veda of the Indians to the Zend-Avesta of Zoroaster; from the mysterious ceremonies of Egypt to the oracles of Greece and Rome."

Guldenstubbé was under a mistake in supposing that he was the first in modern times to get direct writing. It came with the earliest American phenomena in 1848. It was quite common in the manifestations at the Rev. Dr. Phelps's house in Stratford, Conn., in 1850–51, as related by him in a letter to me which I published at the time in the *Boston Transcript;* and innumerable instances occurred at Hydesville, Rochester, Buffalo, and Auburn, in the United States, before the date of the Paris phenomena.

Guldenstubbé proceeds to say: "A marvellous discovery was made by the author at Paris, Aug. 13, 1856, the day when the first experiences, crowned with success, took

4

place : it is that of the direct writing of spirits *withou any intermediary whatever;* that is to say, without either medium or inanimate object." (Here he assumes that he himself was not a medium.) " This marvellous phenomenon confirms what Moses says (Exod. xxxi. 18 ; xxxii. 15, 16 ; xxxiv. 28 ; xxiv. 12 ; Deut. iv. 13 ; v. 22 ; ix. 10 ; x. 1–5) concerning the direct revelation of the Decalogue ; and what Daniel recounts on the subject of the marvellous writing on the wall, which took place during the feast of King Belshazzar (Daniel v. 5, &c.).

" The discovery of writing directly supernatural (?) is so much the more precious, because it can be proved by experiment repeated at will by the author in presence of the incredulous, who can themselves furnish the paper, to avoid the absurd objection which a skeptical materialism has put forward, that the paper used may have been chemically prepared. It is precisely in the application of the experimental method to direct supernatural (?) phenomena or miracles, that reside the originality and the validity of this discovery, which has no precedent in the annals of humanity ; for hitherto it has not been a quality of miracles to admit of reiteration. In order to prove their reality it has been necessary to be content with the testimony of those who have witnessed them.

" In our day, when all the sciences proceed by the experimental method, the most clearly verified results of observation, and the most ample testimony, hardly suffice, when an extraordinary phenomenon, not to be explained by known physical laws, is in question. Man, spoiled by the palpable experiences of the physicists, no more attaches faith to historical testimony, above all when it pertains to mysterious phenomena revealing the existence of powers invisible and superior to the forces and the laws of inert matter.

" To-day, in moral concerns as well as in the exact sciences, our age demands facts; and here we give them in abundance. More than five hundred experiences have been had since the memorable 13th of August, 1856, by the author and his two friends, Count D' Ourches and Gen. Baron de Bréwern. More than fifty persons, supplying their own paper, have been enabled to verify the astonishing phenomenon of direct writing by invisible intelligences.

"Most of our experiences took place in the Hall of Antiques in the Louvre, in the Cathedral of St. Denis, and in the different churches and cemeteries of Paris, as well as in the author's own apartments, *Rue du Chemin de Versailles*, 74.

" The lettered public are well aware that the natural sciences did not make any veritable progress until questions by the experimental method were addressed to Nature. So it is with Spiritualism : this science of invisible causes can only become a positive science in the same experimental way. We must have recourse to this method to beat down and reduce to silence the arrogance of those physicists who have presumed in our day to encroach even upon the domain of the moral sciences and the higher philosophy. Surely there is nothing more absurd than to see physicists assume the position of competent judges on a question of metaphysics and psychology."

Guldenstubbé, we have seen, did not regard himself as a medium, though the pneumatographic and other psycho-physical phenomena occurred in his presence. Perhaps it is on what he claims to be their non-medial character that he bases his pretensions as a discoverer. He tells us that his first experience in getting spirit-writings was preceded by the incessant prayer that he might be instrumental in proving the immortality of the soul. He put some letter-paper and a sharpened lead-pencil in a little locked box, the key of which he always carried about his person. To no one did he confide his intention. He waited twelve days in vain. Not the least trace of a pencil was there on the paper.

But what was his astonishment when he remarked, on the memorable day already named, certain mysterious characters traced on the paper. Ten times during the same day, at intervals of half an hour, he got the same experience, substituting at every trial new pieces of paper. Every time the result was a success.

On the 14th of August, 1856, he got the same phenomenon twenty times by leaving the box open, and not allowing it to be out of his sight. It was then that he saw that the characters and words in the Esthonian language were formed or engraved on the paper without a movement of the pencil. From that moment, seeing that a pencil was superfluous, he ceased to put it on the paper; he would simply place a blank sheet of paper either on the table at his own lodgings, or on the pedestal of some antique statue or urn at the Louvre, at Saint Denis, and other churches. It was the same in the experiences got in the different cemeteries of Paris.

After having proved satisfactorily to himself the phenomenon of direct writing by more than thirty trials, he communicated the secret to Count D'Ourches, a well-known investigator. The Count witnessed the phenomenon more than forty times, sometimes at his own apartments, sometimes at the Baron's, sometimes at the Louvre, and on the benches which surround the monuments of Pascal and of Racine in the Montmartre cemetery. Subsequently, in the month of October, the Count, without the co-operation of Guldenstubbé, got several direct writings from supposed spirits; among the rest one from his mother, who had left this life twenty years before.

Sixty-seven fac-similes of writings got by our author are given in his book. As to the question, *What means do the spirits employ in writing?* he tells us that the phenomenon proves that the spirit must act directly upon matter, *probably by mere jorce of will.* The celerity with which writings are produced, often quicker than human thought, is a confirmation of this theory, which fully accords with my own experience. I have known a message of fifty-two words to be written on a slate in less than fifteen seconds. Generally, where it is desired that the sound of the movement of the pencil shall be heard, the pencil may be used; but this is not always known to be the case.

"During the first fortnight, dating from the day of my discovery of direct writing," writes Guldenstubbé, "the tables on which the spirits wrote would move about alone, and come to rejoin the author in another room, after having traversed several apartments. The tables moved sometimes slowly, sometimes with astonishing rapidity; the author would try to bar their progress sometimes with chairs, but they would make *détours* in continuing their course in the same direction. On one occasion he saw a little round table, on which the spirits had been accustomed to write in his presence, transported through the air from one end of a chamber to the other. . . .

"Nevertheless, though the effects of the influence of freed spirits may correspond with those of spirits incarnate, it must be confessed that their means must differ from ours, in being no longer fettered by material impediments. It is probable that the action and influence of spirits offer some analogy with the phenomenon of creation; spirits being finite images of God, who is the Absolute Spirit *par excellence.* Surely, in a state of existence where time is merged in eternity, and space is comprised in infinity, there cannot be a question of means and appliances to produce any material effect whatever, such as direct writing, &c. The creative will is alone sufficient in acting on inert matter (*Mens agitat molem*). The spirit of man, after having been released from the physical body by death, and after having cast off the obstructions of matter, enters into a state less imperfect. It is, then, rational to suppose that his power over the elements of nature and .his knowledge of the laws which govern them should be enlarged.

" It is, however, possible that the spirits who envelop themselves often with a subtile substance, an ethereal body, according to all the sacred traditions of antiquity (which explains the objective reality of apparitions), may concentre, by their force of will and by the aid of this subtile body, a current of electricity upon any object whatever, such as a sheet of paper; and then the letters are formed on it, just as the light of the sun makes an impression of objects on the daguerreotype plate. And so Moses, in reference to the tables of the Decalogue (Exod. xxxii. 15, 16), says: ' The tables were written on both their sides; on the one side, and on the other, were they written. And the tables were the work of God, and the writing was the writing of God, graven upon the tables.' The greater part of my direct writing from spirits would seem to be done with the lead-pencil; in some thirty, blue or black ink seems to have been used."

On the question of the communications being a reflex of the mind of the supposed mediums, Guldenstubbé says: " My own experience proves amply that the reflex of thoughts must pass for nothing in the phenomenon. In the first place, generally the spirit whom we desire does not present himself for writing; another comes, on whom we have by no means thought, and whose name even is sometimes unknown to us. As to sympathetic spirits, they come hardly ever during these experiences. The spirits have often written whole pages, sometimes with a lead-pencil, sometimes with ink, when I have been busied with other matters. The notion of reflex action contradicts my five hundred experiences, for I have generally made no attempt to evoke any particular spirit."

He gives the names of twenty eye-witnesses to the phenomenon of pneumatography; and says he could give the names of fifty. "No reasoning," he tells us, "can persuade us that a fact, once thoroughly proved, has not existed; surely, no Christian ought to refuse such a proof, at once moral and material, of the immortality of the soul, as is given us in direct spirit-writing. The marvellous facts I have adduced are analogous with the phenomena upon which all the positive religions, all the sacred traditions, and all the mythologies of all nations, are based.*

"My conclusions are in accord with the beliefs of sixteen centuries. It is only the 18th and the 19th that have professed ideas diametrically opposed to Spiritualism. . . . I hold that I have laid the first foundations of a positive science of Spiritualism, based upon irrefutable facts. . . . Surely a day will come when humanity will turn with a compassionate disdain from those materialistic physicists, who believe themselves to be the sole depositaries of the laws of nature, of which they only know the material appearances.

"Unhappily the *demonphobia* of priests and pastors *on one side*, and the materialism, skepticism, rationalism, and excessive study of the sciences claimed as exact, *on the other side*, have almost deracinated the germ of the religious sense in the heart of man. Truly there is but one direct phenomenon, at once intelligent and material, independent of the will and the imagination, such as the direct writing of spirits, whom one had neither evoked nor invoked, which can serve as a proof undeniable of a supersensuous world."

With great stores of erudition at his command, Guldenstubbé shows how almost all the great philosophers of

---

* For a confirmation of this statement, so far as it relates to the Hebrew and Christian religions, see Dr. Eugene Crowell's "Primitive Christianity and Modern Spiritualism," (Carleton, New York, 1874.)

ancient times were Spiritualists. Even Aristotle tells us
that invisible beings are as substantial as the visible ; that
the former have bodies, though these may be very subtile
and ethereal ; and it is a fact, recognized by the most advanced modern scholars, that the greatest minds of Greece
admitted the objective reality of apparitions and phantoms ; and that they further believed that spirits and preternatural beings could communicate with mortals. " The
approaching triumph of Spiritualism," he says, " ought to
fill with joy the hearts of all religious persons ; and yet, is
it so? On the contrary, our professedly orthodox Christians, blinded by their *demonphobia*, regret this prospective
defeat of materialism, the deadly adversary of all religions."

I have translated freely from Guldenstubbé's book, because his testimony is that of a scholar, a philosopher, a
man of great purity and integrity of character, and one
who at the same time got his proofs of psycho-physical
phenomena independently, without any medial aid whatever, unless we insist that he himself must have been a
sensitive. We have abundant proof, too, that these phenomena were not *subjective*, confined to his own inner experience, but were such as could be proved to any witness
of sound body and mind.

His unique testimony, strengthened as it is by the depo-
sitions of honorable witnesses, is therefore of high value
as corroborating those still sufficient proofs which we get
through mediums whose necessities compel them to receive
money for the exhibition of supersensual power, and who
are mostly inferior to him in moral and mental culture.
Moreover, his full belief in the non-medial character of the
phenomena in his presence enhances their importance. If
a medium, he was an unconscious one. He was wholly disinterested in his efforts to spread the truth. He does not
seem to have been subject to trances or to states when his

own watchful and healthy consciousness was impaired or invaded. We hear of no peculiar sensations, no twitchings or contortions as the accompaniment of his manifestations. He rightly claimed that he was entitled to the respectful attention of all genuine truth-seekers and men of science.

The fact that such a man got the remarkable phenomenon of direct writing, under such conditions, and proved it conclusively to the satisfaction of fifty investigators, ought to carry peculiar weight; for it will be seen from the internal evidence of his own writings that he was a sincere, enlightened thinker, a philosopher, and an earnest seeker after the highest truth that can interest a human being; and as he was far above the need of taking pay for any of his exhibitions, or of seeking any material advantage therefrom, we must regard him as a witness whose words are exempt from any questionable adulteration whatever.

In his last pamphlet (1879) I. II. Fichte remarks that notwithstanding his own age and his exemption from the controversies of the day, he feels it his duty to bear testimony to the great fact of Spiritualism, and he thinks it the duty of every man, " with equally earnest convictions," to do the same; that Spiritualism is " the ratification of the belief in the immortality of the soul by means of the evidences of psychical experience." He refers to the Slade phenomena as having been " observed under conditions that preclude all imposture or prestidigitation," and as " being decisive for the cause of Spiritualism in Germany." He tells us " there is no retreat from what has been gained, and that the advance of the great fact is fully secured." *

---

* In his work *Réalité des Esprits*, Guldenstubbé speaks of "the tendency to *naturalize* the *objective* miracles of the Bible, and to sacrifice them to the pretended miracles, moral and *subjective*, of the regeneration of humanity according

Fichte anticipates the greatest possible benefit to the cause of morality and religion from a knowledge of immortality, and writes : "The proof that the future state is a continuation of the present, and to be affected by all earthly experiences, and by our fundamental sentiments and affections while here, whether pleasant or grievous, empowers us to meet the moral obligations of life, entirely abstracted from considerations of future reward or punishment. Here, in the earth-life, we have it in our power to seize and shape our future destination. Certainly is this a serious revelation at a time when mankind has long since been accustomed to displace their care for the future from their daily routine, as a consideration not affecting their interests."

These are strong words from the venerable German sage, just as he was about to take leave of the present stage of being ; words that will not be unfruitful in influencing the developments of future belief.

The late Sergeant E. W. Cox, a respected London lawyer and judge (1809–1879), President of the British Psychological Society, but who was not till a very short time before his sudden death a Spiritualist in the full sense, got satisfactory proofs of independent writing through Henry Slade, and wrote of it, August 8th, 1876 : "I can only say that I was in the full possession of my senses ; that I was wide awake ; that it was in broad daylight; that Dr Slade was under my observation the whole time, and could not have moved hand or foot without being detected by me."

Dr. H. B. Storer, of Boston, Mass., writes, October, 1877, in a published letter, that his own experience with Watkins was "in perfect agreement with the phenomenal and spiritual character of the manifestations," described as experienced by myself.

to the limited ideas of I. H. Fichte." That Fichte should have been converted to a knowledge of super-sensual phenomena by the man who had thus assailed his earlier philosophy, is creditable to his candor, as well as to the character of those proofs by which Guldenstubbé wrought his conversion.

Dr. A. S. Hayward, of Boston, writes, October 31, 1877 :

"While at Lake Pleasant camp-meeting, I introduced Mr. Watkins to Dr. Cottrell of Kansas. Mr. W. asked Dr. C. if he was a Spiritualist. The reply was : ' I am an investigator.' He then went to the tent of Mr. Watkins, and a sitting was had with highly satisfactory results. Two slates were placed together, with a small bit of pencil between them, and were held firmly by Dr. C. Soon the pencil was heard writing, and on opening, the following message was found : ' My dear husband, you may try to deceive the medium, but you cannot deceive your wife. You are a good Spiritualist.' Dr. C. was one of the oldest Spiritualists in the country, and his remark was merely intended to keep the medium in ignorance of facts that might color any communication received."

Mr. Joseph Beals, of Greenfield, Mass., testifies as follows :

"Last year (1877) I procured two slates, washed them off clean, placed a small bit of pencil between them, then put screws through the two frames, one on each side, and screwed them tightly together. This was done in my office. I then took them down to the American House, where Mr. Watkins was stopping, and we sat down, on opposite sides, at a table, and held the slates between us, he holding one end and I the other. Soon we heard writing. When it was through I turned the screws back and found three names written — my father's, my brother's, and Mrs. A. W. Slade's ; and these words : ' We are all here.' "

Mr. John Wetherbee, of Boston, a friend and neighbor of mine, took two new slates, and before he left the shop where he bought them, bored holes in the frames, put between them a bit of slate-pencil, tied them firmly together with twine, and sealed the knots. He then took the tied slates to Watkins, and kept charge of them, never permitting them to go out of his sight. The room was as light as a clear afternoon sun could make it. The slates were clean, and the medium never touched or saw the inside of them.

Yet under these conditions Mr. Wetherbee got a written, consistent message, with the name of a departed relative attached. In his published account (1877) he says:

"I know, as well as I know that the sun has shone to-day, *first*, that the slates were new and clean; *secondly*, that no one in the room or out of the room (the only occupants being the medium and myself) wrote the communication on the slate; and, *thirdly*, that it must have been done by an invisible, intelligent being or beings, and could not have been done in any other conceivable way. I make this statement as strongly as I know how, and my oath shall be attached if needed."

Mr. Wetherbee reiterates all this (June 5, 1880), and writes: "I know I was awake and sound in my mind, and no visible being was doing the work that was then going on in the space between the two slates under my hands."

Mr. Joseph Beals, whose personal testimony I have already quoted, relates that Mr. T. T. Timayenis, a modern Greek by birth, a teacher of the Greek language in the Collegiate Institute, Springfield, Mass., told him that he "obtained from Watkins, in original characters of Romaic, the name of his grandfather, and three lines of Greek words, correctly spelled, and with accents and breathings correctly placed." He also stated that his "grandfather's name was very peculiar, and almost unpronounceable by English lips. The slate was in full view all the time, and Watkins merely touched one corner of it with his fingers."

Wishing to confirm this account, I requested my friend and correspondent, Mrs. Louisa Andrews of Springfield, Mass., to call on Mr. Timayenis (1878), and get him to verify it, which he did most explicitly. He was not a Spiritualist, but he declared that the phenomenon was wholly inexplicable. Any one who has seen the somewhat illiterate letters written by Watkins (I have several of them) will deride the idea that he had so qualified himself in Greek as to be prepared for an accidental and wholly unexpected meeting with Mr. Timayenis. Judging the experiment by the principles of human science, the Greek message, under the conditions, must have been written by an intelligence and a power outside of the medium's own physical organism.

The testimony of my brother, James Otis Sargent, will be found in the volume entitled "Psychography," published in London in 1878. The sitting took place September 19, 1877. The witness says: . . . . "The slates were now cleaned again, the bit of pencil was placed between them, and I held them at arm's length, Watkins not touching them or me. On opening them I found a short communication, signed with another of the names I had written. . . . . Here the séance ended. It took place in broad daylight. I watched every movement of the medium, and there was no possibility of fraud." On this occasion Watkins read the names, &c. on five paper pellets, which had been written on and folded while he was out of the room — doing this while my brother held the pellets, one by one, tightly grasped in his hand.

There was a communication in the *Banner of Light* of June 19, 1880, from a person known to the editor, the substance of which may be thus related : — A. B., who had never been in Boston before, had never seen Watkins, nor had Watkins seen him, went to the medium's rooms, 2 Lovering Place, Boston, early in June, and asked for a sitting. Watkins went out of the room, and A. B. wrote six questions on little slips of paper *belonging to himself*, which he rolled into small ballots as tightly as possible, and placed on the table. Among them he placed a ballot on which was a question written by an absent friend — both the question and the answer to it being unknown to A. B. This ballot A. B. had marked.

Watkins comes in, does not once touch the ballots, but tells A. B. to mix them up, and then point to them slowly.

This he did ; and at the touch of the fourth ballot, which
was the marked one, Watkins tells him to take it up, which
A. B. does, closing his hand so that the medium shall not
see the ballot. Watkins walks about the room, looking
very flushed and excited, and at last cries out " Pin-cushion."
A note is made of this by A. B., and there is a long pause.
Then Watkins, looking dazed and confused, says, " They
speak of a Katharine." This was the name of A. B.'s
friend who had written the question. Another long pause,
and then, with a pleased, bright expression, Watkins ex-
claims, " Yes, I remember now ; it was something I made
for you." Here he stopped, seemed to be trying to grasp
some impression, and at last said, " It was something to
go round the neck ; I don't know what you call it — a tie
or something."

A. B. did not open the ballot, but told him that he could
not say whether this was correct or not, but would let him
know. When A. B. saw his friend he found that the question was, " Where is the pin-cushion you made me at Otter
River, and what else did you make me?" The answer to
the second part of this question was what the medium had
given, " Necktie."

The remarkable points in this experiment are these : The
ballot, untouched by the medium, contained a question addressed by an absent friend of A. B. to some departed
acquaintance, and both the question and the answer to it
were unknown to A. B. Let us set aside as not pertinent
to our present inquiry the remarkable clairvoyant power
manifested by Watkins, of being able to read the inscription on a tightly rolled-up ballot, (which he had never
touched, and which was not written on in his presence,) so
that he could give the leading word on it, " Pin-cushion."
But by what conceivable power did he get at the second
part of the answer, where the word was not written on the
ballot, and where it was not in the mind of A. B., who was

not the person to whom his friend's question seems to have been addressed?

Here is the puzzle. If there was mind-reading, then some transcendent power in Watkins must have gone a journey of miles to the Katharine who wrote the question, and got out of her mind the word " tie," or " necktie," or " something to go round the neck." This is one way of solving the mystery. Another solution is, that the deceased individual, to whom the question was addressed, was, in her capacity of spirit, enabled to impress corresponding spiritual faculties in Watkins with the needed words, until his normal consciousness could grasp them and prompt their utterance. Which is the easier solution of the two? Or are they not both equally insoluble?

While at Lake Pleasant, Mass. (August 25th, 1877), Watkins submitted his mediumship to a crucial testing on the public platform. Two new slates were bought by Mr. Joseph Beals. A committee of three, two of them not believers, were chosen by the audience for the test. They were Eben Ripley, Daniel D. Wiley, and F. L. Sargent. These gentlemen, after making a careful examination of the slates brought by Mr. Beals, between which a bit of slate-pencil was placed, held them by one end, while Watkins held them by the other. It was broad daylight. Soon the scratch of a pencil was heard, and on taking off the top slate the committee found that a message of forty-seven words had been written on the lower surface. They united in declaring that they could see no possible chance for any deception in the manifestation; that there was no possibility of a substitution of slates, or of chemical writing. At Mr. Beals's request they all wrote their names on the slate, and he had it (1879) in his keeping. The communication got is as follows: " My dear friends : As we approach the natural from our spiritual homes, we find our old love for our friends is still strong within us, for father, mother, brother, sister. God and the angel-world bless all, is the wish of this control. MRS. A. W. SLADE."

Mr. Giles B. Stebbins, of Detroit, a man every way estimable, vigilant, and judicial in his investigations, got a remarkable communication through independent writing in Chicago, December, 1878,—Mrs. Simpson, a French woman from New Orleans, imperfectly acquainted with the English language, being the medium. She had met Mr. Stebbins only the night before, and knew nothing of him or his family; yet there came to him this message, signed with the name of his departed uncle, Calvin Stebbins, of Wilbraham, Mass.: "I find no hell or baby's skulls, as we used to talk of. I find over here common sense and justice. Each man makes his own destiny. God has not destined any one to heaven or hell. Ah! Giles, the abyss is bridged, and we are fortifying the arches under the bridge daily, daily."

All this was far above the capacity of the medium, and so characteristic that it is impossible for Mr. Stebbins to believe that it could have come from her unassisted mind. He got writing while he himself held the slate under the table, the medium merely touching the end which projected out, so that her hand was in full sight.

The only way to evade the overwhelming testimony to the great fact of pneumatography is to deny it flatly, and to maintain, as some scientific specialists do, that no amount of human testimony can establish an occurrence so extraordinary. This is the position held by Messrs. Carpenter, Lankester, Beard, Hammond, Youmans, and others, claiming to be men of science. Dismissing such a fact as impossible in the nature of things, they would stamp it out as no proper subject for investigation, but only one for wrathful and contemptuous rejection by all men of science.

"We are not bound to examine into facts so diametrically opposed to our notions of the possible in nature," is

the argument by which they would discredit the attested
phenomenon before they have taken the trouble to enter
upon a patient, practical study of its reality. "Human
testimony is worth nothing in such a case," says Dr George
M. Beard. "We must not believe our senses in such a
case," says Dr. W. B. Carpenter.

It is not the wary man of science who mocks and scolds
at any well-attested phenomenon. He may be a scientific
expert in some one or two departments ; but he knows that
this does not qualify him to assume dictatorship in regard
to facts of which he has had little or no experience, and
which perhaps his prejudices forbid him to examine. Because the false may be mixed up with the true, the absurd
with the genuine, the bad with the good, — the unpleasant
fact does not justify the philosopher in spurning the whole
as valueless. "To abandon these spiritual phenomena to
credulity," says Victor Hugo, "is to commit a treason
against human reason. Nevertheless we see them always
rejected, and always reappearing. They date not their
advent from yesterday."

In regard to the phenomenon of independent writing, we
could accumulate testimony till it should fill volumes as
capacious as the British Cyclopædia ; but those who do not
find reasons in what we have adduced for considering the
subject as at least worthy of being investigated before it is
condemned, would not be moved from their position by any
amount of testimony, however conclusive.

In a little volume entitled " Psychography, by M. A.
Oxon," published in London in 1878, and for sale in Boston and Chicago, the sincere inquirer will find an excellent
summary of evidence establishing the phenomenon. Not
the least valuable is that of Samuel Bellachini, the court
conjurer at Berlin, given in the form of an affidavit before
Gustav Haagen, a public notary, December 6, 1877, and entered in his register under the number 482. In this document

Bellachini declares that the phenomenal occurrences in Slade's presence have been thoroughly examined by him "with the minutest observation and investigation of the surroundings, including the table." He says: "I have not, in the smallest instance, found anything to be produced by means of prestidigitative manifestations, or by mechanical apparatus;" and he declares that "any explanation of the experiments which took place, under the circumstances and conditions then obtaining, by any reference to prestidigitation, to be absolutely impossible."

Now if there is any man who can be called an "expert" in the matter of detecting fraud in an experiment made in broadest daylight, involving the question of direct writing, independent of any human delusion or trick, it must be the experienced juggler. It is difficult to see how a specialist in any of the exact sciences is better qualified to judge of the genuineness of the phenomenon than any man of good common sense, in the full possession of all his faculties, vigilant and calm. A chemist, it is true, might find out whether any chemical preparation had been used on the slate; but the possibility of such a trick is ruled out when we use (as I have repeatedly done) our own slates, fastened together while the inner surfaces cannot be touched by the medium, and the slates are never for a moment out of the sight of the witness.

One can hardly realize, until he sees it, the conclusiveness of the manifestation as a proof of direct writing by some psychical or spiritual power, apart from any visible organism, exercising intelligent force. What escape is there from the conclusion? We must either assume that there is an undiscovered force emitted by the human organism, and performing intelligent acts independently of the normal consciousness, or we are thrown back upon the hypothesis of independent spirit action.

Dr. George Wyld, of London, in his "Theosophy and

the Higher Life" (Trübner & Co., 1880), remarks: "With regard to slate-writing, there is no order of spiritual phenomena which impresses me more powerfully. Slade and his slate-writing were to me objects of absorbing interest. All was done in the light and above-board. The evidence that the writing was produced by a spiritual intelligence, without the intervention of human hands, was overwhelming; and in his presence the materialism of three thousand years was refuted in five minutes. When, therefore, brutal and intolerant ignorance seized Slade, and dragged him into a police court, I felt prepared to run any risk, and incur any responsibility in his defence."

Dr. Wyld is of opinion that the " psychic force " producing the phenomena can be exercised by some human beings in the body, but that much more easily and frequently the souls of departed human beings can exercise the same force. He held the theory at one time that the unconscious spirit of the medium may often produce the direct writing; but in relation to this question he finally says: "I have come much more round to the theory that most of the mediumistic phenomena are produced by foreign spirits." This is generally the conclusion of those who have had the largest and longest experience in studying and testing the phenomena.

It is a sign of the advancing intelligence of the times that Dr. Wyld is able to say (1880) in regard to his unpopular investigations: "For one friend I have lost, I have gained twenty better friends, and even my worldly prosperity has been greatly thereby increased."

CHAPTER II.

A SCIENTIFIC BASIS. — FURTHER TESTIMONY. — SPIRITUAL PROOFS. — THE MATERIALISTIC THEORY CONTRADICTED BY FACTS.

THE theory of the Materialist is, that the aggregation of certain material molecules, developing into an organism, is sufficient to explain the phenomena of life and mind; that there is no more of mystery in the evolution of the phenomenon *man* from a few particles of matter hardly visible with the aid of a microscope, and undistinguishable from the little glutinous speck that grows into a nettle or a tadpole, — than there is in the evolution of an oak-tree from an acorn. And this last half of the assertion may be true.

Tyndall, who is not in the habit of giving comfort to Spiritualists, has the candor to admit that the gap between molecules and the phenomena of mind is not bridged by any theory of materialism. While he believes that "matter contains within itself the promise and potency of all terrestrial life," he prudently adds, "*How it came to have this power*, is a question on which I never ventured an opinion."

Thus he would seem to favor the ancient doctrine of the Hylozoists, that life and matter are inseparable: a doctrine that has been held in various forms. It crops out in "the ultimate particles, material and having life," of Straton of Lampsacus; in the theories of the followers of Plotinus; in the assertion of Spinoza that all things are alive in different degrees; in the monadology of Leibnitz; and in the theory of divine influx of Swedenborg. So we find Tyndall in good company; and he must not be classed with Huxley, who, while he admits that his organism has "certain mental functions," believes they are "dependent on its molecular composition, and come to an end" when he dies.

That an intelligence, whether originating in this sphere of being or coming from some other, can exist and manifest life independently of a brain and nervous system, is what materialism, claiming to represent the most advanced science of the day, repudiates as an impossibility. But Spiritualism, as I have shown, gives direct evidence that intelligence *can* clearly manifest itself independently of any visible organism. In the words of the Rev. H. R. Haweis of England: "It offers to produce intelligence of some kind acting upon matter, and yet unconnected with a brain and nervous system. If this could be proved, the materialist argument would at once fall; for if intelligence similar to ours exists, and can operate outside the usual organized conditions, our souls *may* — we do not say *must* — do the same: — God is conceivable, and intelligence ceases to be the mere product of blind force and matter specially organized."

The facts I have verified by my experience have satisfied me that it *has* been proved that an intelligence operating at a distance of twenty-two feet from any known medium, and of more than fifteen feet from any other human being, may produce a written message on a slate. The theory that there are latent powers in the human subject that, unconsciously to him, can accomplish such an effect, involves the theory that there are powers independent of material organs, and which are not dependent on a visible material body for their potential activity. So that which-ever theory may prevail, the cause of Spiritualism is secure.

In the *Times* of Chicago, July, 1880, there is a graphic account of his experiences by Professor V. B. Denslow, not a Spiritualist, but who had four sittings in that city with Henry Slade, and one or two with Mrs. Simpson. From it I quote the following passages :

"I next sat with Mr. Slade at his own rooms. We entered the back parlor, no other person being in the room, and the doors were closed. I examined the carpet, table, and wall, all of which were ordinary and honest. I did not search Slade's pockets, nor, as the letter in the New York *Nation* recommended, did I look for concealed magnets thrust under his skin. The sequel will show that such precautions on my part would have been as futile as a means of discovering the mode in which the slate-writing was done, as the thrusting of 'magnets' into or under one's skin would be as a means of writing between two slates. Nor is it material whether there was one slate or fifty slates in the room, as, in the mode in which the writing was done, the theory of substitution of slates cuts no figure. But according to my best observation the room contained but two slates at the time, both of which lay on the table, and both of which I examined on both sides at the outset, and they contained no writing. Nor were there any springs about the slates by which, as suggested by one imaginative 'spirit exposer' in California, a roll of muslin indistinguishable from the surface of the slate was unfurled and spread over the slate. All such complicated and impracticable devices only bring out into strong contrast the simplicity yet certainty of the occult power which was now to perform the writing."

Professor Denslow got the slate-writing in a way which he fully describes, and which satisfied him as a proof that slate-writing could be done in Slade's presence "without any contact between any living person and the pencil that wrote." He says :

"I have read, with a sincere desire to get some light from it, Mr. Howells' careful analysis in · The Undiscovered Country,' of the various stages of lunacy which induced his 'Dr. Boynton' to look for spirit manifestations where they were not to be found, but I do not see that they shed any light whatever on a case where slate-writing is clearly done without the possibility of physical contact between any living person and the pencil. I have also read Dr. George M. Beard's efforts to connect the word 'hysteria' with these singular phenomena, but I fail to see wherein they apply to such a case. My health was never so good, and my mind never more calm, than when observing these phenomena. I am as free from hysteria as Dr. Beard, and from lunacy as Mr. Howells, and so 'in like manner 'were each and all of the twenty ladies and gentlemen who at various times have witnessed these phenomena in my presence, or have described to me their nature immediately afterward. So far, I have seen as much intelligence, as much skepticism, as much calm, healthy acumen, learning, and culture, as much familiarity with scientific methods and with sleight-of-hand, as the most querulous could wish, or as either Beard or Howells possesses, brought to bear on the simple problem, which it would seem a child ought to be able to solve, of detecting whether any human being was in physical contact with the pencil when it wrote. They all say no such contact was possible. . . . . .

" Independent slate-writing has never been a characteristic of hysterics. Hysterical persons may believe they see what they do not see, but the principle of illusion has no application in this case, as fifty persons in the room at the time would all have seen the writing alike when it had been done, and all would have heard the pencil doing it. I did not see the pencil make its mark, and therefore there is no fact in the entire phenomena to which the principle of illusion can apply. The use of the word *hysteria*, therefore, where no illusion of the senses is alleged, is merely the impudence of ignorance. It explains nothing, and designates nothing. When I examined the slates before the writing, no illusion theory applies, because nothing had yet occurred. When I examined them after the writing was over, no illusion theory applies, since the writing was undoubtedly there, and any one of a million persons, if they saw the slate at all, would have seen and read it alike. The only part of the fact in relation to which the illusion theory can apply is, that I suppose I held the slate-surface, where physical contact with the pencil on the part of some human writer would be impossible, when, in reality, I did not. But what is so easy as to hold a slate in broad daylight, where no human being can write on it, especially in a room where there is only one other person. To suppose that I cannot do that, or that I cannot know decisively when I do or do not so hold it, is part of the sheer insanity of impudence. It indicates that those who so assert have become infidels to the integrity of the human intellect, and have lost their power to remain loyal to the evidences of the senses, — an assertion which involves no less than an absolute abdication of the throne of human reason.

"Nor does the theory of sleight-of-hand apply, because in all cases of sleight-of-hand the *hand* of the operator is in communication with the thing done, and a chief share of the difficulty is created by keeping this magical hand in such a state of swift and diversified motion that the observer could not follow it. In this case, however, both of Slade's hands were motionless, plainly in sight. A sleight-of-hand man who never uses his hands, but whose hands lie flat on a table while everything is doing, would, indeed, be a wonder, unless he had an assistant, and Slade had none.

"What I had thus far seen with Slade did not differ essentially from what I had already seen with Mrs. Simpson who resides permanently in this city, except that Mrs. Simpson reads easily any question her visitor may write on the slate, without having that visual access to the slate which would be necessary to enable an ordinary person to read it. This, Slade tells me, he does not.

"In another respect, Mrs. Simpson's slate-writing is characterized by an incident that does not appear in Slade's. This is the fact that the bit of pencil is placed on a slate, and a goblet filled with water is placed over it, so that apparently the pencil should be confined in its writing within the hollow space left by the concave bottom of the goblet, which space would be about the size of a silver dollar. But on placing the slate underneath the table, Mrs. Simpson holding one side of the slate and the observer the other, so that the top of the goblet rests steadily and firmly against the under side of the table, the pencil is heard to write in long lines across the slate, as freely as if the goblet were not there, and on removing slate and goblet from under the table, without the possibility that either could have changed its relative position during the operation, or could have been removed by so much as a hair's-breadth from each other, the writing is found to begin on the slate at a point outside the space covered by the goblet, to cross the slate again and again in half a dozen lines, none of which pay any regard to the physical obstacle afforded by the solid contact of the goblet with the slate, so that each line begins to the left of where the goblet stands, passes directly under it with unbroken writing, and reappears at the right of the goblet as if the goblet had not been there.

"When I saw this with Mrs. Simpson, the conditions precluded deceit or sleight-of-hand as absolutely as in the case of Slade. But one other person was in the room, and he sat some twelve feet away. I had examined the carpets for trap-doors, and think I am competent to say there were none, and had there been twenty they would have been of no service, as I held the goblet and slate so firmly and steadily while under the table, that I knew that neither table, slate, nor goblet moved relatively to each other while the writing was being done. Not only was the writing done without possibility of any human person being in contact with the pencil while it was doing, but it was done by some agency which disregarded solid glass as an obstacle, and wrote as easily on a surface covered with it as on a bare surface. This, of course, raises the question why it should have used the pencil at all; but I am not answering questions, but asking them. Moreover, at the end of the writing the bit of pencil was neither in the hollow space in which it had been placed underneath the goblet, nor was it anywhere on the slate; but it was at the bottom of the water on the inside of the goblet, and was worn by the writing it appeared to have done. The physically impossible fact, therefore, of passing one solid substance directly through another, without violence to either, occurred some six or eight times within ten minutes.

"After I had been forty minutes in the room, and knew that neither when I entered, nor since, had there been any other flowers in the room than a growing fuchsia near the door, Mrs. Simpson undertook to produce a flower. Placing the goblet of water on the slate, in like manner as was done for the slate-writing, but with no pencil, after, perhaps, five minutes of apparent strong electro-nervous excitement in the arm which was holding her side of the slate, Mrs. Simpson told me to withdraw the goblet from under the table, and in the act of doing so, the fragrance of the hyacinth filled the room, and inside the goblet was a fresh, rich, unstained hyacinth flower of twenty-two petals, just plucked from the stem, and which I took home with me and kept till it withered — perhaps a week.

" Prior to my third session with Slade, I was present at the residence of Colonel Bundy, when some sixteen persons of indisputable intelligence and some of them of special critical power, including Judge Barnum and Mrs. Barnum, Dr. Jewell, of Evanston, editor of the best reputed journal of nervous diseases in this country and one of the foremost medical journals of the world ; Mr. and Mrs. W. K. Starett, of *The Western Magazine*, Mr. and Mrs. Perry, Mr. Gage, Mrs. Willard, Dr. and Mrs. Dickson, and several others, all witnessed substantially the same method of slate-writing I have described, and none of whom were able to detect any mode by which any living person could have communicated the moving force of the pencil which did the writing. Of course, in all these slate-writings there is no concealment, no turning down of lights, and the slates are always in the hands of the observers, and not of Slade."

After describing with scientific precision some partial experiments in materialization with Slade, Professor Denslow remarks :

" I think I have sufficient acquaintance with the instrumentalities by which spectral and illusory effects are mechanically produced, to say that the use of the means essential to the production of these effects were in this case simply impossible, and that were they possible, such other effects when produced bear virtually no resemblance whatever to the effects which I saw."

In conclusion, he remarks frankly and forcibly :

" Here are facts which, whatever their nature, whether they consist in proofs of stupendous psychological influence of one human mind over others, or whether they are a *lusus naturœ*, derivable from electric influence, or whether they are a window opening from our earthly life into a spirit-world, deserve to be candidly stated by all who have seen them. Even if they are impositions on the human mind, it is the duty of scientific men to study the laws governing the production of such impositions, and to prove the fact by producing the same phenomena themselves, coupled with proof that they do not produce them by spirit agency. The more cautious we are in building theories upon these phenomena, and the more patient we are in developing the phenomena themselves until they evolve their own theories irresistibly, the greater will be the value both of our facts and theories when obtained. As for theories, it will be time enough for me to state mine when I have formed one."

Guldenstubbé is not too sanguine when he declares that the proof by direct writing is the crowning evidence of the existence and activity of a principle assuring us that there is not only a spirit in man, using his material organism, but a spirit outside of him using some invisible organism or instrument for producing effects upon matter. "These immaterial beings," you say, "cannot move matter." But how do we know that they are in all respects immaterial? Are there not finer forces and finer grades of matter than we can distinguish by the unaided bodily senses? Photography proves the fact even to the materialist. And how do we know that what is immaterial to our coarse mortal senses, is immaterial to one in whom the spiritual senses are developed? Moreover, when we say that what is immaterial cannot move matter, do we not say what no scientific or philosophical analysis has yet been able to prove?

The Rev. Samuel Watson, of Tennessee, late of the Methodist Church, a gentleman sincere and estimable in all the relations of life, says: "I have seen the double slate held by skeptics, and truthful messages were written on both slates when thus confined together." The same writer says: "Spirit manifestations constitute the basis upon which the whole fabric of Christianity has been built. Primitive Christianity, as taught by its founder, and pure Spiritualism are identical."

In confirmation of this, the testimony of the three principal founders of Methodism, John Wesley, Adam Clark, and Richard Watson, is adduced. Clark distinctly expresses his belief that spirits may "have intercourse with this world, and become visible to mortals."

Referring to the case of the reappearance of Samuel, (1 Sam. xxviii. 11), Richard Watson says: "It answers all the objections which were ever raised, or can be raised, from the philosophy of the case, against the possibility of the appearance of departed spirits."

That John Wesley was not only a believer, but that he was medially sensitive, would seem to be apparent from passages in which he relates that on three occasions he saw spirits. In every instance their appearance was followed by news of the death of each person at the time he appeared. Referring to one who died in Jamaica, Wesley remarks in a foot-note: "So a spirit finds no difficulty in travelling three or four thousand miles in a moment."

The manifestations in the Wesley family in England, commencing in 1716, resemble in all respects the phenomena of our own day. They continued with some members of the family for over thirty years. Robert Southey, in his " Life of Wesley," regards them, as do modern Spiritualists, as being " in the ordinary course of nature"; and he says: " An author who, in this age, relates such a story and treats it as not utterly incredible and absurd, must expect to be ridiculed; but the testimony upon which it rests is far too strong to be set aside because of the strangeness of the relation."

Priestley, who tried to reconcile his effete system of materialism with a belief in future rewards and punishments, refers to the Wesleyan phenomena as among the most striking on record; though he made an abortive attempt to explain them by natural causes; but they remain as inexplicable as ever by any theory outside of the spiritual.

Oberlin (1740–1826), Protestant pastor in the Ban de la

Roche, part of the former province of Alsace, labored earnestly to raise the condition of his people. They were nearly all Lutherans and Spiritualists. He tried hard to overcome what he regarded as their superstition, and preached forcibly against it; but at last the demoustrable, objective facts became too strong for him, and his opposition ended by his becoming a Spiritualist himself. The dead, he tells us, frequently re-appeared, especially after that well-known and terrible accident which buried several villages (the fall of the Rossberg in 1806). Soon afterwards, as Oberlin expressed it, "many had their spiritual sight opened," and recognized the apparitions of different victims of the disaster. His own deceased wife was often, for years, visible to his sight, watching over him, and holding communion with him. Oberlin left a "large pile of papers" on the subject, under the title of "*Journal des Apparitions et Instructions par rêves*" (Journal of Apparitions and Instructions through dreams). They were committed to M. Matter, who told Robert Dale Owen of the fact in Paris, May, 1859.

The conditions under which clairvoyance and direct writing have been verified, are of such a character that no medium's recreancy, or claim to have deceived, can now be of the slightest avail in invalidating the evidences. Until he can instruct you or me how to do the same things by the exercise of our natural powers, he may be set down as insincere. If a medium, without touching or having touched a slate, can cause writing, indicating clairvoyance, to appear on it, as I hold it in my hand, he must either produce the writing by his own unconsciously exercised abnormal powers, in a way he is impotent to explain, or it must be produced by some foreign, unknown, intelligent force. In either case it is a force operating outside of any visible organism.

As early as 1848, Dr. E. C. Rogers, a gentleman personally known to me, broached the theory that the powers manifested in the phenomena lie within the sphere of the human organization and of simple mundane agencies. He wrote a book enforcing his views. Recently this theory has been borrowed by a German writer as applicable to the phenomena through Henry Slade. But the inquiry is pertinently put: If a spiritually-endowed human agent, while hampered by his material environment, can perform acts independent of material limitations, is it not a fair inference that he can do more and better when the same spiritual powers are released by the dissolution of the physical husk?

In the majority of these supposed manifestations from spirits, it is indeed difficult to arrive at a scientific certainty as to the identity of a form-manifestation, whether partial or entire; but, as a correspondent of the *London Spiritualist* aptly remarks: "Supposing that all the evidences of spirit identity could be swept away, the common phenomenon of a living hand or head, the duplicate in appearance of that of the medium, appearing at one part of the room, while the medium is in a dead trance at the other, would of itself be extremely suggestive. The question might well arise in the mind of the observer, whether, when the dead body of a friend is in the coffin, the living counterpart may not be somewhere else."

"I can never forget," writes Dr. George Wyld, of London (1880), "the overwhelming sensations I experienced on first seeing and touching these hands — warm, sensitive, *detached* hands — which grasped my hand with the perfect reality of human hands, and yet dissolved from the grasp as no human hands could do."

Pneumatography gives us evidence of an intelligent force producing written messages at a distance of more than twenty feet from the medium; and Clairvoyance gives us evidence of a supersensual, intelligent faculty, able to read what no human pair of eyes could possibly detect. Of these facts I am as certain as of any fact of human existence. They are known to hundreds of thousands of competent witnesses at the present day. The legitimate inference is, that there is a natural and a spiritual organism, common to all men, but that the spiritual manifests itself only under certain abnormal or exceptional conditions.

Having satisfied ourselves of intelligent, ultra-corporeal action, independent of mortal muscles, of a palpably material brain, or of any known physical effort, we may rationally conclude that it is not limited to our two great typical phenomena, but that its range is co-extensive with life itself, and that this life is by no means dependent for its continuance on a visibly material organism. Other transcendent phenomena lend ample confirmation to this view, and prove that the manifestations of life and mind are as various as they are inexplicable unless we hypothecate a force very different from that which our material organism can normally supply. From a single bone Cuvier could infer the osteology of the animal to which it belonged. So from one thoroughly demonstrated phenomenon of Spiritualism the great fact of an intelligent force, independent of a visible organism, may be scientifically inferred.

It is true that the various phenomena have occurred in all ages of the world, of which we have any account. But since 1848 they seem to have been epidemic rather than sporadic. In that year the raps occurred in the Fox family at Hydesville, N. Y., and Kate Fox, then a mere child, discovered by questioning them that they betrayed intelligence. From that time the modern phenomena have multiplied and increased in importance: —

With many mediums there were raps and knocks, answering questions and spelling out messages; in other cases, tables rising up on two legs, pounded on the floor their revelations. Dials, with movable hands, were used, which pointed out letters and answered questions without apparent human aid. The hands of mediums, acting convulsively, and, as they averred, without volition, wrote things beyond their knowledge. In these writings, produced often with incredible speed, the chirography was sometimes reversed, so that to read them one had to read the reflection in a mirror. They were done under circumstances that clearly proved abnormal action. Some mediums would write different messages with both hands at a time, and without any consciousness of what they were writing. There were speaking mediums who declared themselves to be merely passive instruments of the spirits. Some would represent with amazing fidelity the actions, voices, and appearance of persons long deceased, and whom they had never seen. There were drawing mediums, who, blindfolded, drew accurate portraits of the departed, and this with incredible celerity. Sometimes stigmata would appear in raised red lines upon the skin of the medium, indicating too the power of clairvoyance. Ponderous bodies, as heavy dining-tables and piano-fortes, would be raised from the floor. Writings and pictures were produced without visible hands. Luminous appearances were frequent. Persons were touched by invisible and sometimes visible hands. Various musical instruments were played on without visible agency. In my own library I have had a large bass-viol skilfully played on by some unknown force in the dark, when the medium's hands were held, and there was no possibility of collusion or deception. Voices were often heard that did not proceed from the medium. Persons were lifted to the ceiling under circumstances that left no doubt as to the reality of the mysterious levitation. Phantom faces, as well as full-form manifestations, would be produced when fraud or hallucination was out of the question.

All the most important of these phenomena I have myself witnessed under conditions, which, if not sufficiently rigorous to induce me to place them by the side of the pneumatographic and clairvoyant phenomena as established facts of science, were yet sufficient to cause me to accept them in my own estimation as equally proved.

Let him who would undervalue the immense significance of our phenomena ask himself why it is, then, that they are denounced so arrogantly and repudiated so angrily by a large majority of the leading physicists and materialists of the day. Why is it, except that they see that if our facts are accepted as true, they must work the utter overthrow of all Sadducean and materialistic systems.

In his report of the phenomena through Slade, Zöllner, the eminent German professor of physical astronomy, testifies as follows:

"On the evening of November 16, 1877, I placed in a room which Slade had never entered, a card-table and four chairs. After Professor Fechner, Professor Braune, Slade, and I had taken our places, and laid our hands upon the table, a knocking in the table was heard. Writing was given in the usual way upon a slate bought by myself two hours before, and which I had also marked. . . . The book-slate, after being first cleaned, and a crumb of pencil laid between, was then closed and held by Slade over the head of Professor Braune. The noise of writing was soon heard, and when the slate was opened, a long message was found upon it. Whilst this was going on, suddenly a bed behind a screen began to move, and came about two feet away from the wall, shoving the screen with it. Slade was more than four feet from the bed, had his back turned to it, and his legs crossed."

Here is Zöllner's account of an experiment in which matter was made to disappear and reappear:

"At about half-past eleven o'clock, in bright sunlight, I became, wholly without expectation or preparation, a witness of a very extraordinary phenomenon. I had, as usual, taken my place with Slade at a card-table. Opposite me, and near the card-table, stood a small round stand. Something like a minute may have passed after Slade and I had seated ourselves and placed our hands, one above the other, together, when the round stand began slowly to sway to and fro.　We both saw it clearly.　The motions were soon more extensive, and, meanwhile, the whole stand drew near to the card-table, and placed itself under the latter, with its three feet turned toward me.　I, and as it seemed also Mr. Slade, did not know in what way the phenomena were to be further developed.　For perhaps a minute nothing at all happened.　Slade was about to use his slate and pencil to ask the spirits whether we were to expect anything, when I resolved to take a nearer view of the round stand which was lying, as I thought, under the card-table.　To my greatest amazement, and Slade's also, we found the space under the card-table perfectly empty.　Nowhere in the rest of the chamber could we find the stand which a minute previously had been before our eyes.　After five or six minutes spent in breathless waiting for the reappearance of the stand, Slade claimed that he saw appearances of lights of which I, as usual, could see nothing.　Looking with more and more anxiety and astonishment in different directions in the air above me, Slade asked me if I did not see the appearance of large lights, and while I answered the question with a decided negative, I turned my head in the direction of the ceiling of the chamber, and suddenly saw, at a height of about five feet, the lost table, with the legs directed upward into the air, float downward rapidly upon the top of the card-table."　(Zöllner, vol. ii., part 2, p. 917.)

The following is the Rev. Joseph Cook's account of one of the experiments with Slade, at which Zöllner and other German professors were present:

"A professor of Leipzig University buys a book-slate himself, and ties it up, or locks it, or screws it together, first having cleansed it and carefully removed any chemical preparation on it.　He does not allow it to go out of his hands during the experiment.　It is watched by men of trained habits of observation, while writing appears on its interior surface.　An elaborate scientific work from the foremost university in the world contains plates illustrating writing produced in this manner. . . . . Very often the subject-matter of the writing found on the slates is beyond the knowledge of the psychic.　Greek has been written on slates, and found to be accurate, when the psychic knew nothing of the language.　It is thought by Zöllner and his associates to be demonstrably impossible to produce these results by fraud. . . . . Zöllner undertakes to face all Germany with experiments like these. He affirms that Weber, Fechner, and Scheibner agree with him, and Leipzig University keeps him in his place.

"The mechanical theory of matter is exploded if Zöllner's alleged facts can be proved to be real, but here are grave experts who unite in assuring the world that these events occurred under their own eye-sight. Here is the Court Conjurer, who says he can do nothing of the kind. I hold in my hand a volume by Fichte, and he says, quoting these experiments, and naming the professors who performed them, that he could himself, if he were authorized, give in addition to these names many others in Germany, who by the experiments at Leipzig had been convinced of the reality of the facts, and of their worthiness to be made the subject of scientific research. (Fichte, *Der neuere Spiritualismus*. Leipzig: Brockhaus. 1878. p. 104.)"

The Leipzig experiment of tying knots in an endless cord was repeated by my correspondent, Dr. T. L. Nichols, 32 Fopstone-road, London, in April, 1878. In his description he says: " It is certain that no mortal man could have tied these knots — equally certain that all the philosophers and all the magicians of Europe cannot now untie them under the same conditions."

Zöllner illustrates his experiment by a large plate, showing the condition of the cord, and that no theory of legerdemain can explain what was accomplished.

. That the psychic force is under the control of spirits, as well as of men under certain abnormal conditions, is the rational conclusion. It was the conclusion of Cicero, of Plutarch, and of St. Augustine.

The Rev. Joseph Cook draws a distinction between the superhuman and the supernatural: a theological speculation which no one can gainsay, since it does not belong to the domain of the demonstrable. The doings, however marvellous, of all finite spirits, may not be supernatural except in the sense that they may be empowered by the only Being superior to Nature, because its Author. Transcendental Physics, initiated by the renewed attention of modern times to psychical phenomena, are in perfect harmony with the dominant teachings of the Bible in respect to the nature of man and the power of spirits.

The accomplished Hindoo preacher and medium, Baboo Chund Mittra, in an address delivered at Calcutta, January, 1879, advocating the scientific claims of Spiritualism, remarked: "The God of science is my God; he who in all ages works wonders, and continually exhibits his wisdom, power, and love throughout the amplitudes of nature. All science is religion, and all religion is science. There is as much science in prayer as in the locomotive engine; as much science in inspiration as in the microscope and telegraph wire."

Mrs. Sarah Helen Whitman, (1802–1878,) the lady who was once betrothed to the poet Poe, and with whom I had a good deal of correspondence on the subject of Spiritualism, remarked, among her other acute observations on the subject: "The occult psychical energies that lie folded up within us, are pointing to a rich and unexplored domain of our mysterious inner life; and the knowledge of this winged, expansive nature, that has long lain dimly dreaming within its chrysalis, is revealed to us precisely at the epoch when the rapid progress of physical science threatened to banish the last faint vestiges of our faith in spiritual causation and spiritual influence."

The New York *Scientific American*, unfriendly to Spiritualism, makes this admission: "If true, it will become the one grand event of the world's history, and will give an imperishable lustre of glory to the nineteenth century. . . . . If the pretensions of Spiritualism have a rational foundation, no more important work has been offered to men than their verification."

To ask for the *cui bono* of such a revelation — to insinuate that we do not need it — is at once to ignore the growing unbelief of the times, and to mock at the most sacred hopes and religious intuitions of the majority of mankind.

This universe, be sure, is not an infinite contrivance for the production and swift extinction of sentient, loving, intelligent life ; — it is not a stupendous vestibule to a charnel-house, — where affection, friendship, science, and art find congenial and progressive recipients for a few fleeting moments, and man is admitted to a glimpse of a possible happiness and growth, and then plunged into the blackness of annihilation ; — a world where life and mind are given only to be withdrawn, as if in mockery, and truth and goodness are as evanescent as falsehood and evil.

Spiritualism, by its objective, supersensual, and verifiable facts, declares to us that this pessimistic view of things is radically wrong ; that all this grand display of suns and systems is not " a tale told by an idiot, signifying nothing ; " that the infinite magnitude and variety of the universe ought to impress us as an earnest of our immortality — for what are all these wonders without minds to study and enjoy them ? — that states of consciousness may subside and give place to other states, but that they are all reproducible, and in that sense, eternal, since memory holds forever in its occult receptacles all the impressions it takes ; — and that a present good is an inalienable good forever, never to be lost by the soul that once felt its power ; — that love is a divine principle of our nature which grows by giving, expands by imparting, and is the spring of a fresh and everlasting joy ; — that death is merely a release from an organism for which the soul has ready a far nobler, though to our coarse mortal senses, invisible, substitute ; — that we are not orphans — nay, worse than orphans — flung out by a blind, remorseless Fate, our only parent, into an alien universe, but that we are destined to have the freedom of every remotest planet, all intelligences forming one grand confraternity, interchanging love and knowledge ; that there is a conscious, a loving and omniscient Omnipotence presiding over all the details of this stupendous complex ; and that by beneficent and eternal laws every soul will gravitate, in the life to come, where it belongs, where it can best find what is congenial to the disposition it has formed here, and there continue till it can rise, by proper gradations and its own sincere efforts, to more worthy conditions, and take in at length a realization of the ineffable grandeur and the splendid possibilities of its inheritance, and aspire and strive accordingly.

Such are the views which Spiritualism, broadly and faithfully studied, suggests and justifies. The certainties presented, in our two representative and fully-established facts, make credible analogous phenomena, fully attested, but not so easy of flawless exposition. The phenomena of direct writing and of clairvoyance have been chosen for a scientific basis, because there is not a flaw, nor a conceivable doubt, in the experimental method by which they have been and are daily certified and confirmed.

There may be other phenomena more surprising, and to an acquaintance with which a thorough conviction of these may safely introduce us ; but there are none that we know of which appeal more directly to the senses and the reason of the scientific investigator for their confirmation. Should all the mediums for direct writing be detected in tricks, they would not invalidate these phenomena until it could be proved that any skilful juggler, exercising no medial power, could produce the same under the same conditions. This, in the nature of things, cannot be done, since they involve the exercise of a faculty at once abnormal and transcendent, and are inexplicable without it.

CHAPTER III.

REPLY TO THE OBJECTIONS OF PROFESSOR WUNDT.

ALL objections to the scientific investigation of a fact of nature must have ignorance or superstition at their root. Professor Wilhelm Wundt, of Leipzig, eminent as a metaphysical writer, is the author of a work on " The Axioms of Physics and their Relation to the Principle of Causality." The subject is one which could hardly be treated exhaustively without some knowledge of those occult causes of motion which operate in the phenomena of Spiritualism. Of these he seems to be ignorant. It is a great error of specialists in science to suppose that the chief claim of a belief in immortality to their attention is that it rests on the emotions.

Because a man is proficient in one branch of science, it does not follow that his authority is of much value in another, with which his acquaintance is superficial. He may be an excellent geologist, and yet unqualified to decide a question in regard to the habits of bees. He may be a subtile logician like Mill, or an accomplished physiologist like Huxley, and yet a poor authority in musical science, and a mere blunderer when, after a slight examination, he would throw discredit on certain psychical phenomena, to which others, who have given to the subject the study of half a lifetime, may testify. The following reply to the objections raised by Professor Wundt to the prosecution of our investigations as matters of scientific interest, will explain itself: —

Your " Open Letter " to Professor Hermann Ulrici, of Halle, on " Spiritualism as a Scientific Question," has been translated and published in the " American Popular Science Monthly " for September, 1879. It appears that Ulrici, from whose views you dissent, had arrived at the conviction that the reality of certain facts, attested by eminent men of science, can no longer be doubted, and that Spiritualism, so called, has thus become *a scientific question of the highest importance.*

It also appears that there were present at the *séances* held with Henry Slade at Leipzic in 1877, besides those professors who became convinced of the actuality of the spiritualistic phenomena, certain other members of the university, who did not appear to share this conviction. Of these latter you were one ; and Ulrici, it would seem, in his " *Zeitschrift für Philosophie und philosophische Kritik,*" called upon the dissenters to state publicly what they saw ; why they doubt the objective reality of what they saw ; and why they feel compelled to assume jugglery, deceit, or illusion.

On this last point your mind, if I may judge from your language, is still in a state of indecision. There are passages in which you seem to admit frankly the objectivity and inexplicable character of the phenomena ; and there are others in which you suggest " jugglery " as the solution, and charge the medium with untruthfulness in claiming to be a passive instrument. The two reasons on which you found this charge so obviously proceed from an ignorance of the facts and theories pertaining to medial development, that they can be very readily confuted.

Meanwhile the proofs of your hesitancy are these : — In your second paragraph, addressing Ulrici, you say : " For merely subjective phantasms of the observers, these phenomena, as you justly remark, cannot be held ; their objectivity and reality in the ordinary sense of the word will in fact be questioned by no man who may even have read only your short description."

Again, in paragraph 15, you write: "If you ask me now whether I am in a condition to express a conjecture as to how these experiments were performed, I answer, No. At the same time, however, I must state that phenomena of this sort lie entirely outside the domain of the special-training which I have acquired during my scientific career." And in the same paragraph you remark: "You will certainly find it justifiable, if I do not go into hypotheses as to how the phenomena produced by Mr. Slade were brought about."

After these ingenuous concessions to the truth, I was certainly surprised to find you, in paragraph 16, suddenly breaking through these wise limitations of your candor, and suggesting the old and ten thousand times exploded theory of jugglery; for you say: "As to the experiments which I saw myself, I believe that they will not fail to produce upon every unprejudiced reader who has ever seen skilful prestidigitations the impression of well-managed feats of jugglery." And again: "I cannot find that any one of the *experiments* which I saw with Mr. Slade was above the powers of a good juggler."

Yet in the paragraph before, you had confessed you were not "in a condition to express a conjecture as to how these experiments were performed." Such inconsistencies are lamentably out of place in what assumes to be a rigorous examination of a scientific question. They suggest the impression that you have not really yet made up your mind on the subject.

There is an obstacle in the way of your theory of jugglery, and you try to remove it in a somewhat off-hand and cavalier manner. The important testimony of Bellachini (see page 65 of this volume) you dismiss in three lines with the evasive remark, that you would acknowledge him as an authority, if you "could premise in his case that *he had a conception of the scientific scope of the question.*" Under this euphuism, what lies concealed? What but an imputation on the veracity of the affiant? What is inattention to the "scientific scope of a question" addressed to an expert, but inattention to the truth of a question? You intimate that Bellachini was careless as to the truth of what he solemnly asserts in regard to a matter he was employed to investigate. His professional reputation was risked in his being outwitted by a competing juggler; and yet because, with the courage of an honest man, he declares that there was no prestidigitation possible in the inexplicable occurrences at the Slade *séances*, you, to give countenance to your own vacillating second thoughts on the subject, presume to impugn his truthfulness.

In arguing against the claims of Spiritualism to scientific recognition, you put these two questions: (1) *What are the characterizing marks of a scientific authority?* (2) *What influence may we concede to outside authority upon our own knowledge?*

You say, with truth: "The highest degree of credibility is not sufficient to make any man a scientific authority; there is requisite to this a special professional, and indeed a technical *training*, which must have approved itself by superior accomplishments in the province concerned." . . . (Precisely such a training as Bellachini had for detecting a trick, if there was one!) "In order to be able to speak with authority concerning any phenomena, one must possess a thorough, critical knowledge of the same."

Influenced by considerations like these, I might reasonably maintain that investigators, thoroughly acquainted with our phenomena, are more competent to judge of them, than any specialist in some other branch of science. You are here sustained in your views by the very class whose belief you would stamp as unscientific.

You further say: "Authorities in the present case, therefore, are only such persons as either possess mediumistic powers, or, without claiming to be bearers of such properties, are able to produce phenomena of the same nature."

Here you show a profound ignorance of the nature of the medial manifestations. The persons who, without possessing medial power, are "able to produce phenomena of the same nature" in the same way that they are produced in the presence of mediums, are as yet a wholly imaginary class. There have been, ever since the year 1847, charlatans and swindlers, or else renegade mediums, who have pretended to be exposers of medial phenomena; but in no one trifling instance have these impostors been able to explain, outside of the spiritual hypothesis, any one actual phenomenon in such a way that it could be produced by non-medial persons as it is through genuine mediums. I defy any man to prove the contrary. The pretended exposers have at times fooled eminent opponents of Spiritualism, like Huxley and Carpenter, both in England and America; but they have never taken the first step towards enlightening a person, really and practically acquainted with the subject, as to the *modus operandi*. This shows that you are clearly right in your remark, that "in order to be able to speak with authority concerning any phenomena, one must possess a thorough, critical knowledge of the same."

Your notion that mediums themselves are authorities as to the phenomena, or that they possess a thorough, critical knowledge of the same, is true only in a few remarkable instances, and in those only to a limited extent. The most powerful mediums are almost always, while the phenomena are going on, in a state of trance or nervous exaltation wholly unfitted for critical observation. That they sometimes believe they are under the influence of some spirit who may discourse through their lips on the character of the phenomena and try to explain them, is quite true; but such testimony is not accepted as scientific, except so far as it satisfies human reason. Your statement, therefore, as to what is authority in the case is wholly fallacious, and merely betrays your ignorance of the whole subject.

The two general questions which I have quoted, and which you yourself undertake to answer, lead you into an assumption, upon which the whole weight of your argument, as to the non-scientific character of the claims of Spiritualism, is made to depend. But the assumption is grossly arbitrary and fallacious; it is expressed by you in various forms, of which I select the following:

(1) There rules in nature neither freak nor accident. . . . On the contrary, the most conspicuous characteristic of these phenomena lies precisely in the fact that in their presence the laws of nature seem to be abrogated.

(2) The laws of gravitation, of electricity, of light, and of heat are altogether, as we are assured, of a purely hypothetical validity; they have authority so long as the inexplicable, spiritualistic something does not cross them.

(3) On the one side stands the authority of the whole history of science, the totality of all known natural laws, which have not only been discovered under the presupposition of a universal causality, but have also without exception confirmed the same.

(4) On the other side stands the authority of a few certainly most eminent naturalists, who . . . announce the discovery that causality has a flaw, and that we must consequently abandon our former view of nature.

Your complaint that the laws of nature are abrogated by the phenomena is as irrational and inane as were the objections of those persons who, when telescopes and microscopes were invented, denounced them as atheistic innovations; or as were the outcries of those who opposed the theory of the rotundity of the earth and the existence of the antipodes as unscientific. How could men be supposed to walk with their heads down in space like flies on a ceiling !

In order to make a show of a scientific reason for your objection, you are obliged to assume what science gives you no authority to assume, namely, that there are no such beings as spirits, invisible to human sight, but exercising wonderful, though limited, powers over matter. I offset your mere hypothesis with another, which is, that there *are* such beings in existence; and I assert that there are proofs of it. Since there is no proof whatever to the contrary, your reiteration of the assertion that our facts clash with the laws of nature, is the mere repetition of a conjecture of your own, having no scientific validity whatever.

You assume that when a man is lifted to the ceiling by no known human means or appliances, the law of gravitation is violated. But, with a purely arbitrary indifference, you leave out of sight entirely the possibility that the levitation may be effected by the power of spirits, substantially organized, though invisible to our coarse natural senses: in which case the law of gravitation is no more violated than it is when a man turns a somerset. If the `` laws of gravitation, of electricity, of light, and of heat " (2) may be, to a limited extent, modified or suspended by human art, why may not spirits have a similar, though greatly superior power, and exercise it without any breach either of the laws of nature or the principles of causality? Your charge that these laws have a `` purely hypothetical validity " in the estimation of Spiritualists, is directly opposed to the truth; for we believe that all phenomena whatever are in accordance with natural law.

This cry that the laws of nature are contravened if our phenomena are true, has been common for the last thirty-five years. It is the chief ammunition of Mr. Youmans, of the *Popular Science Monthly*, in his war against Spiritualism; and though it has been confuted thousands of times by well-known Spiritualists, such as Robert Chambers, Alfred R. Wallace, Professor De Morgan, and Robert Dale Owen, it is now gravely put forth in your letter as if it were a new and stunning objection.

The man of imperfect science postulates "an inflexible order of nature;" but how does he know that there are not higher laws of nature, which he has not yet discovered, but to which other laws are subordinate? It has been justly said of him, that when he assumes that Nature must do so and so because she has done so and so up to this time, he puts a subjective, metaphysical will behind his physical order of things.

My esteemed correspondent, Alfred Russell Wallace, must be well known to the German readers of Darwin's works as an eminent English naturalist He is also an outspoken Spiritualist. He has treated with his usual acuteness this constantly recurring objection (revived by you) of a contravention of the laws of nature. He says:

"One common fallacy appears to me to run through all the arguments against facts deemed miraculous, when it is asserted that they violate, or invade, or subvert the laws of nature. This is really assuming the very point to be decided, for if the disputed fact did happen, it could only be in accordance with the laws of nature, since the only complete definition of the ' laws of nature ' is, that they are the laws which regulate all phenomena.

" To refuse to admit what in other cases would be absolutely conclusive evidence of a fact, because it cannot be explained by those laws of nature with which we are now acquainted, is really to maintain that we have complete knowledge of those laws, and can determine beforehand what is or is not possible.

" I assert, without fear of contradiction, that whenever the scientific men of any age have denied the facts of investigation on *à priori* grounds, they have always been wrong. . . . When Castallet informed Réaumur that he had reared perfect silkworms from the eggs laid by a virgin moth, the answer was, *Ex nihilo nihil fit;* and the fact was disbelieved.   It was contrary to one of the widest and best established laws of nature; yet it is now universally admitted to be true, and the supposed law ceases to be universal."

You will thus see that your alarm lest the laws of nature should be "done away with," is quite gratuitous. The laws of nature, in her seen as well as her unseen spheres, will probably continue to be as secure and inflexible as they have been hitherto, undisturbed by the anxieties and misconstructions of fallible professors.

You tell us (3) that " the authority of the whole history of science, the totality of all known natural laws," confirm without exception "the presupposition of a universal causality."   This presupposition is made justifiable by Spiritualism; but it is not the authoritative declaration of absolute science.   That one Mind rules in the universe is a legitimate inference from all the science we have thus far attained to; but science cannot assert this inference as a part of itself.   It cannot transcend phenomena and enter the realm of causality, without leaving its own domain, and invading another where it cannot exist as science.   Indeed, your views of a universal causality, "confirmed by the authority of the whole history of science," are quite opposed to the conclusions of the great majority of the scientific naturalists of our day.

Professor Newcomb, one of the leading men of science in America, in an address delivered recently at St. Louis before the American Scientific Association, contradicts, in the following words, your whole statement. He says: " The entire course of nature is a series of mechanical sequences, *from which all interference from outside causation is entirely excluded.*" In this view (which I do not accept), most of the physicists of our day concur.

Even Kant tells us that the idea of cause, and also the

belief that every commencing phenomenon implies the operation of a cause, are merely forms of our understanding, subjective conditions of human thought. You must have been well aware, too, that Hume is far from admitting your assertion. He contends that all we see or know is mere succession, antecedent and consequent; that having seen things in this relation, we associate them together, and imagining that there is some *vinculum* or connection between them, we call the one the cause, and the other the effect. Thus your claim that your views in regard to causation are a part of science does not hold good,—since speculations as to primary causation transcend phenomena which are the limits to which human science is confined.

Your assertion (4) that the eminent naturalists who satisfied themselves of the objectivity and genuineness of the Slade phenomena "announce that causality has a flaw," is an unwarrantable perversion or an erroneous paraphrase of their language, made to suit your own peculiar purpose. The statement falls along with your other assumptions.

You criticise the conditions under which the medial phenomena are produced; but as these conditions can be intelligently judged only by a person long and practically acquainted with the subject, I shall not pause here to consider them. Nor is it necessary for me to analyze your account of your own *séance* with Mr. Slade, at which various "experiments" occurred, concerning which you confess that you cannot "express a conjecture" as to how they were done.

Referring to your own inability to explain the experiments, and to Mr. Slade's inability to disclose the *modus operandi*, you remark:

"What was surprising to me in the matter, however, and what will also surprise you, is that Mr. Slade also refused to give any information of this kind. *He is a medium, he is an experimenter*, and he must therefore know

under what conditions the phenomena have their origin.
He asserts that he knows nothing of them, but that his
relation is a perfectly passive one.   The latter, however, is
plainly untrue, since the phenomena generally appear only
in the *séances* held by him, and also, as a rule, in the order
in which he wishes to produce them."

That you, a philosopher and a man of science, should
venture to discourse upon a great, complex, and momentous subject, occupying at this moment the attention of
millions in all parts of the world, and requiring a great
amount of study and investigation for its proper understanding, — with the very rudiments of which subject, if
we may judge from the baseless vituperation in the preceding paragraph, you are as yet unacquainted, — is indeed a matter of surprise.   You make a medium the
equivalent of an " experimenter."   In this you exalt your
own crude and random theory above the empirical knowledge of all those who have long and faithfully investigated
the subject of mediumship.   A medium is not regarded as
the real "experimenter"; and Slade, if he is a medium,
tells the truth in saying that his relation is a passive one.
Both your reasons for charging him with mendacity are
plainly the promptings of ignorance.   They are frivolous,
and they are erroneous.   One of your reasons is that "the
phenomena generally appear only in the *séances* held by
him."   On the contrary, phenomena, some of them more
surprising than those in his presence, and under conditions
more satisfactory, have been given in America by Watkins,
Powell, Phillips, Mrs. Simpson, and by some private mediums who decline to take money for the exhibition.

Your second reason, namely, that the phenomena appear,
" as a rule, in the order in which he wishes to produce
them," is an assumption which, while it may be true in
what it asserts, is false in what it omits.   The theory is,
that if Slade wishes to produce phenomena in a certain

order, it is because the impressions he gets from his so-called "controls" incline him to choose that order. Your two reasons for charging untruthfulness on him do not stand the first incision of intelligent analysis.

You wind up your abuse of Slade (whose uniform honesty I neither vouch for nor deny) with the remark, that this question of the reality or non-reality of the spiritualistic phenomena would be for you "an extremely painful one," if you "had to regard as excluded every possible explanation of the phenomena in a natural way; in a way which leaves the universal law of causation untouched."

Causation again! Violation of nature again! My dear philosopher, be comforted. The appearance of a spirit in this mundane sphere, if it actually occurs, must be a purely natural fact, since nature embraces all demonstrable phenomena. The "universal law of causation" is no more violated or threatened by such a fact than it is when a balloon goes up in the air, or when a painless surgical operation is performed while the patient is under the effect of chloroform. May it not be that it is because you look through such a haze of mediæval apprehension and dread, that Spiritualism assumes the amorphous aspect, the sinister colors, it does, in your eyes?

You admit, for the sake of argument, that view of Ulrici and of most Spiritualists, which regards the manifesting spirits as those of our deceased fellow-men, who advise us in this way of their survival and their condition after death; and you ask, "What significance have the phenomena then?"

Ulrici, it appears, has ventured the opinion that their significance lies, above all else, in the fact that nothing could more powerfully strengthen our faith in a supreme moral government of the world, nothing more surely counteract the materialism and indifferentism of the time, than the certainty of immortality.

The same view was held by the late I. H. Fichte, of Stuttgard (an illustrious and venerable name!), who anticipated great benefit to the cause of religion and morality from an enlightened Spiritualism.   His words are: "Here in the earth-life we have it in our power to seize our future destination."   And he considered this a very serious revelation at a time when mankind have long since become accustomed to displace their care for the future from their daily routine, as a consideration not affecting their interests.

These anticipations are in full accord with those held by most Spiritualists, and seem to me eminently reasonable and apt.   Imagine a time when generations of well-born children shall be brought up in the confident knowledge of immortality; when the laws of pre-natal and post-natal influence shall be understood and heeded; when a man shall realize that what he thinks and does, he thinks and does for eternity, — and shall be sensible that a cloud of witnesses, the great and good of the past, as well as his own departed relatives and friends, not to speak of the Supreme Intelligence itself, have his inmost thoughts and most secret acts literally within their ken; — and I can conceive of no possible evangel more likely to control a man for good, strengthen the best and most elevating impulses by which he is actuated, and keep him reverently loyal to divine law as expressed in his own organization and the facts of the universe.   What can be more touching and noble than the written prayer of the young prince imperial, slain by the Zulu savages in 1879, and whose father, Louis Napoleon, like himself, was a Spiritualist: "Grant, O God, that my heart may be penetrated with the conviction that those whom I love, and who are deceased, can see all my actions.   Help me that my life shall be worthy of their witness, and my innermost thought shall never make them blush."

From considerations like these you dissent with emphatic

energy. You tell us that Ulrici acknowledges, indeed, that the written communications of the spirits "have a very insignificant content," and that their other performances also seem to be substantially to no purpose; but that he consoles himself with the thought that "*the principle of development will also find its application in the other life*, so that the souls of the dead only gradually attain the highest perfection of knowledge and will."

A doctrine so rational and just, so consistent with all the analogies revealed in psychological investigation, and so reconcilable with all that we can conceive of divine goodness, love, and wisdom, would seem to commend itself to a philosopher of liberal religious proclivities. But you repudiate it as if the spectral aspect of the old vicarious doctrine had interposed to warn you off. You say: "Here, unfortunately, I must oppose your conclusions in the most decided manner. I hold these conclusions to be as false as they are dangerous, and of this I will endeavor to convince you and your readers."

Your endeavor is a most signal failure, made the more manifest by the solemn confidence with which you introduce it. The Spiritual doctrine is in harmony with all the lofty religious thought of the age, even among those who do not recognize Spiritualism. Your own thought is mediæval and retrograde. You begin by charging upon Ulrici the assumption that phenomena, similar to those of Spiritualism, "have never been observed in former times." And you really seem to think that you have made a discovery, of which Spiritualists have been ignorant up to this time, and that you will bring them to confusion by your superior sagacity. But the ignorance is all on your side, since you assume what is contrary to notorious facts.

Instead of supposing that "similar phenomena have never been observed in former times," Spiritualists have from the first maintained, as one of the most important of their credentials, the striking fact that the present phenomena are corroborated and illustrated by those of all past ages. We find them in the mythologies and oracles of the ancients; in the Hebrew and Christian Scriptures; nay, even in the evidences given in Mr. E. B. Tylor's "Primitive Culture," of the universality of the spiritual belief among savage tribes, as far back as history or the knowledge got from prehistoric facts, revealed in geological investigations, can go.

You refer to the history of witchcraft up to the 17th century as if you thought that you were enlightening Spiritualists in regard to the analogy between many of its phenomena and those of the present time. But you will find that the real facts of witchcraft, disengaged from much that was purely chimerical, fancifully subjective, or wantonly false, are accepted by Spiritualists as part of their own phenomena.

In a work,* originally published in 1868, I say : " The annals of the race are full of these phenomena, back to the first dawn of authentic history. They have been interrogated and examined in a different spirit during the last quarter of a century; and that is the only respect in which they can be said to differ from many of the phenomena of witchcraft, necromancy, somnambulism, mesmerism, &c., so long known and disputed."

Blackstone, the great English legal authority (1723–80), says, in his Commentaries : " To deny the possibility, nay, actual existence of witchcraft and sorcery, is at once flatly to contradict the revealed Word of God; . . . and the thing itself is a truth to which every nation in the world hath borne testimony, either by examples seemingly well attested, or by prohibitory laws, which, at least, suppose' the possibility of commerce with evil spirits."

---

* See " Planchette, or the Despair of Science," p. 8. A seventh edition of the work was published by Roberts Brothers, Boston, in 1880.

Mr. Lecky, in his " History of Rationalism" (1864), shows that the wisest men in Europe shared in the belief of the witchcraft phenomena. For hundreds of years no man of any account rejected it. Lord Bacon could not divest himself of it. Shakespeare accepted it, as did the most enlightened of his contemporaries. Glanvil, Henry More, Sir Thomas Browne, and other eminent thinkers, strenuously asserted it.

You refer to these phenomena as " lamentable expressions of a corrupting superstition." A more enlightened acquaintance with well-attested facts would convince you that the superstition was not in the admission of certain objective phenomena, but in the unscientific demonphobia which led men to misinterpret them, to lay a superstitious stress upon the old Hebrew prohibitions, made in ignorance and fear, and to allow the Church to dictate to the Legislature as to the construction to be put on the manifestations. There are " lamentable expressions " of evil in human nature; and there may be " lamentable expressions " of evil among spirits, who are but the continuations of human nature into another stage of being.

And now you and other men of science are repeating the bad work which the priestly power, aided by the civil, did in former times. You are laboring to give the impression that these phenomena are not in the order of nature, and that therefore they must either be repudiated as not occurring, or else regarded with that sort of horror which the idea of the uncanny and the unnatural awakens.

The witchcraft frenzy, bursting beyond the limits of genuine phenomena, led to the grossest falsehoods, the most grotesque exaggerations, and the most merciless persecutions; and this for the simple reason that men, women, and children, who wished to bring an enemy to destruction, or, for some profitable reason, to put him out of the way, found a very simple means by fixing upon him or her the

suspicion of practising witchcraft.   But what chance could
the counterfeit have had if there had not been a basis of
the genuine?

If there had been but a few eminent men in those days,
practically acquainted with the great facts of somnambulism,
mesmerism, and modern Spiritualism, in their purely scientific bearings, they could have arrested the whole terrible
delusion.   And if any such outbreak should occur again,
the men who will appease the public alarm, and eliminate
from the manifestations every element of superstition, would
be, not the doctors and philosophers, who, like yourself,
are now making the outcry that the phenomena violate
natural laws, but the men who have carefully studied and
witnessed them, and who know that they actually occur
under certain abnormal conditions.

You may smile at the thought that any such " delusion "
should prevail in this scientific age ; but you must be imperfectly acquainted with the facts if you do not know that
phenomena in complete analogy with those of witchcraft
have occurred sporadically up to the present time.   In
many families the stone-throwing manifestations, levita-
tions, bell-ringing, the dressing-up of grotesque figures,
mocking messages written independently of human agency,
have occurred under circumstances that bar out the theory
of human fraud.

If you wish to become acquainted with a thoroughly
authenticated history of occurrences indicating the *diablerie*
of modern witchcraft, I would refer you to the account of
those which took place in the house of the Rev. Dr. Phelps,
at Stratford, Conn., from March, 1850, to December, 1851.
You will find a full report of the case in " Modern Spiritualism, by E. Capron," (Boston, 1855,) a work of candor
and ability.   In the year 1850 I had a letter on the subject
from Dr. Phelps himself, and published it in the " Boston
Daily Transcript," which I was editing at the time.   It

fully authenticates the accounts of mysterious writings without human aid, the dressing-up of figures, the movement of objects, the throwing of stones, etc. Dr. Phelps was a man highly respected, sincere, and intelligent. The phenomena were confirmed as supra-human by the most ample testimony. IIis clear and thoroughly-tested facts have never been disproved, and they have been corroborated by many similar occurrences of more recent date.

The "lamentable expressions of a corrupting superstition" were, you must remember, not confined to the lowly and obscure. The leading divines, lawyers, and legislators were under its influence. Their error was not in believing, but in misinterpreting facts. Do you imagine they would have countenanced the atrocities perpetrated on innocent persons, unless they had become convinced, by observation and by testimony, of certain objective phenomena, which in their ignorance and alarm they construed as unnatural? Suddenly a reaction took place. In Boston, several believers publicly underwent penance in church, for their impious and merciless credulity. It was as if the community had awakened all at once from a dreadful nightmare. One day witchcraft seemed a fixed fact, and the next it was spurned and trodden out. Unquestionably, with much that was fanatical and false, much that was true was also stricken from the popular belief. From one extreme men went to the other, and a public opinion adverse to the phenomena, real and spurious, checked the development of mediums for the next century and a half.

You put this question to Ulrici: "What conception must we form of the condition of our deceased fellow-men, if your view is correct?" And you think that he can urge "no material objections" against certain conclusions of your own, the first of which is as follows:

"*Physically* the souls of our dead fall into the bondage of certain living men, the so-called mediums. These mediums are, at present at any rate, not very widely spread, and appear to belong almost exclusively to the American nationality.   At the command of the mediums, the souls execute mechanical performances, which bear throughout the character of purposelessness ; they knock, lift tables and chairs, play harmoniums, &c."

Here is a series of charges, every one of which is, to put it mildly, a mistake :   (1) The spirits are *not* in bondage to the mediums. By what logical process a *medium* can be converted into a *principal*, you do not explain.   (2) The mediums are *not* " almost exclusively " American.   Home, one of the earliest of the famous mediums, was a Scotchman ; Mr. Williams, Mr. Eglinton, Miss Florence Cook, Miss Wood, Mrs. Guppy, Mr. Duguid, Mrs. Esperance, Dr. Monck, and some twenty others of note, are all English or Scotch.   (3) The souls do *not*, " at the command of the mediums," execute mechanical performances.   The phenomena are *not* producible at the will of the medium. (4) The performances do *not* " bear throughout the character of purposelessness."

You say that to knock or move a table is a " purposeless " act. Suppose you were shut up in an enclosure from which you could not escape, and wished to make it known to the outside world of your friends that you were still alive ; — would it be so very " purposeless " an act for you to try by knocks or movements to make the fact of your existence known? The spirit, limited to certain conditions, sees that the friends he has left behind on earth believe that death is the end of being. Would any knock, movement, or musical sound, by which he could try to dispel the delusion, be a " purposeless " or undignified act? George Herbert tells us that he who " sweeps a room," in accordance with the divine sense of duty, dignifies the act. May not the *motive* transfigure the character of the spirit's humble attempt to gain recognition by a knock or the moving of a table?

The independent movement may be a very trivial act in itself, but when it is done without the application of any known human or mechanical force, it becomes so important in the eyes of Faraday, Haeckel, Youmans, and other physicists, as to assume the character of a miracle, which they must repudiate. Can an incredible act be a wholly purposeless act?

Your whole letter illustrates the importance of studying a subject thoroughly before undertaking to pronounce upon it. You say: "The assumption that the beings of some other world unknown to us would naturally resemble us, not only in their bodily constitution, but also in their dress, has to me only a very slight probability." Slight or not, your notions of the probable must give way to facts. The spirits or angels of the Bible come in the form of human beings, suitably clad; and the modern materialization phenomena show that spirits can often create for themselves some characteristic or emblematic garb, or at least what appears such to human senses. In nearly all the best authenticated accounts of apparitions, the spirit has come robed either in garments similar to those of the earth-life, or in "raiment shining, exceeding white as snow; so as no fuller on earth can white them."

If you had ever given a day's faithful study to the subject, you would have learned that the forms and the clothing, in which the materializing spirits appear, are assumed transiently, often for the simple purpose of identification. They are not regarded as the abiding forms and clothing of the spirit. You make merry over the notion that a male spirit should appear with a foot deformed by a tight shoe; and you facetiously remark: "The thought that hard-hearted shoemakers might, even in the next world, continue their attempts to improve the anatomical structure of our feet, gives me great uneasiness."

Such facetiousness can amuse only the ignorant; for it

is founded on a gross, unspiritual misconception. Admit that a spirit can present a palpable and tangible representation of the earth-body, or of any part of it as it was at a certain period of its mortal existence : it does not follow that the spirit is itself "transformed into matter," as you wildly imagine.

Of the spiritual body, the Rev. Joseph Cook (who is not a Spiritualist), remarks : "It is a body, which apparently makes nothing of passing through what we call ordinary matter. Our Lord had that body after his resurrection. He appeared suddenly in the midst of his disciples, although the doors were shut. . . . . We must not forget that this conclusion is proclaimed in the name of the philosophy of the severest sort. The verdict is scientific ; it happens also to be biblical."

Because it was Christ's spiritual body that passed into the room with shut doors, it does not follow that it was his spiritual body which became visible to his disciples. He had, as a spirit, the power of improvising and externalizing a material representation of the earth-body with its wounds. The history of modern Spiritualism is full of similar phenomena. Christ came to show that death is a delusion, and that man is potentially a man still, after the dissolution of all that is mortal of him.

Another spirit wishes to show that he has intelligence ; that his affections are unchanged ; that he has not lost his love of music. So he sends loving messages ; so he plays on the harmonium a tune, known, perhaps, as his favorite, to some one present. Shall we condemn it as a purposeless act? You say :

" The *moral* condition of the souls seems to be relatively the most favorable. According to all the evidence, the character of harmlessness cannot be denied them. It shows itself particularly in the fact that they hold it to be necessary to make excuses for proceedings of a somewhat brutal nature, in case of becoming guilty of such — as, for instance, the destruction of a bed-screen, with a politeness which, in a ghost, is certainly deserving of acknowledgment. This harmlessness, therefore, gives us a right to expect something good of their other moral qualities, concerning which nothing particular is known."

Upon this you remark: "Pardon me if I seem to joke." You may rest assured that no apology is needed; your jocular allusions are of so mild and harmless a quality, that their point is not felt by any one versed in Spiritualism. A bed-screen was destroyed, and the operating forces (to which you choose to give the name of *ghosts*) politely made excuses. "This harmlessness," you say, gives you "a right to expect something good of their other moral qualities, *concerning which nothing particular is known.*" Known by *yourself*, — you should have added. The "other moral qualities" of the supposed spirits have been expressed in a multiplicity of forms. As the theory is that there are all grades of good and bad, stupid and intelligent, in spirit-life as well as in this, we get just what we ought to expect, if our expectations are based on well-established facts.

You charge Ulrici with "suddenly throwing overboard all principles of scientific investigation, in order to find in the revelations of rapping spirits the means of supplement-ing our insight into the order of the world;" and you ask, in your consternation, "Whence is the scientific investi-gator to get courage and perseverance for his work, if the laws of nature, according to the prospect which you open, are approaching a point where they shall be done away with?"

I have already answered your constantly-recurring ques-tion on this point. Let me answer it again, since it ex-presses the great objection of those scientific specialists, who become very unscientific the moment the subject of Spiritualism comes up. From the connection of the phe-

nomena with physiological conditions, they appear to be as
purely a part of nature as the phenomena of the living
organism. When an instrument is played on without human
agency, when a medium is lifted to the ceiling, when independent writing is produced under conditions without a
flaw, when objects are independently moved from place to
place in broad daylight, when human forms appear palpably,—the manifestations have their objective as well as
their subjective side. They are as much entitled to scientific
scrutiny as any other phenomena in nature ; and to say that
they are supernatural, is plainly to prejudge the question
ignorantly.

The reputation of the late Baden Powell (1796–1850)
of England, is perhaps not unknown to you. He was
Savilian professor of geometry at Oxford, and a profoundly
scientific thinker. He believed that spiritual phenomena
would be recognized as a part of the domain of nature, and
become a subject for philosophic investigation. His prediction has been already verified, as the writings of Wallace,
Varley, Crookes, Fichte, Franz Hoffman, Zöllner, Boutlerof, Hare, Wagner, and other men of science, amply show.
Referring to supersensual phenomena, Powell says : " In
such cases, science has not yet advanced to any generaliza-
tions ; results only are presented, which have not as yet
been traced to laws ; yet no inductive inquirer for a moment
doubts that these classes of phenomena are *all really connected by some great principle of order.* If, then, some
peculiar manifestations should appear of a more extraordinary character, still less apparently reducible to any known
principles, *it could not be doubted by any philosophic mind
that they were in reality harmonious and conspiring parts of
some higher series of causes as yet undiscovered.* The most
formidable outstanding apparent anomalies will, at some
future time, undoubtedly be found to merge in great and
harmonious laws, the connection will be fully made out,

and the claims of order, continuity, and analogy, eventually vindicated."

This is the large and liberal scientific view. Let it assuage your alarm, my dear professor. It is a full and conclusive reply to the objections of supernaturalism, violation of nature's laws, etc., brought by yourself, and by many before you, who passed sentence on Spiritualism before they had studied it.

You say, that " the worst enemy of morality has always been superstition." Most true. But whence came the superstition during the witchcraft craze of the sixteenth and seventeenth centuries? It was a superstition, I repeat, that affected eminent divines like Mather, judges like Sewall, and magistrates like Sir William Phipps : inciting them to countenance the persecutions with which persons suspected of witchcraft were visited. The superstition sprang from an ignorant misconstruction of actual phenomena, and was encouraged by the bibliolatry, the bigotry, and the fear influencing the action of priests and their dupes. In ostracising these now common phenomena as unnatural or supernatural, you and your co-workers are doing what you can to discourage a scientific investigation into their origin. To the developments of the present day you are opposing the same hindrances and superstitions which prevented a thoroughly scientific inquiry into the witchcraft manifestations. You would stop what you call the " spiritualistic nuisances " prevailing in America ; and by this you do not mean that you would stop the abuses and the credulities, springing from an unscientific manner of dealing with the facts, but the facts themselves. You would repudiate the whole great inquiry as something contrary to the order of nature and the laws of Divine Causation. Possibly you and your helpers may succeed in checking the phenomena, and in putting off their investigation for another century ; but I am encouraged by the signs of the times to believe that you

will be defeated.   The Sibyl presents her books anew.
Shall we reject them all?

The following passage from your letter is somewhat
obscure and equivocal ; but I will try to do it justice :

" The moral barbarism produced in its time by the belief
in witchcraft, would have been precisely the same if there
had been real witches.   *We can, therefore, leave the question
entirely alone, whether or not you have ground to believe in
the Spiritualistic phenomena.*   We can content ourselves
with considering the question, whether the objects of your
belief show the characteristic signs which we find in those
objects of belief which, according to the testimony of history and of social psychology, we must call prejudicial to
the moral development of man.   This question, after the
intimate relation which we have shown to exist between
spiritualism and the most corrupt forms of so-called superstition, can only be answered in the affirmative."

What if some disbeliever in Christianity, referring to the
Inquisition, or to the atrocities of Philip II. of Spain, all
instituted in the interests of religion, — or to the obscenities
of the Anabaptists and other sects, — should say : " The
moral barbarism produced in its time by the belief in
Christianity. would have been precisely the same if Christianity had been true.   We can, therefore, leave the question of the truth of Christianity entirely alone.   We can
content ourselves with asking, Was it found prejudicial to
the moral development of man?   This question can only be
answered in the affirmative."

Plausible as this may seem, would it not be repudiated
by Christians generally as a view narrow and unjust?
Because the phenomena of witchcraft, regarded from the
standpoint of ignorance and religious terror, were productive of evil, does it follow that they would not be productive of good, because productive of knowledge. if regarded
and studied with scientific coolness and philosophic precision, abstracted from all superstition, all religious super-

fluity, all chimerical dread of a violation of nature's order?

Among the "demoralizing influences" of Spiritualism, you instance "the danger of estrangement from earnest work, devoted to the service of science or of a practical calling." But the theory is, that after a proper amount of investigation and discussion by competent persons, the facts of Spiritualism will be as well understood and as freely admitted as the facts of chemistry or anatomy ; that coming generations will be educated in a knowledge of the facts. If this view is correct, it will only be a few specialists with a taste for the study, who will be "estranged from earnest work" in other directions. Your alarm here, too, is wholly supererogatory.

You say : "Of far greater importance are the unworthy conceptions of the condition of the spirit after death, which these phenomena awaken, and which find their analogy only in the so-called *animism* of the most degraded races." Twelve lines farther on you remark :

"Astonishingly, however, you see in Spiritualism nothing less than a contrivance of Providence for counteracting the materialism of the present. This is to me the most incomprehensible part of your essay. I see in Spiritualism, on the contrary, a sign of the materialism and the barbarism of our time. From early times, as you well know, materialism has had two forms ; the one denies the spiritual, the other transforms it into matter. The latter form is the older. From the *animism* of the popular mythologies, it passes into philosophy, in order to be by the latter gradually overcome. As civilized barbarism can experience relapses into all forms of primitive conditions, so it is not spared from this also. That, in your person, philosophy too has shared in this relapse, I count most melancholy."

The essential question is not, What does this or that man, however eminent, imagine will be the effects? — but, Is it a fact of nature? If that is once settled in the affirmative, the true wisdom is to leave the results to Providence.

You assume that it is " an unworthy conception of the condition of the spirit after death," to suppose that it may manifest many of the low traits of character which it manifested in the earth-life. I assume that the identity of the individual would not be preserved, unless this were not only possible but probable. But the question is not, Are these things esthetically agreeable? but, Are they true?

You are grieved because eminent men see in these phenomena what you are pleased to call " a contrivance of Providence for counteracting the materialism of the present." What is there irreverent or irrational in the opinion? Just as a materialistic science dreamed it was having things its own way,—driving God and Spirit out of men's minds, and educating a generation of unbelievers in regard to a future life and the realities of the unseen world,—just at this critical moment, when faith in aught but matter and motion seemed to be dying out of the hearts of men,—up starts this ill-favored, this perplexing and exasperating Spiritualism — this marplot — this *enfant terrible* — and attracts, I know not how many, deserters from the ranks of a Sadducean materialism. It has already carried the full assurance of immortality to millions of minds all over the world. It has converted many from the direst unbelief; and in thirty-three years it has permeated humanity to an extent unparalleled in the history of creeds. If there are such beings as spirits, is it so very incredible that the present phenomena have been providentially permitted?

You see in Spiritualism " a sign of the materialism and barbarism of our times." Here again the essential question is, Are the phenomena true? If so, the scientific recognition of them is simply a sign of the advancing intelligence of our times. The facts appeal to different minds in different ways, according to our state of receptivity. That a mischievous construction is put on them by many, is merely to say that every great gift or truth from God may be misconstrued or abused. The vine is a divine gift, but from its fruit a maddening beverage may be distilled. That a good and profitable construction is put on the phenomena by many, has been proved by their changed lives and characters, and by their rising to a comprehension of the immense significance of an immortal life.

What you call "the *animism*** of the popular mythologies," is simply a belief in the objectivity of apparitions; which, as an apparition is *something that appears*, would seem to be a not wholly unreasonable theory. Transferred to our own day, in Europe and America, the belief becomes, in your opinion, "civilized barbarism." Now, if you had studied with proper attention the subject in regard to which you affect an oracular tone, you would have learned that this same *animism*, with the variations attributable to different intellectual grades, permeates the entire pneumatology of the Hebrew and Christian Scriptures; that it was held and illustrated in his own person by Christ; believed in by his apostles, and by John the Revelator; and that it was most distinctly the faith of the early Christian fathers, down to the fifth century, as the writings of Tertullian, Origen, and others indicate.

What these "degraded races," of whose animism you have such a horror, really believed, in respect to immortality, was clearly based on certain objective facts, very common in our own day, and which our new psycho-physical science is destined to study and co-ordinate: — facts tending to show that the spirit is the man himself; that his personality is permanent. But that new organisms may be evolved as adaptations to the progressive stages of his existence is, perhaps, among the possibilities.

If you choose, like some of the English atheists, Leslie

---

* A word appropriated by Mr. E. B. Tylor, in his "Primitive Culture," to express the recognition, throughout all the races of mankind, of the soul as a distinct entity.

Stephen, the late Professor Clifford, and others, to denounce this belief as merely "a grosser sort of materialism," you are simply giving a bad name to what the great seers of all the ages have intuitively accepted. There is nothing in this belief which the most advanced science can stamp as unscientific. It violates no principle of chemistry, mechanics, or physics generally. The hypothesis of a supersensual organism, developed *pari-passu* with the physical, and acting between it and the life inflowing from the Divine Source of all things, is not only a purely rational conception, but one corroborated by innumerable facts.

The pneumatology of Spiritualism, like that of the Bible, the North American Indians, and other "degraded races," teaches us that apparitions of deceased persons may be (1) either those visible only to the spiritual senses of the medium or seer; or (2) those that are visible to the normal senses of a promiscuous assemblage, like that which saw Christ enter the room with closed doors. In both cases, the question whether the apparition is composed of what our human senses recognize as matter, is left open. The fact that an apparition may be not only visible but tangible would seem to justify the belief that the spirit has power to use some grade of evanescent materiality in presenting a simulacrum of its earth-body. It is not at all likely that the "degraded races" trouble themselves with the distinction between material substance and spiritual substance. But what they can see and touch they believe in as something having form and substance of some kind, and as occupying space. And in this they are plainly right—however it may affect you as "materialism."

In regard to the constituent nature of the so-called spiritual body we do not presume to dogmatize. Whether mind is an organism or the result of an organism, is not the question. All that Spiritualism teaches on the subject is that the spirit or soul is not an abstract, thinking principle, but the accompaniment .or expression of a distinct substance and form, dwelling in the physical body, and independent of it when that body dies.

The act of clairvoyance involves the existence of a spiritual faculty inhering in something distinct from gross, visible matter. If man is ever to exist after the dissolution of the terrestrial body, then must he be already, in his terrestrial life, a spirit though circumscribed by organs adapting him to it; and he should be able to manifest, under certain conditions, foregleams of his spiritual and immortal nature. That he does this we have the proofs.

Whether matter and spirit are distinct in their ultimate essence is a question the solution of which does not affect the facts on which the Spiritual theory is grounded. But when you charge it upon Spiritualism that it " transforms the Spiritual into matter," you again misrepresent the fact. On the contrary, it makes mind, Spirit, the Master of matter, exercising a power over it so inconceivable to our finite faculties, that Zöllner has to resort to Kant's hard hypothesis of a fifth dimension in space in order to bring the seeming miracle within the sphere of an obscure scientific solution.

That which underlies both matter and spirit, and is their substance, " fulgurates " forth, or flows forth, as Leibnitz and Swedenborg both teach, from the Divine Substance; but we do not confound the Spiritual principle which controls matter with matter itself; nor do we confound the Spirit-body with the Spirit itself.

You must be aware that the two greatest philosophers that Germany has produced, Leibnitz and Kant, were to a great extent sharers in the belief which you account as " most melancholy." Leibnitz insisted that in regard to every finite intelligence, the soul is necessarily always clothed with a material body, more or less attenuated, — (pure animism of the " degraded races !") ; — and that it finds in its spiritual body of the Pauline type fresh organs of consciousness. Kant predicted that there will come a day when it will be demonstrated that there is "a communion actual and indissoluble" between the world of spirits and the human soul throughout its terrestrial existence. (The animism of the lower races again !) It is true that Kant speaks of spirits in this connection as "immaterial natures ;" but that does not conflict with the application of the notion that they may require substantial organisms through which to express such natures, and realize the wealth of God's universe, visible and invisible. I. H. Fichte, shortly before he died, in 1879, wrote of our phenomena : "Belief in the immortality of the soul is ratified by these evidences of psychical experience."

Augustine (A. D. 430) and Thomas Aquinas (A. D. 1274) both wrote in favor of the soul's immateriality ; but the former postulated a subtile corporeal substance, the germ or equivalent of a body like that, for belief in which you charge the "degraded races" with "animism." Aquinas, deriving his doctrine from the Neo-Platonists, teaches that there are immaterial forms (*formæ separatæ*), and that these are individualized by themselves, since they have no need, for their existence, of a form-receiving substratum. The fallacy of this view is clearly exposed by Duns Scotus, and some of the earlier opponents of Thomas.

It was not till his theory was taught by Descartes (1640) that it had much influence on the popular belief. Then the Pauline doctrine of a spiritual body being superseded largely in the minds of scholars, the common belief became "small by degrees" till it subsided into a vacuum of skepticism, justifying this remark by Mr. W. R. Greg in regard to the doctrine of immortality : "Let it rest in the vague, if you would have it rest unshaken."

Is it because we Spiritualists do not allow it to "*rest in the vague,*" but re-assert the rational Pauline doctrine, and bring it forward as an inference of science, that you call its adoption by such philosophers as I. H. Fichte, Franz Hoffman, and others, a " relapse "?

Tylor, in his " Primitive Culture," tells us that the " animism of the degraded races," into which you fear we are " relapsing," was the conception of an " apparition-soul or ghost-soul, its substance impalpable and invisible." Are we, then, quite sure, that even in their notions of the soul's organism in a future life, they were so " grossly materialistic " as you charge them with being?

Professor Müller tells us that even " the same people who believed in fetiches cherished at the same time very pure, very exalted, very true sentiments of the Deity." He says: " We may consider ourselves safe against the fetich-worship of the poor negroes; but there are few of us, if any, who have not their own fetiches, or their own idols, whether in their churches or in their hearts." He assures us that no tribe or nation has yet been met with, destitute of belief in higher beings than man.

What you call " the unworthy conceptions of the condition of the spirit after death" attach no more to Spiritualism than to any other form of belief in a future state. An intelligence claiming to be that of a returned spirit, being asked if life in the spirit-world was at all analogous to life in this, replied: " Somewhat;" and added: " We live more in the ideal." Now that we should carry our best ideals with us, and be affected thereby, it is perfectly rational to suppose, if we are to preserve our identity unimpaired, Spiritualism teaches that each one gravitates where he belongs; that we reap as we sow; that the controlling affections, tastes, and acts of this life affect our future condition; or, in the words of the venerable I. H. Fichte, " The future life is a continuation of the present, and will be affected by our experiences and our prevailing thoughts and affections here." This you call "an un-worthy conception." To my mind it is the worthiest possible conception, for the simple reason that it is the most consistent, rational, and just, as well as a conception the most analogous with our present mental or psychical constitution.

The North American Indian's idea of an Elysium is that of a grand hunting-ground. Possibly it is just as rational as the idea, held by certain Christians, that heaven is a place where the elect shall eternally strike golden harps to the praise of the Triune Being, or lie on "Immanuel's bosom." But it is not a mere conception or erroneous speculation that is to largely affect our future condition; it is the real dominant love that we have made a part of our innermost nature, and which is likely to cling to us until, according to the analogies of this present life, we can, by our own force of will and of habit, aided perhaps by influences from friendly spirits or from the Fountain of all grace and truth, cast it off for something higher and better. For Spiritualism does not hold that the mistakes and evils of this life are to be eternally irreparable, or that God is the keeper of an everlasting insane asylum.

You think it "most pernicious" that the "Spiritualistic system" should make men, "of, at the very least, most ordinary intellectual and spiritual endowments, the bearers of *supernatural* powers, thereby sealing them as the chosen instruments of Providence."

Ah, my dear sir, it would seem that Providence does not always work according to our poor finite notions of what is most fit. We have somewhat higher authority than yours or mine for believing that "the foolishness of God is wiser than men; and the weakness of God is stronger than men;" that "God hath chosen the foolish things of the world to confound the wise; and God hath chosen the weak things of the world to confound the things which are mighty; and base things of the world, and things which are despised, hath God chosen, *yea*, and things which are not, to bring to naught things that are; that no flesh should glory in his presence."

You speak of "spiritual endowments," and it is evident that you mean by the phrase what we understand by *spirit-ual-mindedness*. If you had acquainted yourself with the phenomena before trying to discredit them, you would have learned that medial sensitiveness to effects from supposed spirits does not depend on the moral or intellectual superiority of the medium over other men; that some of the most powerful mediums are the least entitled to the credit of being "spiritually-minded;" that they are often persons as readily swayed by bad influences, by coarse sensual appetites, as by good and pure, and that the instances are rare in which a medium for certain objective phenomena is at the same time a philosopher and a saint.

All this may seem quite wrong to you and to me. It would perhaps be much more convincing if a philosopher and man of character like yourself should be selected as the instrument of these phenomena, rather than a man like Henry Slade, who knows little or nothing of "Causation," or "the Conservation of Energy." That such a person should be medially endowed, and you, the author of "Axioms of Physics," should not be qualified, by the development of some occult faculty in your nature, to read what is written on a tightly-folded pellet, or to get direct writing on a locked slate, is indeed hard to explain. It looks as if Providence were unacquainted with your reputation in Leipzig. How we can reconcile this with the attribute of omniscience I do not see any better than you.

What you call the "materialization of ghosts" is an offence to you. The phenomenon would seem to be quite analogous with that related of Christ, where, after his crucifixion, he entered the room with closed doors, and showed the wounds in his side to the doubting disciple, just as "materializing spirits" now exhibit the personal deformities which marked their earthly bodies,—and all for the single purpose of identification.   That a spirit should have such a power over matter as to be able to extemporize a visible and palpable *simulacrum* of any part of its earthly form, would seem to exalt rather than belittle our conception of the power of spirits.   Will you explain why the Spiritualism that attributes such a conditioned power to a finite spirit, is any more "grossly materialistic" than the theology which ascribes to the Infinite Spirit an unconditioned power over all material things?

The very fact that the medium cannot command at pleasure, and for the purpose of gain, the influences through which the phenomena take place, is a full explanation of the conscious frauds to which he may sometimes resort. The medium does not command the spirit; it is the supposed spirit, who voluntarily comes to produce certain effects which may satisfy the observer that an intelligent force, not always animating a visible body, is at work.

The paramount question, according to your estimate, is not whether the phenomena are real, undeniable facts, "divine disclosures,"—but whether they are supposed by philosophers like yourself to be "prejudicial" to our social welfare.   Truly this would seem to be an attitude of mind hardly favorable to the discussion of the scientific claims of Spiritualism.   Ought any persistent fact of the cosmos to be ignored because, in our human weakness, we may regard it as "prejudicial" to some interest of our own?   Shall we place our own judgment in the matter above that of the Author of Nature?   "Shall mortal man be more just than God?   Shall a man be more pure than his Maker?"   One would think that the very possibility of injury from a fact of nature ought to incite a generous lover of his race to a most thorough investigation.   Is it not the glory of real science that it is impartial and neutral; that it asks not whether a phenomenon is "prejudicial" or beneficial, but works for the truth, though the heavens fall?

You say, "We can leave the question entirely alone" whether there is "a ground for belief" in our phenomena. These words clearly embody your thought; and that thought is not scientific but jesuitical.

Perhaps you will reply, that admitting our phenomena to be true, we are not justified in drawing from them the inference we do. But what we ask is, not that you shall admit our inferences, but our facts. The inferences can take care of themselves. But here, too, you would block the progress of science. The axioms on which all science rests are inferences. In the words of the late Thomas M. Herbert, "All science and human life would be impossible unless we accepted the deliverance of consciousness *when it carries us beyond phenomena.* . . . . . Science transcends phenomena at every step; the whole fabric of human knowledge would collapse, unless the testimony of consciousness was accepted to facts not found amongst phenomena, *but inferred from them.*"

We are forced every day to accept inferences relating to what transcends phenomena, if we are to recognize the past history of the world, or anything externally presented to us. Phenomena, then, and conceptions derived from them — i. e., inferences, — are all that we can know directly, and both are but "symbols of inaccessible realities."

In regard to the direct writing of supposed spirits, you remark: "Intellectually the soul falls into a condition which, so far as we can conclude from the character of the writing upon slates, can only be described as lamentable. These writings belong throughout to the domain of higher or lower stupidity, chiefly lower — i. e., they are absolutely without sense."

The mischiefs from Spiritualism, like those from witchcraft, arise, as I have already asserted, from a misinterpretation of the facts. The novice, naturally excited by the transcendent character of the phenomena, forms an exaggerated estimate of the wisdom and reliability of those who have passed from this into the next stage of being. Shakspeare, who was well acquainted with the traditional demonology of his day, makes Hamlet at first mistrust the spirit he has seen, as one who is abusing him to damn him. The doubt was apt and proper. When we have learned to regard spirits not as ghastly monstrosities outside of nature, but as our human fellow-beings, changed only through their relations to a new and untried sphere of life, we may possibly shake off these injurious misconceptions.

One of the great lessons that Spiritualism has to teach, is that death makes no instant change in the moral or intellectual condition of man. The bearings of this knowledge on human morality are obvious. The fool will not at once become a sage, nor the clown a gentleman, nor the thief an honest man. Each will talk, and feel, and act very much as he did on earth.

But your remark as to the direct writings on slates is an error. I have had a good deal of experience in them, and on no one occasion have I received a message that could be called stupid. They have been apt and well-written replies to general questions, and though often unsatisfactory in withholding clear proofs of identity, they have frequently indicated an intelligence far beyond that of the medium. Writings in languages unknown to him are often got. I have related elsewhere the experience of Mr. Timayenis, the Greek, and of Mr. Giles B. Stebbins. Such instances are not unfrequent. There are numerous facts that contradict the theory that the direct writing comes *always* from the mind of the medium. That it may sometimes be colored by medial impressions, is probable. To assert in a general way that these pneumatographic communications are " absolutely without sense" is a declaration without sense, because without truth. Supposing your assertion to be true, how would you explain the fact, without classing the mediums themselves (to whom, I suppose, you would credit the *tricks*) as belonging to "the domain of higher or lower stupidity"? This would be notoriously contrary to the truth.

When communications come indirectly through mediums, and signed with the name of some eminent person, it is true that they often belie the assumption by the style. The theory that there are impostors in the spirit-world as well as in this, is consistent with all the facts of pneumatology throughout the ages.

But the intellectual state of the medium may sometimes be in fault. Centuries ago Plutarch, who was well acquainted with supersensual phenomena, remarked that "the greatest number of Apollo's oracles were, in respect both to metre and expression, tasteless and full of errors." The same remark applies to nearly all the modern medial poetry. But Plutarch did not question the spiritual derivation of certain oracles because of their faulty style. One of the characters of the dialogue, in which he discusses the subject, is made to say: "Voice and sound, expression and metre, do not belong to Apollo, but to the prophetess; he only inspires her with the images and conceptions, and inflames her soul so that it can see the future."

Some few of the psychographic communications have been worthy of the literary powers of a Fénélon, a Channing, or even a Wundt. The instances may be rare; but not more so than instances of eminent genius are rare among human beings in this life.

Let me come to the last of your objections. You tell us that Spiritualism is a superstition; and you add:

"Superstition defies every opposition and attack. Driven from one position, it is at once ready in another. It were almost chimerical to hope that science will ever completely root it out. Nothing could darken such a hope more than the appearance of superstition in scientific circles themselves. Science, striking off one head from the monstrous hydra, is obliged to see a new one start out in another place, a head which even assumes her own face."

Now, sir, when you give us to understand that a fact of nature ought not to be investigated because it may prove "prejudicial" to human welfare, does the superstition lie on your side, or on that of those who, reverently believing that all the operations of nature have a divine meaning, are willing to give their best energies to the investigation of the truth? You warn us off from a scientific study of certain phenomena, and in the same breath you tell us that Science "must cope with Modern Superstition."

Cope with it, how? Unscientifically? By refusing to investigate the grounds of what you call a superstition? Such is the strange inconsistency suggested by your language! Nay, you go further. You insinuate that well-known phenomena, which have not been scientifically discredited after thirty-three years of testing, though quite inexplicable to yourself, will *probably* turn out to be mere juggling tricks. You bring against a well-tested medium charges of mendacity and imposture, founded wholly on an ignorance of the history and nature of medial manifestations. Upon the good faith of the " court-artist," Bellachini, you cast an aspersion because he manfully confessed he could detect no sleight-of-hand trick in the phenomena through Slade.

Before you can rule out Spiritualism as a non-scientific question, you must prove that our two basic facts of clairvoyance and direct writing are not established. This it is impossible for you to do. You yourself have confessed your inability to explain them, and your suggestion of jugglery is merely the exploded superstition of the last thirty-three years. There is now daily testimony of the most unimpeachable kind to the occurrence of these phenomena under various conditions, and in various forms. While I write this paragraph, I take up a paper that came to me by mail an hour ago, and find in it a communication from Mr. S. B. Nichols, of 467 Waverly Avenue, Brooklyn, N. Y., a careful observer and a gentleman long known to me by reputation, in which he tells us of his visit, July 14, 1880, to Mr. A. Phillips, at 133 East 36th Street, New York city. "I found," he says, " a young man of some twenty-five summers, prepossessing in appearance, who said that he could guarantee nothing. Sometimes there were failures under the best conditions. I did not make myself known, and he had no means of knowing whether I was a believer or a skeptic."

Mr. Nichols got the direct writing several times on clean slates, and, as Guldenstubbé did on paper, without the use of a pencil. He says: " The medium did not touch the slates after they had been placed in position. When the raps were heard, I opened the slates and found written upon one of them in a legible hand : ' No doubt you think this easily accomplished. You just try it, and you will find out.'"

Mr. Nichols bought two large slates of his own, and of the experiment with these he says :

" I placed my own double slate on the shelf to the table ; also the medium's small slates on the top of mine. On my own slate was written, 'If you were alone, we can come. JAMES.' On the small slates was written, ' If you will sit alone for a little while each evening, we will make ourselves manifest. I am MARTHA.'

" I next put a clean, whole sheet of commercial note-paper between my own slates, and put it on the shelf to the table, and my foot upon it. While the writing was being done I could feel the vibrations distinctly on the inside of this sheet of paper, without pencil crumb, or anything that could scratch or make a mark. On the paper or slates was written :

" 'Would that I had the power to give you further evidences. JAMES NICHOLS.'

" During these various experiments, the medium was walking about the room, and did not touch my slates unless in my presence, and then only casually. Three of the names were of persons who once lived here in this mortal life, and have passed to the other world. If this writing was not produced by a conscious individuality disembodied, whence the power? And whence the individuality?"

Scarcely had I read the above account, than, turning to another column of the paper, I read the following statement by a writer (not a Spiritualist), taken from the *Denver* (Colorado) *Daily News* of July, 1880. The genuineness of the phenomena through Mrs. A. R. Simpson, to whom he refers, had been previously tested repeatedly by personal friends of my own in Chicago:

" Mrs. Simpson handed two slates to the reporter, also a needle and some thread, then leaving the room, requested him to sew the two slates together through the binding on the border. This was done effectually, the two slates being securely sewed together, and the outsides marked to show that they could not possibly be separated without the fact being known. After a few seconds, during which the writer never let go of the slates, he was requested to cut them apart. When this was done, writing was found upon the inside slate, in answer to a question that had been put in the usual way, by writing, and folding it up in a paper."

In this double experiment there was manifested not only direct writing, but the power of reading what was written on a paper, folded so that by no means known to physical science could it be read. Here was a double guaranty of genuineness. Nothing could have been written beforehand by some occult chemical means on the slate; for the writing was in answer to a question written on the spot by the sitter, and the paper was folded so that no writing on it could be read by human eyesight. The clairvoyance was proved by the answer on the slate, and the direct writing was proved not only by the conditions, but by its being in reply to what was contained in a paper not yet unfolded.

The San Francisco *Sunday Chronicle* of September, 1879, says that Mrs. E. W. Lennett, at 817 Bush Street, in that city, is a remarkable medium for independent slate-writing. It tells us that a skeptic recently took to her a covered, double slate, joined by hinges, put on one of the inside surfaces, with his own hand, a bit of slate-pencil, folded the slates together, and held them with both hands. The medium, without even stopping the conversation in which she was engaged, also took hold of the slate with one hand, and immediately the pencil could be heard scratching over the surface of the slate within. When the pencil ceased, and the slate was opened, the entire side of one slate was filled with writing in a plain, bold hand, in English, while the other was partially filled with writing in French, a language the medium is entirely unacquainted with, but which the gentleman in question thoroughly understood. As a still further test, the medium gave him the slate to hold in his own hands, *without her being in contact with it in any way*, when the result was the same as before, the slate being filled with writing.

Will you say that all this host of witnesses are fooled, or that they lie? A simple experiment of your own would soon prove to you that you were in just the same predicament — for your honesty would force you, in spite of your bitter prejudices, to testify to the truth.

Spiritualism, even if true, you think ought to be dismissed from scientific consideration as immoral in its tendency. It is not necessary for me here to discuss the question, whether Spiritualism, being a cosmical fact, is moral or not in its tendency. I should as soon think of questioning the morality of the interstellar ether, or of the principle of gravitation. "Truth before all things," should be the motto of the man of science. Yet your objection, impertinent as it is, is a common one; and we often hear the question put in regard to Spiritualism, "What is the use of it?"

The questions, "What is the use of the human race?" "What is the use of the universe?" would be quite as much to the purpose. If falsehood and depravity are manifested by spirits, so they are by the whole human family. If incitements to evil come from the spirit-world, so they do from this. The only question for science to settle is, Do these claimed phenomena occur? And in failing to place this as the scientific limit to your argument, you show that you are an untrustworthy guide on a subject which you affect to treat from the scientific point of view.

If our phenomena are destined to change the notions of scientific men as to the constitution of matter, or as to a seeming infraction of laws which may be subject to a hitherto unrecognized spiritual law, then you must accommodate your notions to the facts, and not think to get rid of the latter by crying out against them as interruptions of the sequences of nature.

If these apparent interruptions are permitted by the great Orderer, let us summon the faith that will enable us to see in them a dispensation nothing less than divine. No matter how low, how distasteful, or how apparently immoral they may seem to our finite and unprepared minds, let us be sure they mean something for our good which it is our business to find out, however difficult the problem may seem at first. It is the absence of a wise faith in God and nature, which prompts these despairing cries of a violation of natural law, or of a loosening of moral restrictions. Order and law prevail in all that may seem chaotic to your distorted view of the spirit-world; and your fears that all is going to the bad, if Spiritualism is allowed to vindicate its claims to scientific attention, are chimerical and gratuitous, if not blasphemous.

The aim of the philosophy of Ulrici is " to demonstrate on the basis of facts that to the soul, in contradistinction to nature, not simply *independent existence*, but also the supremacy belongs, both of right and in fact." Can you wonder then that he welcomed the facts of Spiritualism, and, seeing the gravity of the testimony, asked for it a scientific investigation?

" The testimony," says Challis, Professor of Astronomy, Cambridge, England, " has been so abundant and consentaneous, that either the facts must be admitted to be such as are reported, or the possibility of certifying facts by human testimony must be given up."

Your easy cry of *jugglery* has been doing service ever since 1847. Bellachini, Houdin, Hamilton, Hermann, Jacobs,* Rhys, and other eminent professors of the conjuring art, have declared that medial phenomena are not explicable by the theory of prestidigitation; yet you fall back on it as if it were your only way of retreat from the Spiritual theory. Why not employ your great abilities, your learning, and your meditative powers in bringing forward some other theory in explanation, which may at least have the merit of novelty and of reason? If you will do it, you will do what the sages of all the centuries have been unable to accomplish. Let this be an incentive to your ambition.

---

* Jacobs, a well-known German professor, says (1880), that, after having thoroughly examined what are termed Spiritual phenomena, he can declare — though he can imitate a great many of the more startling exhibitions of power accorded us by the disembodied — that what he is enabled to do as a sleight-of-hand performer " has nothing in common with Spiritualism."

CHAPTER IV.

CLAIRVOYANCE A SPIRITUAL FACULTY.—TRANCE-SPEAKING.— UNSCIENTIFIC OBJECTIONS OF SPECIALISTS IN SCIENCE. — MORE TESTIMONY.

WE are told that the Spiritualist is the victim of an illusion; that he has none of the "wariness" becoming the scientific mind; that he "seeks for comfort at the expense of truth;" that "sentiment and imagination have made that true to him which is not true; whereas the spirit of science is that attitude of mind which abhors delusion as the most colossal of errors."

It is only the self-complacency of ignorance that could invent such objections. Imagine men like Zöllner and his professional associates, all trained and accomplished physicists, watching the movements of a glass bell under the table, and being so deficient in "wariness" as to testify to seeing what they did not see, and to hearing what they did not hear, and to touching what they did not touch!

"It is from no dread of annihilation," says Alfred R. Wallace, "that I have gone into this subject of Spiritualism. I came to the inquiry utterly unbiased by hopes or fears, because I knew that my belief could not affect the reality, and with an ingrained prejudice against even such a word as *spirit*, which I have hardly yet overcome."

Dr. John Elliotson, F.R.S., one of the most scientific of English physicians, and for several years editor of *The Zoist* in London, had advocated extreme Sadducean and materialistic views almost to the end of his life, although he was well acquainted with some of the lower phenomena of mesmerism. One little proof of supersensual power which he got through D. D. Home, in France, wholly revolutionized his opinions, and he became an earnest Spiritualist.

In the year 1868, in company with my friend, Wm. White, of London, author of a candid Life of Swedenborg, I called on Elliotson's friend and colleague, Dr. Ashburner, at the house of the latter in London, opposite Hyde Park Gate. He had been one of the Queen's physicians. He described to me in touching terms the softening effects upon Elliotson's character of his new convictions. Ashburner is the author of some remarkable works, giving his experiences in Spiritualism. I found him, though blind, serenely happy in his old age in the possession of a great, inspiring truth, of which he had satisfied himself fully.

J. F. Deleuze, the experienced student of mesmerism and somnambulism, says that the power of seeing at a distance, prevision, the communication of thought without the aid of external signs, are sufficient proofs of the spirituality of the soul. He marvels at the materialism of Dr. Georget, who had acquainted himself with some of the phenomena. Georget was the author of the much-esteemed " Physiology of the Nervous System " (1821), in which extreme materialistic views were maintained. But the transcendent facts of somnambulism came fast and thick, and fairly wrested from him his materialism. In his last will and testament he solemnly says, referring to the above-named volume from his pen :

" This work had scarcely appeared, when renewed meditations on a very extraordinary phenomenon, somnambulism, no longer permitted me to entertain doubts of the existence within us, and external to us, of an intelligent principle, altogether different from material existences : in a word, of the soul and God. With respect to this I have a profound conviction, founded upon facts which I believe to be incontestable. This declaration will not see the light till a period when its sincerity will not be doubted, nor my intentions suspected. As I cannot publish it myself, I request those persons who may read it, on opening this will, that is to say, after my death, to give it all possible publicity."

Georget will probably be set aside by our opponents as a man who got his convictions " by suppressing the skeptical intellect, not by satisfying it." Having first manifested his sincerity in his skeptical utterances, he will be charged with insincerity or incompetence in frankly admitting that new facts had convinced him of his error.

And what is this clairvoyance to which Georget refers? In its connection with mesmeric somnambulism, it was first announced by Puysegur in 1784. As far as I have admitted it as part of a scientific basis, it is the exercise of the supersensual faculty of penetrating opaque and dense matter as if by the faculty of sight. But it does more. It detects our unuttered, undeveloped thoughts ; it goes back along the past, and describes what is hidden ; nay, the proofs are overwhelming that it may pierce the future, and predict coming events from the shadows they cast before.

What is it that sees without the physical eyes, and without the assistance of light? What is normal sight? It is not the vibrating ether — it is not the external eye — that sees. It is the soul using the eye as an instrument, and the light as a condition. Prove once that sight can exist without the use of light, sensation, or any physical organ of vision, and you prove an abnormal, supersensual, spiritual faculty ; — a proof which puts an end to the theory of materialism, and which, through its affinity with analogous or corresponding facts, justifies its introduction as part of a scientific basis for the spiritual theory.

"Thus it is," says Mr. R. H. Brown, (1868,) "that clairvoyance furnishes the most conclusive answer to the materialists, and presents the most satisfactory proof of

the existence of the soul, separate from the body ; — residing within it, generally employing its organs for the reception of ideas, but at times acting independently of those
organs, and obtaining information without their aid. By
clairvoyance we thus show the truth of the first proposition
upon which Spiritualism rests, — the existence of a dual
nature in man, a soul as well as a body."

The same writer proceeds to argue, that if the mind *sees*
without the aid of light or of the optic nerve, it must have
some other medium by which the simple impression of sight
can be individualized, and presented distinct and separate
from all other impressions ; there must be a spiritual organ
of sight besides a physical. And if there is a spiritual
organ of sight, there must also be a spiritual organ for the
individualization of all the other impressions. In nature,
each part is adapted to all the other parts, and the existence of one part presupposes the existence of all the other
parts. If there is a spiritual organ of sight, there must also
be a complete spiritual organization or body, interfused
with and permeating the physical body. And this is what
Spiritualism asserts.

" Nature, our wise and powerful mother, fore-adapts
everything for the conditions amid which she intends it
shall live. How shall we escape the conclusion, that by
adapting the soul to another state of being, and endowing
it for that purpose with the power to exist, act, think, see,
and hear, without the aid of the body, and separated from
it, Nature has given us her solemn and sacred guaranty
that we shall live hereafter?"

There are some, even among those called scientific, who
are so blinded by theories as to be impervious to facts.
Even among Spiritualists there are those who would undervalue the importance of our objective phenomena. But all
the great advances in human invention and discovery have
been made through attention to facts ; — and some of them

facts as humble as the falling of an apple, or the swinging
of a lamp. To undervalue the slightest manifestation from
a spiritual source is a folly, no matter whether it be a simple
rap, or a message written by some force unknown. Even
if it only discloses to us the frivolity of the manifesting
agent, it is knowledge gained. I confess that a simple,
flawless experiment in direct writing is to me more impressive
than all the speculative discourses by so-called trance-
speakers, in which no objective, scientific proof is given of
preterhuman power.

In this I do not disparage the trance-speaker. There is
place for him, too; and when the influence impelling him
is that of wisdom and reason, I can listen to him with profit.
But it is often impossible to distinguish between what
comes from the occult powers, the unconscious reminis-
cences, of the trance-speaker himself, and that which may
come from some prompting spirit. The flowery fluency of
a trance-speaker must not be taken as a proof of power;
rather is it an evidence of weakness. Even granting that
such mediums speak from some foreign spirit's inspiration,
that spirit may be inferior to many a mortal in sound judgment and intelligence. The spirits that assume great
names, and influence the medium to talk in a style that
revolts our sense of truth, of good taste, and of identity,
must be brought to the bar of our highest reason, and
judged by its verdict. That spirits, as well as mortals, may
deceive; that they may be influenced by vanity or ambition,
and may afflict us by verbose twaddle, is one of the facts
which Modern Spiritualism daily discloses; and in this it is
doing good service, if we only have the wit to see it: for
the fact explodes some ancient and respectable errors in
regard to the spirit-world.

The absence of these considerations leads to deplorable
credulities. That spirits may sometimes play gross hoaxes
on unsuspecting-mortals, is made probable by the history

of fanaticism in all ages, and our modern experiences go far to confirm it as a fact. Henry More, (1614–1687,) the Platonic philosopher and learned Spiritualist, who was himself a medium for certain physical phenomena, once remarked: "There are as great fools in the spirit-world as there ever were in this." Of the spirits that came through Madame Hauffe, the "Seeress of Prevorst," Dr. Kerner (1826) relates that some of them were "foolish and trifling," and some "much poorer and more destitute than spirits in this life ever showed themselves;" and he remarks of this seemingly undivine order of things, "What I here in the dust, with the eye of a mole, regard as so great a disharmony, will hereafter, when the scales fall from my mole's-eye, appear as harmony."

The importance attached to the utterances of "trance-speakers" by uncritical or inexperienced Spiritualists, has justly excited the ridicule of those who detect in mere prolixity and florid verbiage very human failings. Where the utterance or the knowledge can be fairly hypothecated as coming from the medium, exercising abnormal powers, the idea of the intervention of a foreign spirit ought to be dismissed.

In a discourse delivered in London, July 11, 1880, by Mrs. Richmond, the gifted American "trance-speaker," I find this remark: "To say, therefore, there has been an accurate scientific basis of Spiritualism, is to say *that which is impossible.*" Here is an assertion which our facts plainly contradict, and which the so-called "controls" themselves of Mrs. Richmond contradict in other parts of their discourse.

If the facts of clairvoyance and direct writing have really occurred, and are reproducible, are they not as much facts of science as the neutralization of an acid by an alkali, or the appearance of the aurora borealis?

"Spiritualism," say these so-called controls, "cannot be

a science. It is more than science; it is beyond human comprehension *in the physical sense.* It is that which, *demonstrating its presence to the senses,* leaves the knowledge of its methods entirely outside the human senses."

Are there not other facts of nature besides Spiritualism, which, " demonstrating their presence to the senses, leave the knowledge of their methods entirely outside the human senses?" Does not crystallography do the same? Do we yet know the " methods " by which comets and the aurora borealis come into existence? Must not a fact that " demonstrates its presence to the senses" possess the first great essential of a fact of science, however ignorant we may remain as to all its methods and causes? See how loosely these " controls" contradict themselves! In one sentence we are told, " That which you chiefly have to mind is to *know* that you have the truth." In another sentence these same " controls " assert in regard to spiritual phenomena, " The very testimony upon which you seek to establish a truth evades you in an hour, and the very evidence that you were prepared to swear by has the next moment turned against you."

What shall we say to an unreasoned generalization like this? If it were true, there would be no tenable truth in Spiritualism. We should have to keep abandoning our facts as fast as they were grasped. Is there any person who, once having come intelligently into possession of our facts, has been known to deny them? The construction put on them may vary; but the facts themselves, once thoroughly tested, are the mind's inalienable acquisition. How will the following passage from the same discourse bear the probe of critical analysis?

" There has been test after test; there have been evidences piled mountains high, *but these are immeasurably greater than science.*" (That is, too great to be *known !*) " They are immeasurably beyond the scope of scientific thought to-day; they are immeasurably beyond the reach and grasp of any human school of thought," (Are not many admitted facts beyond human explanation?) "and must belong forever to that region of super-science upon which the truths are founded, and for which they builded their strongholds. If we trust to science to demonstrate Spiritualism it will pass away to-morrow," (Then let it pass!) "and be enrolled among the failures of each succeeding age. If we trust to the scientific man, he will catalogue it his own way, place it where he chooses in his laboratory— a manifestation without a letter, body without spirit, a law without a source of existence— it will become one of the phenomenal phases of the universe, which the scientific world to-day declares is without an intelligent source of being."

"If we trust to the scientific man!" But the scientific man is in this case the individual Spiritualist himself, who has studied certain phenomena, objective and subjective, till they are to him facts of science, of which he is as well assured as of any fact in hydraulics or in chemistry. Has not Spiritualism won its millions without the aid of scienific specialists in other branches?

Immediately after the paragraph last quoted, as if the "controls" were fooling their medium, and compelling her unconsciously to keep confuting their words, they say:

"It (Spiritualism) has a source of being, spiritual and intelligent. Its methods are also working its way to humanity, according to their needs and condition; *it manifests itself through the senses,* because you require it. To those who have spiritual vision, it speaks in the spirit; to those who have the power of inspiration, there is no need of outward sign and token. But to the dumb and dull human sense, they must needs have a sign and token. It breaks through the barriers, the material walls that surround you, and says, ' If you will have the physical voice, here it is; if you will have the physical hand, here it is.' "

Having been told that Spiritualism "manifests itself through the senses" because we require it; and also that what we "chiefly have to mind is to *know*" that we "have the truth," — by what logical consequence are we debarred from proving the truth by all the tests that science (which is *knowledge*) can apply?

I could go further in exposing the inconsistencies of this crude and shallow, though ludicrously oracular discourse; but the game is hardly worth the candle. What I have said I mean as no reflection on the lady medium herself, who is undoubtedly a person of rare ability: my criticism applies to the "controls," under whose influence she would sometimes seem to speak. That she has often, while believing herself to be controlled, spoken wisely and well I do not doubt. But she must know that there is hardly a prominent investigator at this time who has not committed himself to the demonstrable and scientific character of *some*, at least, of our phenomena.

Who is the scientific expert? There is no one who can be a master of all the sciences. In order to partially acquaint himself with only one or two, he must give the best part of his life to study. The scientific expert in regard to elements and their compounds is the chemist; and so the scientific expert in regard to the subtile phenomena of Spiritualism is the man who has given the most thought, time, and intelligence to the study of them, — who has corrected the most mistakes in his experience, and revised hasty conclusions the most thoroughly.

The conscious-automaton theory of Huxley, Clifford, and others, who affect the tone of extreme science, is that the mind is pure mechanism; that thoughts follow one another in a certain order; that feeling is not to be taken into the account: to which Professor James replies:

"Many persons nowadays seem to think that any conclusion must be very scientific if the arguments in favor of it are all derived from the twitching of frogs' legs, — especially if the frogs are decapitated, — and that on the other hand any doctrine chiefly vouched for by the feelings of human beings, with heads on their shoulders, must be benighted and superstitious. They seem to think, too, that any vagary or whim, however unverified, of a scientific man must needs form an integral part of science itself; that when Huxley, for example, has ruled feeling out of the game of life, and called it a mere bystander, a supernumerary, the matter is settled."

This eager deglutition of everything materialistic as peculiarly scientific is deplorable indeed. The truth is that the deductions from science, and from all that relates to the functions of the human mind, are alike the results of our thinking upon the phenomena which life and nature present. No mode of thinking, except false, illogical thinking, can be in conflict with genuine science and its teachings.

Professor Tyndall, who, in spite of his attempts to defame the subject, seems to be at heart a good Spiritualist, has favored us with an account of his investigations into our facts. It appears that at a certain séance, a lady said that the introduction of a magnet would make her terribly ill, and that she would instantly know of the presence of one on entering a room. The ingenious professor had brought with him a magnet in his pocket; and yet the lady owned that she was particularly well. *Ergo*, all this testimony by Wallace, Crookes, Zöllner, and the rest of us, is disproved, and Spiritualism must be dismissed as nothing but "intellectual whoredom!"

Again: Professor Tyndall had a séance with a certain "warm-hearted old gentleman," who imagined that a table was moved by spirits, when all the while Tyndall himself was causing it to vibrate. "Believing," he says. "that the disclosure of the secret would provoke anger, I kept it to myself." So it would seem that the "warm-hearted old gentleman" took it for granted that the eminent physicist was as honorable and sincere as he was himself in the investigation : surely a not unpardonable delusion, and one no more a proof of the old gentleman's imbecility than if he had accepted a spurious guinea from Mr. Tyndall, supposing it to be genuine.

Such experiences have about as much force against Spiritualism as they have against the solar system. And yet the rest of the incidents related by Tyndall as proofs of the thorough manner in which he has *done* Spiritualism, are of no higher importance. Felicitating himself upon the issue of his vast expenditure of sagacity and labor in investigating the question whether there are scientific proofs of spiritual activity, his self-complacent comment is: " This, then, is the result of an attempt, made by a scientific man, to look into the spiritual phenomena ! " I will resist the temptation of any animadversion.

Far different is the temper in which William Crookes, the chemist, approaches the subject. After referring (1870) to the modern phenomena as " occurring to an almost unprecedented extent," he remarks : " That a hitherto unrecognized form of Force exists — whether it be called psychic force or X force is of little consequence — is not with me a matter of opinion, but of absolute knowledge ; but the nature of that force, or the cause which immediately excites its activity, forms a subject on which I do not at present feel competent to offer an opinion."

Such is the wary conclusion of an accomplished man of science who has tested the phenomena laboriously with the aid of an apparatus proper for the work. Mr. Crookes is the discoverer of the new metal, thallium ; also of the supra-gaseous state in which matter exists in high vacua ; and is the deviser of the radiometer. He edits the London *Quarterly Journal of Science.*

" The conditions are such as to render exact results impossible," says an objector. The remark is directly confuted by the experiments of Hare, Crookes, Varley, Boutlerof, Zöllner, Wallace, Cox, Wyld, W. H. Harrison,

Denslow, Ashburner, and more than a hundred more investigators known to science. Any man may obtain "exact results" who will take the trouble to investigate the subject patiently and repeatedly in the presence of tested mediums.

Mr. F. L. H. Willis, a gentleman well known to me, was suspended (1857) from the divinity school of Harvard University on a charge of simulating so-called spiritual phenomena. The character of these in his presence was then patiently examined into by Thomas Wentworth Higginson, well known both in England and America as an accomplished gentleman and scholar, and who tested certain facts to his entire satisfaction. His feet, without the shoes, were grasped by palpable hands; the guitar was played on "accurately and gracefully," while he sang several songs, he first placing the guitar "in such a position as to guard the instrument from possibility of contact," and it being "beyond the reach of any part of Mr. Willis's person." Mr. Higginson, in his affidavit, remarks: "I cannot play the guitar, but I have heard it played a good deal, and I *know* that the accompaniment was an extraordinary thing, apart from the mystery of its origin." He says, in conclusion:

"The question of the 'spiritual origin' is not now raised; it is a simple question of fraud or genuineness. If I have not satisfactory evidence of the genuineness of these phenomena, which I have just described, then there is no such thing as evidence, and all the fabric of natural science may be a mass of imposture. And when I find, on examination. that facts similar to these have been observed by hundreds of intelligent persons, in various places, for several years back, I am disposed humbly to remember the maxim, attributed to Arago, 'He is a rash man who, outside of pure mathematics, pronounces the word *impossible.*'

"THOS. WENTWORTH HIGGINSON."

"*Worcester*, ss., April 15, 1857. Subscribed and sworn to before me.

"HENRY CHAPIN, *Justice of the Peace.*"

Automatic writing and direct spirit-writing occurred in Mr. Willis's presence; and several times there was an *apport* of beautiful and fragrant flowers, under conditions which are fully explained in the life of Mr. Willis (*Banner of Light*, June 7, 1879).

After being fully warned as to the impossible and therefore delusive character of the phenomena; after having the imaginary sources of the delusion pointed out; knowing, too, that all the prejudices of the age and the whole tone of educated thought, are arrayed against the reality of such facts, — we yet see that the conviction of their genuineness is forced every day upon such scientific men as can rise above the prejudices of their fellows, and venture to investigate an ill-reputed truth. And there is not as yet a known instance wherein an investigator of any character or authority has changed his opinion as to the unexplained occurrence of our phenomena. To attribute such convictions to "a diseased faculty of wonder," is simply to mock at the intellectual integrity of the witnesses, among whom are hundreds of eminent men, whose testimony on any other subject would be accepted without question.

"It must be remembered," says Alfred R. Wallace,* the well-known naturalist, "that we have to consider, not absurd beliefs or false influences, but plain matters of fact; and it never has been proved, and cannot be proved, that any large amount of cumulative evidence of disinterested and sensible men was ever obtained for an absolute and entire delusion."

He further says: "I maintain that human testimony increases in value in such an enormous ratio with each additional independent and honest witness, that no fact

* Born in Ulsk, Monmouthshire, in 1822, Mr. Wallace shares with Darwin the honor of originating the doctrine of natural selection. He is one of the most eminent naturalists of the day; and the author of "On Miracles and Modern Spiritualism: Three Essays. London, James Burns, 1875."

ought to be rejected when attested by such a body of evidence as exists for many of the events termed miraculous or supernatural, and which occur now daily among us."

"When Spiritualism," we are told, "will submit to really scientific investigation, it will undoubtedly receive it." The reply is, that it has so submitted, and so received it. It has submitted openly, repeatedly, in broad daylight, where every condition that the investigator could reasonably ask has been granted. Scientific witnesses enough to establish its truth forever have testified to the reality of its phenomena. It has come out triumphant from the ordeal; and no scoffs of so-called scientific journals, no leading articles, however clever and sarcastic, can now affect the impregnable basis of pure science on which it rests.

Darius Lyman, of Washington, D. C., gives some apt illustrations of the capacity of pseudo-science, *not* to know when she is not in the humor:

"If, for example, upon a slate, writing should be produced hundreds of times, under circumstances absolutely precluding any chemical processes, or any mechanical agency other than of a common pencil, that fact would not in the estimate of science be sufficient to justify the inference that a person in intangible presence had produced the writing.

"If a table suspended in mid-air were made to yield intelligible movements in the presence of persons having no agency in the motion, and without the intervention of mechanism appreciable by any ordinary human sense, that fact would not warrant the inference of the presence of an intangible person aiding in the suspension.

"If a well-known tune were played on a piano without the intervention of any mechanism distinct from the instrument, or of any automatic appliances, or the contact of any object of sufficient consistency to be at once visible and tangible, science could not justify the inference that an intangible person did the playing.

"If three persons, the solo occupants of the same chamber and the same house, none of them ventriloquists, should, in such chamber and house converse with an audible voice addressed to all, and if the voice should communicate to each one facts known only to each, that fact, according to science, would not justify the conclusion that the voice proceeded from a person who lacked the attribute of a tangible body, and was not one of the three.

"These supposed illustrations exhibit the attitude of science to the alleged facts of Spiritualism, as understood by Professor Youmans and Dr. Carpenter. No amount of testimony is adequate to verify the alleged facts; no logic known to science is sufficient to warrant an inference from any facts of the existence or intervention of spirits, or the reality of any supersensual world!

"The behavior of the loadstone is thought by scientific men to warrant the inference of a magnetic force; a stroke from the Leyden jar indubitably proves the presence of an electric force; the fall of an apple establishes the reality of the force of gravity. Yet no human sense can directly cognize any one of these forces. They are simply *inferred* from motions of bodies. They belong entirely to the supersensual world. Because they are *impersonal*, though strictly supersensual, science can manage to put on them the seal of its approval.

"But other forces equally supersensual, revealed like gravity and magnetism in insulated cases of the disturbance of the state of solid substances, science cannot recognize, because they are *personal*, and reveal human intelligence and affection existing in modes hitherto undreamed of. There is danger, probably, if science recognizes any such forces upon any testimony, that man may be discovered to be capable of surviving death!"

Mr. John Fiske, the distinguished cosmic philosopher, stigmatizes as "totemism" the spiritual belief of such persons as Franz Hoffman, editor of Baader's philosophical works, Immanuel H. Fichte, son of Kant's great contemporary, Alfred R. Wallace, Frederic Tennyson, Elizabeth Barrett Browning, and not a few others, reputed as clever in their way. Mr. Fiske makes a somewhat elaborate attempt to console us for the absence of all rational proofs of an hereafter, by considerations which I will leave it for my friend, Mr. Lyman, to set forth with his happy combination of science and wit:

" Mr. Fiske flatters the man of science with an attempted proof that no proper spiritual world can be an object of knowledge ; and seeming to feel that such an argument might possibly be too much for the theologian to accept without grimaces, he soothes the latter with arguments tending to reconcile him to a spiritual world according to the taste of *savans*, by showing the strong probabilities in favor of its reality arising from the consideration that a scintilla of actual light can never come from it."

" The upshot of the whole is :   That if there is a spiritual world it is absolutely divorced from matter, and there is no bridge to it for human thought ; and secondly, we cannot even imagine souls except in a sort of physical organism (with which, of course, they have ' no community of nature ') ; and thirdly, if they exist after death, there is, therefore, no possible means of our knowing it in this life. The critic does not enunciate these several propositions, but they underlie his charming rhetoric and logic.

" The comfort afforded to the theologian is not very great ; but after he has secured a spiritual world incommunicably separate from this, he ought to be thankful for small additional favors.   He is saved from the clutches of science in this way : Though a spiritual world must be utterly divorced from all effective connection with this, and is even inconceivable, that inconceivability is no proof of its unreality.   For be it known to the doctors of theology, that (p. 48)—

" ' Since our inability to conceive anything is limited by the extent of our experience, and since human experience is very far from being infinite, it follows that there may be, and in all probability is, (!) an immense region of existence in every way as real as the region which we know, yet concerning which we cannot form the faintest rudiment of a conception.' [Is not this the proper domain of faith?] ' Any hypothesis relating to such a region of existence is not only disproved by the total failure of evidence in its favor, but the total failure of evidence in its favor does not raise even the slightest *primâ facie* presumption against its validity.'

" And let the theological doctor take notice, that ' These considerations apply with great force to the hypothesis of ?

world in which psychical phenomena persist in the absence of material conditions.'   And let him further observe, that 'It is true on the one hand, that we can bring up no scientific evidence in support of such an hypothesis.   But on the other hand, it is equally true that in the very nature of things no such evidence could be expected to be forthcoming; even were there such evidence in abundance, it could not be accessible to us.   The existence of a single soul, or congeries of psychical phenomena, unaccompanied by a material body, would be evidence sufficient to demonstrate the hypothesis.   But in the nature of things, even were there a million such souls round about us, we could not become aware of the existence of one of them, for we have no organ or faculty for the perception of soul apart from the material structure and activities in which it has been manifested throughout the whole course of our experience.'

"So the theologian can understand that the strongest proof we have of a spiritual world incommunicably separate from matter, is that it is neither conceivable nor in the line of the analogies of experience!" . . . .

"The antagonist school of Materialists pure and simple, is alike incapable of accepting the alleged fact of materialization.   The fundamental postulate of this class of persons is, that there can be no *qualities in matter that are not matter*.   Indeed, with them it is absurd to talk of the *qualities* of matter; for the very words, 'qualities of matter,' convey the implication that there is in matter something *not* matter — which would be a very dangerous admission; for that something not matter might possibly be more potent than matter itself.   But aside from this hyperphysical objection of the Materialists to the existence of something latent in matter which is not matter, there is to them a greater one.   And that is, that the alleged materialization of spirits concedes the possibility of the action upon physical substances of *an order of persons who are intrinsically inappreciable by the ordinary senses*.   This concession would, in their view, be a concession of the reality of miracles; and as miracles are impossible, materialization is impossible.

"This objection rests upon a wrong conception of what should be considered a miracle.   Though it is admitted that a miracle is not possible, it is well to define what it should be thought to be, if it were possible. The ordinary definition — a violation of the laws of nature — defines nothing ; for every fact entirely new in human experience, being in conflict with all former experience, is to the observer a violation of the laws of nature. And as the totality of the order of nature can never be known, it cannot be known that something entirely new to that order (so far as experience goes) may not occur. Our definition of a miracle, therefore, should show on its face that it is essentially impossible." . . .

"At first thought, one would be inclined to credit the theologians with a ready predisposition to faith in the fact of materialization. . . . Why, then, is the alleged modern fact of materialization so distressingly offensive to them?

"Because, if a fact, its tendency is to depress human authority in matters of religion, to make every man his own mediator, and thus to do away with that army of clergymen and priests who perform — honestly, it may be — fictitious services of mediation *between God and others than themselves.* There is a very large class whose interest it is to make the access to God, or the gods, as circuitous as possible. Like all middle-men, they do not like compendious methods for the exchange of commodities. But when our invisible friends, called spirits, invest themselves temporarily in the masks of bodies, and *demonstrate that death is dead,* the one stupendous horror of all the ages lays aside its Gorgon head, men gain courage to treat with the Invisible God for themselves, and the reign of the priest, so far as it rests in cowardly superstition, draws to a sensible close. Such a result is alarming to the theologians. The fear of death, and of what follows after, is their capital, and the principal source of their influence over the people. If spirits do appear visibly and tangibly, and if they shall continue to appear, all men will manage their *post mortem* concerns for themselves, and will not look to the 'ambassadors of Christ' for any very reliable instruction in those matters. The materialization of spirits carrying all these dire influences with it, as the seed carries the germ of the future tree, must of course, to the theologians, be unreal." . . .

"The effect upon the fastidious tastes of different

schools of thinkers of the alleged materialization of spirits, has its comic aspects to such as are willing to admit extraordinary facts upon reasonable evidence. The shock such alleged facts must give to all such as sympathize with Mr. Fiske, and who believe in no such spiritual world as can come in connection with matter, is abundantly ludicrous. This class consists of students of the old psychology, who have formed their notions of spirits from speculations on the laws of abstract thought and on the various forms of emotion. With them it is an axiom that matter is always essentially tangible, and that spirit, being the perfect opposite of matter, has no necessary or conceivable contact with it.

"How thoroughly this postulate pervades Mr. Fiske's speculations, will be evident from the extracts from his essay already cited, and particularly from the unction with which he reproduces the famous dictum of Descartes. This school *must* deny the possibility of materialization. For the presence of a material form *in no case* can guarantee the presence of a soul. For according to their logic, there can be no spirit in living contact with matter, nor any matter in vital contact with spirit. As there is no rational evidence for them that a spiritual part animates *living* human beings, the theory that a spiritual force or being can animate a *temporary* form of matter, and dissolve it again in thin air, must be for them in the last degree preposterous. As their conceited ignorance has sounded the utmost possibilities of nature, why should one attempt to convince them of the reality of facts which put all their vain philosophy to shame? Their suffrages for the truth are not worth the trouble of winning."

"There is another class of persons that affect a knowledge of scientific methods, who are quite sure that if a speaking, tangible form should suddenly appear in a closed room, to which no person but the spectators could gain admission, should verify its presence to the senses of sight and touch, should converse in an audible voice on topics familiar only to each witness, and should then as suddenly vanish, there would still be no proof in such a manifestation of the presence of a spirit. How such a reasoner can with any certainty identify a friend on Monday whom he had last seen on the preceding Sunday, passes my comprehension. For the real friend he has never *really seen*. . . .

This pretentious display of doubt in regard to the spiritual agency involved in such a case as is supposed, is of all claims to superior acuteness the most shallow and contemptible."

"All base things have their day. Why should not the prejudice of the *savans*, the bigotry of the theologians, the pretensions of the sciolist, be allowed to have theirs? . . . The wave of the new movement will continue to rise slowly but surely, and it will never retire till all the objections and cavils of the prejudiced many that do not discern the signs of the times are sunk in everlasting oblivion. Our facts depend for their acceptance on no person's patronage; the pressure of ridicule cannot extinguish or thrust them out of view. Steadily increasing in number, variety, and beauty, they are competent to win their own way to general recognition."

In a paper written in reply to Mr. Youmans, of the *Popular Science Monthly*, Mr. Lyman says:

" Professor Youmans acknowledges no spiritual world other than thoughts and emotions correlated to matter, no spiritual world in which moral agents exist intrinsically inappreciable by any of the senses, no spiritual world above the sensuous order. But the non-recognition of such a world is just what, in popular language, constitutes materialism. The popular apprehension has not yet reduced the hemisphere of being opposed to matter to a nebulous mass of sensations, perceptions, conceptions, and feelings." . . .

" The facts of Spiritualism certainly answer to all the criteria of the subjects-matter of any science, as laid down by Professor Youmans. They are such facts as have been, and still are, repeatedly experienced. They are not only accessible to the normal action of the human faculties, but most of them are quite palpable to the senses. The variety in which they occur renders them susceptible of classification and methodized knowledge, and thus suggests that the law of their genesis and evolution can be comprehended." . . .

" Common people believe in a supersensual world, in which moral beings hold intercourse with one another in modes transcending the ordinary reach of the senses; they have never imagined a spiritual world, inhabited only by thoughts, emotions, and volitions floating loose from souls." . . .

"All argument against the occasional intervention of spirits in mundane affairs, on the ground of its impossibility, or its incompatibility with the laws of nature, is simply frivolous. There are no known laws of nature that preclude it. The weight of human experience is against such facts, but that experience is in favor of facts every whit as mysterious. On the contrary, there is a steadily augmenting experience in favor of spiritual intervention coming through phenomena addressed to every sense, and indicating a tendency to issue in an intercourse between ours and the supersensual world, constant, regular, and rigorously conditioned."

Here I would again call attention to the circumstance that I claim for my basis the great verified facts of clairvoyance, as proved in the reading of closely-folded papers, and of direct writing, as proved in the German experiments with Slade, in those of hundreds of well-known persons in England and America, and in my own experiments with Watkins and others. To the phenomena analogous with these, and corroborated by them, I may frequently refer, and assume them as true without including them in my basis. And so, with regard to the Spiritual hypothesis: I shall assume that we have evidences of spirit power, both in the two typical facts, which have been scientifically confirmed, and in others where the proofs have not been so cumulative and direct as we may expect them to be as the developments go on. But it is not for the spiritual hypothesis that I have any concern, since it is one to which all the facts inevitably lead, and without which many of the higher phenomena cannot be explained.

In the *Popular Science Monthly* there recently appeared a paper by Dr. Gairdner, of Edinburgh, in opposition to Spiritualism. Assuming that we have "absolute proof and evidence" in our own souls and bodies of a future for man, he would discredit any attempt to investigate the important phenomena which invite our attention. But he fails to show where the "absolute proof" is to be found, that shall be satisfactory to many earnest and critical minds. No fact can be more notorious than that of the present skepticism and utter unbelief in regard to the immortality of the soul among a large class of intelligent persons. He who shuts his eyes to this fact can do so only by ignoring what is written, published, and preached every day.

Dr. Gairdner naively asks, If such a fact as clairvoyance exists, what is there to prevent a *sensitive* from reading your private papers in your locked drawers? Truly, I know of nothing to prevent it, except the absence of conditions or the lack of power. I have repeatedly known a clairvoyant to detect not only my unspoken thoughts, but to read what I had written on a slip of paper, and then had rolled tightly into a pellet or wad, which he did not even touch except with the point of a pencil. Why he cannot always read a paper that lies folded in my friend's pocket or in a locked drawer, I cannot say. But how our ignorance of one fact can impair our absolute knowledge of another, I also fail to see.

"If clairvoyance is true," says Dr. Gairdner, "there is nothing to prevent a spirit from getting possession of a private paper, and publishing it." And then he adds: "But it has been shown that this cannot be done." The assertion is about as reasonable as it would be to say, that because a prize had been offered to the man who could leap a ditch twenty feet wide, and the prize had not been won, therefore it had been proved that the feat could not be accomplished.

To what does Dr. Gairdner refer as his proof? Why, to the tradition among skeptics that a certain person once placed a hundred-pound note in a sealed envelope in the Bank of England, and promised to give it to any one who could tell the number; but the prize was never won: *therefore*, according to our logical opponent, there is no such thing as clairvoyance; it is "in fact impossible."

The conclusion is of the order styled *fast*. Belief in clairvoyance, the Doctor tells us, comes from "a diseased condition of the faculty of wonder." Truly a luminous discovery, worthy to be recorded in a scientific journal! He should have learned that clairvoyance does not proceed from a simple effort of the will; it is the unforced exercise, often involuntary, of a transcendent spiritual faculty. Schopenhauer, the eccentric German philosopher, relates that he once told his landlady in Milan the numbers of two lottery tickets which she had bought; but when she began to praise him for his wonderful cleverness, he was disconcerted, his passive state was at an end, and he blundered in his attempt to tell the number of the third ticket.

The recollection of a name or of a word cannot be forced by an effort of volition. How often we strive to recall something, and the more we strive the more unattainable seems to be the reminiscence! We give up the pursuit, lapse into a passive state, and then, all at once perhaps, the word, name, or event comes back to us clearly and completely.

The deliverances of the memory are not subject always to the will; and so it is with clairvoyance. Like the kingdom of heaven it does not come "by observation." There is an intelligent power in man, no more under the control of his will than are his involuntary muscles. We know not whence it cometh, nor whither it goeth. It transcends the outward senses; and from it comes the light that enlighteneth every man who comes into the world, even though its revelations may be rejected and contradicted by the speculative intellect, which thinks itself the wiser.

To Locke's proposition that there is nothing in the mind that has not come to it through the senses, Leibnitz made the familiar reply: "Except the mind itself." The reasoning faculty which confirms the experience that the whole is greater than a part, or that a straight line is the shortest distance between two points, is not a derivation from the senses. As Mr. David A. Wasson well remarks: it is as much innate as "the potency of a beard is innate in the boy."

The late Selden J. Finney, philosopher and spiritualist, wisely says: "If an axiom be only subjectively true, then it lies, for it is given as universal and necessary, and hence as objectively true. To deny its objective truth is to contradict the axiom itself. And if it be said that we cannot prove this, I answer, we must take our reason for the ultimate mental sovereign. And even a denial of such trustworthiness is confession of the sovereignty of reason itself; for we are able to deny a mental proposition only by the assumption of a competent authority in mind. We must accept the primary laws and ideas, axioms of reason, as authoritative and supreme, whether or no."

Here is a specimen of what Alexis Didier, the Parisian clairvoyant, could do: — Some years ago, Mme. Celleron, wife of the proprietor of the "Villes de France, rue Vivienne," lost her watch at Neuilly. Presuming that she might have left it in the carriage which conveyed her there, she went to Alexis to make some inquiries in regard to the driver; but as soon as she was in communication with the somnambulist he told her that her watch had been found by a soldier. "Wait," he added, "and I will read the number on his shako — it is 57; this soldier is in garrison at Courbevoie, and his name is Vincent." The lady hastened to Courbevoie, and applied to M. Othenin, chief of battalion, who ordered a general inspection of the companies. But at that moment a soldier came out of the ranks and presented the watch, which he had found near the bridge of Neuilly, adding, that his military duties had prevented his making the proper efforts to find the owner. Upon the officer's demanding his name, he replied Vincent.

In February, 1850, an English lady, once the pupil of the celebrated pianist Chopin, learning that he was ill, and suspecting that he was in want of money, sent him by mail a bank-note for 250 francs. Some months afterwards, while visiting in Paris, she called on her illustrious teacher and asked if the remittance had been received. On Chopin's replying in the negative, the lady, accompanied by Count de Grisimola, called on Alexis, who told her that the letter with its contents would be found at the domicil of the porteress of M. Chopin, in the drawer of a commode, the position of which he indicated. The lady hastened to verify this information, and it was found exact. The letter had been received in the absence of the porteress by a laboring woman, who had put it in the drawer of the commode, and had forgotten to say anything about it.

On one occasion a milliner of the *rue* Neuve-des-Matharius, No. 5, having lost a valuable dog, to which she was much attached, came to Alexis to learn if he could put her in the way of finding it. He directed her to go at once to the St. Germain railroad terminus, where she would recover her dog, which was about to be offered there for sale. She went to the place indicated, but not finding what she sought returned to Alexis, complaining of the false instructions he had given her. "You are right, madame," said he; "I was too precipitate; I announced as occurring at the very moment what was not to take place till some minutes afterwards; return whence you came, and your search will be crowned with success." She did as directed, and this time Alexis had not been in fault in his clairvoyance. His thought had run before the attempt of the fellow who was going to sell the dog. The lady recovered the animal as had been promised.

The following letter will show what estimate the most celebrated of French conjurors, Robert Houdin, put upon the manifestations in the presence of Alexis:

MONSIEUR: As I had the honor of informing you, I had a second séance; that at which I assisted yesterday at Marcillet's was even more marvellous than the first, and left no longer any doubt on my mind as to the lucidity of Alexis. I presented myself at this sitting with the pre-determination of closely watching the game of *écarté* which had astonished me so much. This time I took even greater precautions than at the first trial; for, distrusting myself, I took one of my friends as a companion, whose calm character could appreciate coolly and establish a sort of equi-librium in my judgment.

Here is what passed, and you can judge whether *subtilités* could ever produce effects like those I am about to cite. I unsealed a pack of cards brought by me, and the envelope of which I had marked so that it could not be changed. I shuffled and got the deal. I dealt with all the precautions of a man skilled in the finesse of his art. Useless pre-cautions! Alexis checks me, and pointing out to me one of the cards which I had just placed before him on the table, says, "I have the king!" "But you know nothing about it yet, since the trump-card is not given out." "You will see," he replied. In effect I turned up the eight of dia-monds, and his card was the king of diamonds. The game was continued in rather an odd manner, for he told me in advance the cards which I ought to play, although I had them concealed under the table, and pressed in my hands. At every play he would present one of his own cards with-out turning it up, and it was invariably found to be the card *en rapport* with that which I had myself played.

I have then, returned from this séance as much over-whelmed with astonishment as I could well be, and per-suaded that it is altogether impossible that either chance or address could have produced effects so marvellous.

Recevez, Monsieur, etc.

Signé: ROBERT HOUDIN, May 16, 1847.

To the Marquis de Mirville.

But Alexis, who by flashes could do such marvels, was not unfrequently at fault, according to his own confession. He says: "The chief feature of the somnambulic lucidity is its variability. While the conjuror or juggler, at all moments in the day and before all spectators, will invariably succeed, the somnambulist, endowed with the marvellous power of clairvoyance, will not be lucid with all interviewers and at all moments of the day; for the faculty of lucidity being a crisis painful and abnormal, there may be atmospheric influences or invincible antipathies at work opposing its production, and which seem to paralyze all supersensual manifestations. Intuition, clairvoyance, lucidity, are faculties which the somnambulist gets from the nature of his temperament, and which are rarely developed in force."

Again he says: "The somnambulic lucidity varies in a way to make one despair; success is continually followed by failure; in a word, error succeeds to truth; but when one analyzes the causes of this, no right-minded person will bring up the charge of charlatanism, since the faculty is subject to influences independent of the will and the consciousness of the clairvoyant."

Hudson Tuttle, the estimable medium of Berlin Heights, Ohio, was at one time clairvoyant like Alexis Didier, but never received pay for his revelations. He gives the following account of the sensitive condition in which a clairvoyant finds himself:

"During the physical manifestations I was usually in a half-trance, intensely sensitive and impressible. The least word or jarring question, even when the *intention* was commendable, grated on my nerves like a rasp of fire. No words can convey the least idea of this condition. I can only compare it to that *physical* state which would result if the nerves were all laid bare. It seemed that the nerves of the spirit were in like manner exposed, and the word, or intonation of voice, which in the normal state would pass unnoticed, broke with the roar of thunder, and tore and lacerated the quivering spirit. I remember once a gentleman called for a private sitting.

"Together with my father and mother we sat for an hour, and there was not the least movement of the table, nor was I sensitive. The gentleman withdrew his hands, and in less than a minute the table was promptly raised, and by the alphabet spelled his father's name. The effort seemed to have been very great and exhaustive, and I had become almost unconscious. The name was scarcely pronounced when the gentleman seized the side of the table and began to rock it, saying, 'See, I can move it as well as any one.' Had he discharged an electric battery through my brain the shock would not have been greater or the pain more unendurable. The implication at ordinary times would have passed with a smile, for I had not the least desire or interest to convert any one, but at that moment, when every nerve-fibre was tense and vibrating, they broke at the rude touch, and I awoke with anger, and my speech was hot with indignation. I could not explain to him how or why he had so offended me, for I could not understand myself, and after an hour I was filled with shame that I had so far forgotten myself.

"Mother, blessed soul, came forward with words of explanation, persuasion, and extenuation to the gentleman, and afterwards with balm for my troubled mind, yet it was a long time before I recovered my former serenity, or dared allow myself to fall into the same unguarded sensitive condition. As soon as I felt its approach I would instinctively start back in undefinable terror, fearing again the fiery pain.

"This, you may say, was an exceedingly trifling thing to produce such a result, and mediums should school themselves to bear opposition, disapproval, and criticism. I speak advisedly when I say, that when the medium has gained this condition, his sensitiveness will have become so obtuse he will not be a medium. You say, 'A little thing for so great a disturbance!' You forget that an almost imperceptible mote in the eye causes unbearable pain: yet the eye is not to be compared in its sensitiveness with that of the brain in its spiritualized state."

Object as we may to being under *surveillance*, the fact of clairvoyance persists. It is now daily demonstrated. Wrap ourselves as we may in our own individuality, look down as we may in the arrogance of our self-sufficiency upon surrounding intelligences, we cannot escape from the great fact of the solidarity of all created things. Clairvoyance proves to us that there is no such privilege to be had as perfect privacy; that there is no such thing as absolute independence for any human being. We think we hold a secret in our breast; we flatter ourselves that there is not another individual intelligence in the whole world that knows, or can know, what we would hide. Vain, illusive thought! Our whole moral and physical nature is transparent to higher intelligences. Our secret is known perhaps by others before we know it ourselves.

A Roman Catholic writer, who, as he tells us, could not at one time listen with any patience to the mere mention of our phenomena, has in the *Dublin Review* some apt remarks, of which, however, I can only give the pith in language much abridged. He remarks that a plausible lie soon loses its hold on the credence of men, and at length vanishes utterly and forever. But what has been the fortune of these phenomena? They were received at first not only with disbelief but with derision; they were rejected as untrue, not because not proven, but because incapable of proof, because they were impossible — and, indeed, impossible they are to mere human power and skill. The characteristic of the times is certainly not one of credulity. It was predicted that before the generation that witnessed the rise of these phenomena had died out, they would have disappeared and been forgotten. Well, years have rolled on, and men who once impatiently repudiated the phenomena, having been induced to examine into what was making such a noise in the world, have been led, from mature, and for a time prejudiced examination, to conviction.

In this way have been brought round several of the ablest and most learned men in Europe, physicians, philosophers, theologians, Catholic, Protestant, and free-thinking.

Authority does not prove an *opinion;* but here there is a question of *facts* and of the testimony of the senses, — of facts and testimonies repeated over and over again, beyond the possibility of calculation, in the greater part of Europe and America, not to speak of Australia, and recorded year after year down to the present day. It is quite impossible that about such facts such a cloud of such witnesses should be all deceived.

The charge that Spiritualism is a superstition recoils on its utterers. It is the remedy for all superstitions. Can beliefs founded on absolute and demonstrable *facts* prove less potent in influencing life and character than dogmas and conjectures?

" Spiritualism," says Alfred R. Wallace, " is an experimental science, and affords the only foundation for a true philosophy and a pure religion. It abolishes the terms ' supernatural ' and ' miracle ' by an extension of the sphere of law and the realm of nature ; and in doing so it takes up and explains whatever is true in the superstitions and so-called miracles of all ages. A science of human nature, which teaches that happiness in a future life can be secured by cultivating and developing to the utmost the higher faculties of our intellectual and moral nature, and by no other method, is and must be the natural enemy of all superstitions."

" I have left off believing in deaths so called," writes Philip Pearsall Carpenter, the naturalist, (brother of the Dr. W. B. Carpenter who has fought so against our facts) and goes on to say :

" The spiritual world appears to me close and near. Judging from all accounts, there are only a few hours, or days at most, before the spirit wakes again. I believe my deprivation of home sympathies has made me live more in the spiritual world, from which I feel separated only by a veil of flesh. I feel as though it would never surprise me to find that I had died and was there: it often seems more natural than the present state. In old times, when I believed in an external heaven, and thought we left off being men and became some queer kind of undefined angels, it was not so. Now I feel it to be a waking of the same humanity without the hindrances of flesh. . . . In my intercourse with the Spiritualists it is evident to me that they do not mourn for death like orthodox Christians, whose heaven is more ideal than real. They really do believe that their friends are living happily, and have intercourse with them. About this medium work I care very little: its principal use is to teach the reality of things unseen; and it must be a very imperfect thing at best, because it is only the lowest elements of their nature that can communicate with the highest of ours. But for us all to look on the next state as an absolute continuation of this, only in a far purer and in every way better sphere, is good for us all, and especially for those who have treasures in heaven."

The cause of the unbelief in what is taught in systems of theology, sectarian creeds, and historical assertions, on the subject of immortality, is that the advanced intellect of the age lacks a scientific basis for a full, energizing conviction as to spiritual realities. It is idle to say that men ought to infer from their own natures that they have souls. They still lend too ready an ear on this point to the confident contradictions of an arrogant Materialism, sporting the credentials of science.

But here are the facts of Spiritualism, forcing upon those who will fairly investigate them, the great conviction that spiritual agency can be objectively proved. What folly is it, then, in the friends of religion to reject the aid presented, because there may be much that still seems perplexing, incongruous, and even offensive in the developments?

CHAPTER V

IS SPIRITUAL SCIENCE HOSTILE TO RELIGION?

In a previous chapter I referred to some fanciful theories as to the origin of the belief in immortality among the primitive races of men. I have contended that the belief must have sprung as a corollary from a knowledge of actual phenomena, such as millions have had proved to them in our own day. I am glad to learn from one of the pamphlets of my esteemed friend, Thomas Shorter, of London, that my convictions on this point are supported by the philosophical inferences of so high an authority as the late John Stuart Mill, who wisely says:

"The argument from tradition, or the general belief of the human race, if we accept it as a guide to our own belief, must be accepted entire; if so, we are bound to believe that the souls of human beings not only survive after death, but show themselves as ghosts to the living; for we find no people who have had the one belief without the other. Indeed, it is probable that the former belief originated in the latter, and that primitive men would never have supposed that the soul did not die with the body, if they had not fancied that it visited them after death."

Here we have the subtlest skeptical philosophy corroborating one of our most important positions, namely, that the primitive tribes drew their belief in immortality, not from seeing their faces in the water, or their shadows against the sunlight, as Mr. Spencer supposes, but from seeing actual, objective, recognizable apparitions of deceased persons.

The ground-thought of the system which I. H. Fichte

drew from his knowledge of our phenomena is, according to Professor Franz Hoffman, of Wurtzburg, *a God-given, spiritually-real individualism.* Fichte accepts the facts of modern Spiritualism, and refutes the materialism, the pantheism, and the merely realistic individualism of the day. From the standpoint of psycho-physical science, he argues in favor of the objective nature of the soul itself. It has a certain *where* in space, but is all-present in every part of its space-existence. Its body is the *real*, its consciousness the *ideal* expression of its individuality. From its inner, continuing, invisible body, the separable exterior body must be distinguished.

The inner body is the soul itself *considered in its sense-relations only.* The outer body is the chemical material body, appropriated and then dissolved, and, in death, altogether separable from the imperishable soul. The whole body is the organ of the soul, the instrument of its activity, and consequently a system of organs; and the soul, considered still in its sense-relations only, is *unconscious-rational, body-fashioning force.* Thus the spirit-form is fair or otherwise, according to the character of the individual. To higher spirits the hypocrite unmasks himself by his very aspect. "*There* is no shuffling — *there* the action lies in its true light." Fichte says of our facts:

"Through their inner analogy, one with another, they become credible, and through their frequent recurrence among different peoples of different grades of culture in ancient and modern times, are found to cohere so remarkably that neither the theory of an accidental reception of ever-returning delusions, nor that of a superstition transmitted from generation to generation, can suffice as an explanation. However offensive, therefore, to the ruling notions of the day, they must be admitted to the domain of well-accepted psychical facts."

"No faith," says Leibnitz, "can be real or intelligible unless its foundations are detected in the human reason.

Religion, dissevered from the reason of man, can have no hold or standing-place." It is the glory of Spiritualism that its appeal is to the reason through science; that it gives us the elements of a religion, old as the world, and at once rational, scientific, and emotional. But this religion the individual must himself deduce from our facts, and thus make it truly his own, and not a graft from some other man's tree of life. This being the case, there must be diversity of religious insight.

"Anything becomes religious to us," says Mrs. Louisa Andrews, " which tends, directly or indirectly, to lift the mind above the lower and narrower spheres of thought into a contemplation of realities that are eternal, and by this uplifting to inspire in the heart that ' worship of something afar from the sphere of our sorrow,' which is the soul of all true religion, irrespective of creeds. Spiritualism may do this or it may not. ' The fool sees not the same tree that the wise man sees ;' nor do all the wise necessarily see the same. ' We receive but what we give.' "

The same writer tells us that Spiritualists differ, one from another, in their views in regard to right living and right thinking, as widely as it is possible for men to do; some insisting on a purely moral life, and others ready to sweep away all recognized boundary lines between right and wrong that may interfere with an indulgence of their own unchallenged desires. There are many of the latter class who claim to be Spiritualists ; and where are we to draw the line of exclusion? The influence exerted by Spiritualism having its source in the phenomena, we must not leave these behind as things outgrown, but continue to study them, and draw from them — confirming as they do belief in spiritual, immortal life — such truths as may make us wise unto eternity.

Because many persons do not draw these precious inferences, it does not follow that the repeated demonstration

of spirit power ought not to elevate us by filling us with
the sense of immortality. Even the manifestations of an
evil spirit may have their impressive lesson; though unless
we can do him good, the less we have of his society the
better. "These proofs of spirit existence and energy,"
says Mrs. Andrews, "with all the mysteries involved in
the exercise of unknown forces as they act upon the things
we call material, must, rightly used, be of incalculable
value."

Spiritualism is not, as the ignorant have called it, "a
form of religion." To the pure in heart it is religion itself.
Theodore Parker, though lack of opportunities of investigation left him without personal proof of our facts, intuitively recognized their vast significance; for in his "Notes
for Sermons," he says: "In 1856 it seems more likely that
Spiritualism would become the religion of America than in
156 that Christianity would become the religion of the
Roman empire, or in 756 that Mohammedanism would be
that of the Arabian populations: (1) It has more evidence
for its wonders than any historic form of religion hitherto.
(2) It is thoroughly democratic, with no hierarchy; but
inspiration is open to all. (3) It is no fixed fact — has no
punctum stans — but is a *punctum fluens*. (4) It admits
all the truths of religion and morality in all the world-
sects."

Thus Spiritualism is eclectic. It gives us a basis of
demonstrable truth for our religion. It is remarked by
Henry Thomas Buckle that those who would found their
belief in immortality on their religion, instead of founding
their religion on their belief in immortality, are making a
great mistake. "They imperil," he says, "their own
cause. They make the fundamental depend upon the cas-
ual; they support what is permanent by what is ephem-
eral; and with their books, their dogmas, their traditions,
their rituals, their records, and their other perishable con-

trivances, they seek to prove what was known to the world before these existed, and what, if these were to die away, would still be known, and would remain the common heritage of the human species, and the consolation of myriads yet unborn."

Again he says: "It is to that sense of immortality with which the affections inspire us, that I would appeal for the best proof of the reality of a future life. So surely as we lose what we love, so surely does hope mingle with grief."

I grant that the testimony of the affections is supplementary and important; but it is not the original factor which made the belief in immortality so prevalent even among uncivilized tribes. That belief, as I have shown, had actual phenomena for its basis.

And what is religion? For no word have more definitions been invented. I will give another, acknowledging that it is a limited one: Religion is the sentiment of reverence or of appeal, growing out of a sense of the possibility that there may be in the universe a Power or powers unseen, able to take cognizance of our thoughts and our needs, and to help us spiritually or physically.   .

The religious sentiment is then genuine, legitimate, and almost universal. It will detract nothing from its authority for some Darwinian to tell us of its pedigree, to inform us that, like many traits of character, it is mostly the result of heredity; of the gradual complexity of the brain-cells; that it is a mere evolution from certain experiences, fears, hopes, and imaginations, all of which can be traced through merely material developments, like the physical faculties of man and beast, till by the survival of the fittest, and a progress over long tracts of time, we have arrived at our present state. Grant that this is all so, it does not explain how the original cell or germ should have been endowed with these amazing potentialities, nor does it detract from the legitimacy and the efficacy of the religious sentiment.

Truly does Coleridge say: "A religion — *i. e.*, a true religion — must consist of ideas and facts both; not of ideas alone without facts, for then it would be mere philosophy; nor of facts alone without ideas, of which those facts are the symbols, or out of which they arise, or upon which they are grounded, for then it would be mere history."

Spiritualism fulfils these requirements. Its facts, rightly construed, hold out the loftiest inducements to a noble, beneficent life. It proclaims to us that we think and do in the sight of a host of witnesses; it recognizes the supremacy of law, physical, moral, and spiritual; it looks for no relief from the penalties of sin through the mystical sufferings of another; it teaches no vicarious advantage. It illustrates the efficacy of prayer, but teaches that the power of finite spirits is limited, and that the Divine Benignity is exercised in harmony with laws which it is for us to study and obey. It proves that as we sow we reap, and that man is preparing his future condition while here, by his ruling thoughts, desires, and acts, and is thus his own punisher, his own rewarder.

Thus the religion prompted by the facts of Spiritualism cannot differ largely in any essential point from that of primitive Christianity. This did not spring from the decisions of councils, from the interpretations of students, from the dictation of majorities, from any dogma relative to vicarious atonement, the Trinity, or the nature of salvation. It was born of the knowledge that the Jesus whom they had known and conversed with had reappeared to certain disciples and friends after his crucifixion, and thus given them the assurance and the palpable proof of his own immortality, and indirectly of theirs. Nay, in his visible and tangible presentation of himself he had endeavored to dissipate the fears they associated with disembodied spirits, and had partaken of food to show that he was no mere shadow of his former self, but had that power over matter that he could re-compose a simulacrum of his earth-form, or reduce it to invisibility by a simple act of volition.

This fact of Christ's reappearance was the cardinal doctrine of the early Christians, their common faith and hope. " They had," says Thomas Shorter, " an indubitable assurance that as He lived they should live also. This inspired them with enthusiasm, and a courage to brave torture and death. It was the apparition of Christ that converted Saul the poor persecutor into Paul the apostle, and transformed the heresy of an obscure provincial sect into a universal faith."

We must believe in an absolute, immutable principle of goodness, and in a Divine Intelligence, from which all axiomatic, *à priori* truth must flow down to finite intelligences, if we would unite religion with morality ; for if we are at the mercy of some blind chance, under which what is right to-day may be wrong to-morrow, the cosmos is not likely to be a pleasant abiding-place for an eternity to truth-loving, justice-loving souls. An enlightened Spiritualism conducts the mind, sooner or later, to an enlightened Theism — liberal as the sun and all-embracing as the universe. But it is not dogmatic, since its inferences are those of the scientific mind itself.

The sphere of science, as science herself declares, is the sphere of demonstrable phenomena. Beyond that she does not assume to penetrate. Our Sadducean friends, however, as well as philosophers like Wundt, do not hesitate to enter this forbidden *Beyond* very confidently, as if they were qualified to teach us as to the existence or non-existence of a First Cause. As far as they do this they are indulging in mere speculation. Spiritualism differs from all speculative systems in presenting a body of well-attested phenomena, and a thoroughly scientific synthesis for its basis, since it is from phenomena only, supplemented by axioms and the postulates of reason, that all science is derivable.

Spiritualism, then, in its primitive relations, is the science of pneumatology. What "form of religion" may proceed from it depends on the character, mental, moral, and emotional, of the recipient. He may be, in his own estimation, an atheist; for, as Bishop Butler has remarked, " That we are to live hereafter is just as reconcilable with the scheme of atheism, and as well to be accounted for by it, as that we are now alive is ; and therefore nothing can be more absurd than to argue from that scheme that there can be no future state." I have my doubts, however, whether atheism can ever thrive in the atmosphere of Spiritualism. As pneumatology is tending to be a science, Sadducceism at least is doomed, and its expulsion from minds scientifically trained is merely a question of time.

The inquiry, then, is not whether Spiritualism may be favorable to religion, but whether it is true.   And yet it has been the very life-blood of all the world's serious religions ; and if there is to be a religion of the future, the basis must be a scientific belief in the immortality of man. If we can once realize what Spiritualism makes known to us, that a finite spirit can manifest its existence by exercising a preterhuman power over matter in many intelligent ways, it makes scientifically possible the existence of an Infinite Spirit, conscious, intelligent, and omnipotent, able to create the very principle of matter, to will into existence a universe, and to sustain it by his immutable volition. I admit that this faith must be largely and properly a postulate of the reason ; but Spiritualism, through its marvellous phenomena, vouches for it with the force of all its analogies. It is a familiar fact that there are Spiritualists who, in regard to the question of a supreme Spiritual Orderer, are agnostic, pantheistic, or atheistic. But that Spiritualism lends new authority to the theistic hypothesis, by proving grand spiritual possibilities, transcending all that human effort could accomplish or even comprehend, there can be no reasonable doubt. Establish the fact of this spiritual power over matter; — from what a finite spirit can do, rise to an estimate of what an infinite spirit might do — and the hypothesis of a Supreme Intelligence, filling the earth with the exuberance of his life, and power, and love, becomes something more than a speculation.

To say that religion cannot have science — *i. e.*, a knowledge of the phenomena of nature, including the soul of man — for its basis, is as absurd as it would be to say that mathematics do not require axioms for their foundation. Religion may transcend phenomena and rise into a region which mortal science may not enter; indeed it must do so, the more it ascends to the height of its great argument, the more it expands and draws nearer to the Infinite; but if it have no other basis than the emotions, and reject all that intuition, science, and reason may offer for its justification, it may not soar to that "purer ether, that diviner air," where faith is merged in knowledge.

Religion has its root in the belief or intuitive feeling that within us or external to us is an intelligent, supersensual power that can affect us for good. According to Quatrefages, religion is "a belief in beings superior to man, and capable of exercising good or evil influences upon his destiny; and the conviction that the existence of man is not limited to the present life, but that there remains for him a future beyond the grave."

Any scientific confirmation of such a belief must then be a new force added to it. If we can justify it by an appeal to actual phenomena, it is a gain which no sane man, not desiring annihilation, would forego. This is what Spiritualism enables us to do; and therefore, since science "takes cognizance of phenomena, and endeavors to discover their laws," and consists in "an infallible and unchanging knowledge of phenomena," Spiritualism is a science, though as yet in many respects rudimental.

A critic objecting to the deduction of religion from Spiritualism, remarks, " How absurd, then, to demand that religion shall have a scientific basis ! " He goes on to tell us of the " shifting sands " of science, as if it were something here to-day and gone to-morrow. Plainly he confounds hypothesis with science. His argument rests on a palpable misconception. " Instead then of attempting," he says, " to place religion upon a basis consisting of the *shifting sands* of science, would it not be more logical to attempt to find for it a religious basis ? " But is not that sentence a little tautological? Is is not equivalent to telling us to base religion on religion? Where the " logic " comes in it is difficult to discover.

In a recent number of an American journal devoted to Spiritualism I find the following remarks from a correspondent :

" Religion will eventually become science ; but in doing so it will cease to be religion. Alchemy lost its identity in chemistry ; astrology gave way to astronomy ; and religion, like both alchemy and astrology, being a system which is composed mainly of supposed facts and their imaginary relations, must pass away and be forgotten just as fast as the real facts are discovered and their true relations understood."

As there are innumerable differing definitions of the word *religion*, and as the writer of the above remarks has made a new definition, it would seem somewhat idle to criticise his assumption that religion must fade out as science advances. If, as he says, religion is merely " a system composed mainly of supposed facts and their imaginary relations," then no one will be likely to go into mourning at seeing religion thrust out. But many thoughtful persons have a very different estimate of religion from this. To them it is the very culmination of all truth and all knowledge ; it is science " flushed with emotion."

When Kepler, as one of his grand discoveries flashed

upon his mind, knelt in devout thanksgiving and awe at the realization that he was "re-thinking the thoughts of God," I hardly think he would have been in a mood to admit that science is, or can ever be, the death of religion. It all depends upon what notions one has of religion, and what faculties he has for feeling it.

And so, when this same writer says, "Spiritualism can never develop a religion in any sense," the force of the proposition all depends upon what sort of thing one's Spiritualism is. One man's spiritual proclivities and affinities may lead him into very bad company and into a very low sphere of thought; while another's may surround him with all uplifting influences.

To say that Spiritualism can never "develop a religion in any sense," is about equivalent to saying that human and angelic thought can never develop a religion in any sense. There is no scientific force in the affirmation; it is pure dogmatism, entitled to not the least scientific respect.

One mind may see in certain facts very different "relations" from those that are suggested to another mind. The thought that forced a Kepler down on his knees might be wholly barren and unsuggestive to a Gradgrind or a Haeckel. In Spiritualism we find only what we bring the vision and the faculty for finding. To those who really know its phenomena, it is as much a science even now as astronomy or chemistry. So far is it from being true that science has a tendency to kill out religion, the real truth is, as Newton, Kepler, Copernicus, and Franklin found it, religion becomes all the more religion as the mind advances in positive science.

Are we to suppose that as physiology, anthropology, the laws of parentage, heredity, and embryology, are developed, the natural affections of the human race must die out? Yet such a proposition would be quite as philosophical as the notion that as religion grows more scientific it must dwindle and die.

Religion, pure and undefiled, is not the child of ignorance and superstition ; the more we know and feel, the more truly and purely religious must we become. On from the time of Copernicus science has been revealing to us new marvels, and widening our conceptions of that inscrutable Power that lives in all life. Can the growth of a scientific Spiritualism lead, any more than the growth of the sister sciences, to a less reverent and adoring sense of that Supreme Mind, whose thoughts it is our discipline here, like Kepler's, to " re-think,"—an occupation which an eternity cannot exhaust?

Let no one fear that as man advances in knowledge of the facts of universal nature he will grow less religious, less loving, less reverent, or less aspiring. All history and all human biography prove the contrary. It is the shallow draught that intoxicates the brain ; " but drinking largely sobers us again." It is the half-way, the second-hand philosophers —the men partially informed, confounding science in the state of hypothesis with science in the state of fact — who find science and religion at variance, and imagine that the latter will be compelled to yield the right of way to the former.

All religions have had some form of Spiritualism for their basis. Aptly does Mr. Stainton Moses remark : " As a factor in the religious thought of the age, as a regenerating force operating most strongly within the pale of religious systems that sadly need purifying, I believe it (Spiritualism) to be imperishable in its effects." To ignore the religious significance of Spiritualism — to fail to recognize it as " God's gift to a Sadducean generation "— is to be content with the husk and reject the life-giving grain. All religions still owe to it — in its past forms if not in its present — all they have in them of vitality.

The abstract, attenuated Spiritualism, for which Descartes, among the more modern philosophers, is so largely responsible, still dominates in philosophy, in religion, and in the speculations of leading physicists. Nearly all the attacks on Spiritualism from physicists like Tyndall, or amateur philosophers like Mr. John Fiske or Mr. Frederic Harrison, are grounded on the conception which holds the Cartesian notion in regard to the soul as the only scientific one, since from that to a psychic nonentity the step is easy. These men consider the soul, not as inhering in a substratum, to which death is not a sting and the grave is not a victory, — but as something having not so much substantial existence as the reflection of a form in a mirror. Thought, for them, does not inhere in a supra-physical substance, but in a certain pulpy, cerebral matter, going off in a flux of atoms, and disorganized forever by death. Hence thought, consciousness, emotion, having no other instrument or basis, vanish like a reflected image when the mirror is covered or shivered. To such thinkers, therefore, with their limited or partial science, the immortality of the soul is an absurdity, since to them the individual life and experience are the exclusive property of that compound of charcoal, lime, water, oxygen, nitrogen, and hydrogen, which goes to make up the visible body. Dissolve and dissipate these by death, and the phenomenon, *man*, has an end, body and soul.

No thought is here given to the consideration that all these substances and gases may exist in, or are resolvable into, invisible states, in which their powers and uses may be greatly augmented for spiritual appropriation, if necessary. The following remarks are by I. H. Fichte:

" Certainly this is a serious revelation at a time when an earnest belief in a future for man has been so widely impaired or dismissed. Thus should modern Spiritualism become a monitor and a stimulator for us to recover a firm and abiding assurance of our immortality.

"The causes that have turned the so-called educated class away from this belief in a spiritual organism are far from being irrefutable arguments against its scientific possibility: they are wholly untenable as such. The grounds for an enlarged and improved psychology lie in modern Spiritualism, since its physical phenomena are, in remarkable particulars, analogous to those known long ago. The old has been unexpectedly confirmed by the new, and *vice versâ*.

"The power of the departed to materialize is entirely antagonistic to all conceptions of a pure abstract spirituality as the only ground of *being* in a future state. This new science of *transcendental physics*, the elements of which are presented in materialization and other objective phenomena, is as yet, however, only in its first uncertain beginnings. Belief in the immortality of the soul is ratified by these evidences of psychical experience. It is now known that we may seize our future destination already here in the earth-life. The trite saying, '*Memento mori*,' is now converted into the more serious one, '*Memento vivere*,' which means, 'Remember that you are to live hereafter.' The future state is a continuation of the present, and will be affected by our experiences and our prevailing thoughts and affections here."

Coming from an octogenarian of vast experience in psychological and philosophical studies, a son of that Fichte who was one of the most eminent philosophers and eloquent writers of Germany, and one of the most active of her citizens in her day of disaster, the words I have quoted ought certainly to carry weight. Fichte looks to the advance of modern Spiritualism as an earnest of the revivification of the religious sentiment, and the precursor of a high and purified morality; since a knowledge that we are shaping our future destiny by our acts, thoughts, and affections in this life — a knowledge that we are under the scrutiny of all clairvoyant spirit-intelligences — must, as new generations are bred up to accept this as a revelation of science, exercise a most important influence upon the character and conduct of mankind.

Spiritualism has been referred to as " a new religion." On the contrary, it is the attracting principle, assimilating whatever is essential in all religions, but contradicting nothing that the eminent saints and sages of all the centuries have, in their highest moods, recognized as the eternally true, and subverting nothing of vital truth in any religion. Since Spiritualism is coeval with humanity, there can be nothing new in it, except so far as there is something new in every step made in life and knowledge by the human race, or in every immortal soul that appears on the stage of terrestrial being, and passes on to the spirit-world.

Let it be remembered that Spiritualism is now in a transitional state, and that we cannot expect its full results in a religious respect until its external phenomena are freely accepted by coming generations as facts of science. When the minds of men are once set at rest in regard to these actual occurrences, attention will be more generally directed to the higher, interior, and moral meanings which the subject involves. We may then expect the development of those truths which must give new force to the religious intuitions of our nature.

It would hardly be fair to hold a novelist to a strict philosophical account for the opinions he may seem to favor. His business is to invent — to deal in fiction ; and we cannot always draw the line between what he would seriously teach and what he means simply as a bit of inoffensive character drawing. But the extent to which the *laudatores librorum novorum*, hostile to Spiritualism, have extolled Mr. Howells's " Undiscovered Country " as a just and much-needed analysis of a movement which is fast revolutionizing the minds of men in regard to a future state, induces me to exhibit the grounds of my dissent. If I may believe the eulogistic reviewers, whose praise of his literary ability is doubtless just, he gives his own conclusions in the words of his reformed Spiritualist, "Boynton," in representing him as declaring, that "Spiritualism is a grosser materialism than that which it denies; a materialism that asserts and affirms, and appeals for proof to purely physical phenomena," — and that it is "as thoroughly godless as atheism itself; and no man can accept it upon any other man's word because it has not yet shown its truth in the ameliorated life of men."

I do not for a moment suppose that this senile and vapid abuse of Spiritualism by the imaginary old man conveys the real opinions of Mr. Howells. I do not charge it upon him, as some of his friends have done, that such is the fact. I will therefore reply to him solely in his capacity of a novelist, leaving the question open as to his real views.

The materialism which he makes Boynton charge upon Spiritualism is (1) simply that of the Hebrew and Christian Scriptures. See Gen. xviii., how Abraham entertained three angels; in the 2d verse: "And, lo, three men stood beside him;" and food having been prepared for them, in the 8th verse it is said, "And he stood by them under the tree, and they did eat." In Ezek. ii. 9, we find that a materialized spirit-hand holds out "a roll of a book" . . . "written within and without" by direct spirit-power. The crucified Christ is represented as entering a room with closed doors, and reappearing in so lifelike and palpable a form as to be recognized by his disciples, and to be able to show his wounds, and to say to one of the Twelve who was not present when the Saviour first came, and who doubted the report of the rest, — "Reach hither thy finger, and behold my hands; and reach hither thy hand, and thrust it into my side; and be not faithless, but believing." Is

12

not this the very *ne plus ultra* of what our amiable novelist calls materialism?

With what new force all this narrative is invested, when one can really accept it as in perfect harmony with natural law, and therefore perfectly credible! And when Jesus would cure the apostles of that demonophobia which made them regard a returned human being as something uncanny and unnatural, did he not vindicate his power of materialization, and dissipate their dread, with the remark, "Behold my hands and my feet, that it is I myself: handle me and see; for a spirit hath not flesh and bones, as ye see me have"? And further to impress them with a sense of his existence as the same Jesus they had known, and supped with, he says, "Have ye any meat? And they gave him a piece of broiled fish and of an honeycomb. And he took it, and did eat before them."

All this "grosser materialism" an experienced Spiritualist can accept as thoroughly consistent with facts he has known, either as a witness or through the testimony of others. Truly here indeed *is* "a materialism that asserts and affirms, and appeals for proof to purely physical phenomena." Will our novelist say it was all right centuries ago, but all wrong now?

Spiritualism may be to us either a "gross materialism" or a sublime manifestation of spirit-power, according to the degree and quality of our moral and mental insight and predisposition. But how can the reappearance of Christ affect me as a type and a guaranty of my own immortality unless I can see in it the same process by which other departed human beings can give us tokens of their existence? Was it then simply a reanimated corpse, a monstrous "Frankenstein" that appeared to the Twelve? Or will you say it was that corpse changed into a "glorified body" (a glorified body with wounds!) and refer to the disappearance of the cadaverous remains from the sepulchre as the reason for your theory? If it was a body that could enter a room with closed doors, it was plainly something distinct from the earth-body. Whether Christ, as a human spirit, had that power over matter that he could dissipate and recompose the atoms of his old body, I cannot say; I will say, however, that if he had that power, the presumption is that it is one common to all human spirits. Because I accept so much of the narrative as is reconcilable with known facts, it does not follow that I must accept all the rest. But I find in the Christian Scriptures no passage that justifies the interpretation that the re-materialized body of Christ was a reconstruction of the very particles of matter that formed his physical organism — the same corpse which he had parted from at his crucifixion, so re-animated or " glorified " as to be independent of material obstructions. Immortality must be inferred from a continuation of life quite independent of the corruptible body that is laid in the tomb to mingle with the elements like other corporeal exuviæ which we are all the time casting off.

Whether the spirit has that transcendent power that would enable it to create, independently of its own form, an animated simulacrum of its earthly body, or whether the spirit-body attracts to itself from the atomic spheres of mortals and from the atmosphere the ultimate particles which, by condensation, are made to resemble any material substance, or whether both modes of presentation may be used, are questions which perhaps can be settled only by our own post-mortem experiences.

In giving his readers to infer (2) that the Spiritualist has no other proof than the physical to which to appeal, our novelist shows himself altogether too swift an accuser. What is clairvoyance? What is prevision? What the use of languages unknown to the medium? The intellectual evidences, too various to be summed up? The reminis-

cences, showing that the earth-born affections, transferred
to the unseen world, have been deepened rather than paralyzed? Surely such proofs can be classed as in the highest
sense mental and spiritual.

The charge (3) that Spiritualism may be stigmatized as
being "as thoroughly godless as atheism itself," since "it
has not yet shown its truth in the ameliorated life of men,"
is a *non-sequitur*, to which even a novelist, in the full blast
of his inventive powers, ought not to have resorted. Precisely the same argument might be used against all great
beliefs, including those of Theism, Buddhism, and Christianity. If we are to gauge our estimate of the truth by
the character of its utterers, our creed is likely to be a
very short one.

The novelist makes his representative Spiritualist, Boynton, give up his belief because he learns from an old magazine that there was once a girl in whose presence some of
the minor medial phenomena occurred, for which the investigator sought a natural cause; " and he found that by
insulating the posts of the girl's bedstead — for these things
mostly occurred during her sleep — he controlled them perfectly. She was simply surcharged with electricity."

And this is the novelist's explanation of the whole matter! A surcharge of electricity! The theory was exploded
as far back as 1850 by the experiments of Dr. Hare and
others; and the evocation of it at this late day to eke out
the requirements of a work of fiction would not call for
notice except for the fact that the device has been com-
mended as if it were something more than an extinct conjecture. Electricity has been of no avail in explaining the
medial phenomena. It was used by Wm. Crookes, F.R.S.,
and C. F. Varley, F.R.S., to verify the genuineness of the
form-manifestations at Mr. Luxmore's house, London, early
in March, 1874. This was done by means of a galvanic
battery and cable-testing apparatus, which was so delicate

that any movement whatever on the part of the medium
would be instantly indicated, while it would be impossible
for her to play the part of the spirit without breaking the
circuit and being instantly detected.

. The novelist's attempt to resuscitate the defunct hypothesis of insulation can delude only the ignorant. Among
the objections to Spiritualism he puts into the mouth of his
Boynton is this: "It offers nothing but the barren fact that
we live again." So, then, we are to accept his word for it
that immortality, if a fact, is a barren one; and that Paul
was out in his reckoning when he said, "If in this life only
we have hope, then are we of all men most miserable." A
barren fact! How many there are who would give up life
and fortune if they could once be sure of that barren fact!

"The Immortal Life, by John Weiss," is the title of a
posthumous volume (1880) published in Boston. I knew
the author. He was a man of genius and a strenuous believer in human immortality. But he seems to have had
a great disdain for a belief founded on creeds, traditions,
or historical and psycho-physical facts. He was so willing
to trust to his own estimate of the energy of the primitive
faculties — of the soul itself — to his own inward aspira-
tions towards the immortal life — that he even neglected
to investigate with any thoroughness the phenomena which
would have proved to him that he was wrong in his attitude
of opposition to Modern Spiritualism.

He does not put quite so fine a point on the great question as Matthew Arnold does, who finds "the true basis
for all religious aspiration after immortality" in what he
calls "the strong sense of life from righteousness, capable
of being developed, apparently by progress in righteousness, into something immeasurably stronger." So attenuated and contingent a belief could hardly have suited
Weiss's delicate yet robust mind.

After frankly admitting that "if the soul is going to continue its personal existence, and not be merged into blind currents of forces, or states of motion, it must be furnished with another set of senses correspondent to another set of impressions which result from a new relation between the universe and the soul," — he plants himself in vehement antagonism to the ancient and rational idea of the Spiritualist, that the germ, the embryo, or the psychical organism, *essential to that continuity of personal existence*, is involved in man's present constitution, and is the explanation of those spiritual powers manifested in clairvoyance, in pneumatography, and other proved phenomena.

This is the view of many of the greatest thinkers in the annals of humanity. Professors Stewart and Tait, of Edinburgh, in their "Unseen Universe," a work thoroughly scientific in its plan, tell us that it is only within the last thirty or forty years that there has gradually dawned upon the minds of scientific men the conviction that there is. something besides matter or stuff in the physical universe, which *has at least as much claim as matter to recognition as an objective reality*, though, of course, far less directly obvious to our senses as such, and therefore much later in being detected. Crookes's discovery of the supra-gaseous state of matter in high vacua I have remarked upon elsewhere.

The physicists to whom I have referred arrive logically at the conclusion that there is an invisible universe, from which life as well as matter proceed, and that immortality is possible *without a break of continuity*. Thus they accept the Pauline doctrine of a spiritual body, now existing, either actually or potentially, and making life continuous from the seen to the unseen world ; and they quote with approval this passage from Swedenborg : " A man at death escapes from his material body as from a rent or worn-out vesture, carrying with him every member, faculty, and function complete, with not one wanting, yet the corpse is as heavy as when he dwelt therein." From this it would seem that Swedenborg regarded the nervous fluid as among the so-called imponderables. Why, then, should not the spiritual body belong to the same class?

The spiritual senses, Weiss tells us, do not yet exist. He says:

"They cannot exist; the ground is preoccupied. The soul can be related to but one body at a time, just as it can think but one thought and experience but one feeling at a time; for the most complex internal sensations have a unity, whose place cannot be occupied by another at the same time. There is a natural body and there is a spiritual body, but not both at once; and one cannot overlap and be entangled in the other. The soul must be entirely ignorant of the second body until it has ceased to use the first."

Here is a tissue of plausible assertions without one particle of scientific proof. Cannot a man make use of two senses at once? Cannot I both hear and see you, and shall it be said that the seeing and hearing are not a simultaneous complex thought, but that one must precede the other? Experience contradicts the notion, however stoutly logic may assert it: The faculties and capabilities of the soul are complex. Clairvoyance proves that there is something deeper in us than our external faculties of vision; though of this we may be unconscious in our normal state. Weiss is in error when he argues that one faculty may not "overlap another" as yet latent or undeveloped. The analogies by which he would prove that the soul cannot be simultaneously related to its earth-body and its spirit-body are purely fanciful; and his attempt to correct the apostle Paul, who distinctly tells us that "there is a natural body and there *is*" (not *shall* be) "a spiritual body," is a little presumptuous, seeing that the contradiction is so unsupported by proofs. As well might he say that the worm and the potential chrysalis could not coexist. Is it true, as Weiss asserts, that a man can experience but one feeling at a time? Can he not be simultaneously afflicted by tooth-ache and a twinge of the gout — by frost and fire? "No matter," he says, "how curious the facts of somnam- bulism, of unconscious cerebration, of the magnectic con- dition, and of those which arise from a double hemispheric brain, may be, they are all referable to one material body, and to the soul, its ordinary tenant, who cannot quit with- out killing it — who *cannot have another till that one is killed.*"

Strangely contradictory to these views is the following sentence, which comes in some sixteen lines further on : "Nothing can save the soul from collapsing into the blind forces of the world but the preservation of its identity ; and that cannot be preserved without a frame to hold it, a system of organs by which it can express spiritual func- tion." Well and truly stated ! Stick a pin there. But what is to become of the soul at death unless this "frame to hold it," this "system of organs by which it can ex- press spiritual function," is pre-related to it so that there shall be no unbridged hiatus — so that "the frame to hold it" (the soul) shall not be a foreign body magically sent for its occupancy (at death), but a body with organs in full harmony with all the mental activities, the experiences and developments of its earth-life? In continuous existence there must be an organ for memory, connecting the indi- vidual *with the past*, and in the next place such an organism and such a universe that he can be active in various ways *in the present*. All this is substantially admitted by Pro- fessors Stewart and Tait. And how else is identity to be preserved in the transition from one state of being to an- other? How is the interval to be annulled, unless the soul can carry with it that "system of organs," which, as Weiss tells us, (inconsistently with his objections to a duplex organism,) is essential to its preservation from "a collapse into the blind forces of the world"?

Weiss seems to be of the opinion that the disembodied soul will "*attract*" a suitable body. He says :

"The soul of your friend, then, passes from a frame of flesh into a frame more subtly woven, *without a single corporeal characteristic in it, yet not without the character of matter*. So to speak, blood will still tell ; that is to say, the finer soul will *attract* and use the finer body, just as it does now by the principle of heredity."

Subtly reasoned and partially true ; only one consideration is dropped which vitiates the hypothesis as a whole. Weiss has told us distinctly that the soul's identity " cannot be preserved without a frame to hold it." Yet now he launches his soul (it matters not whether for a moment or for an eternity) into disembodiment, " merges it into blind currents of forces, or states of motion," leaving it to the soul, thus merged and loosened from all its moorings, to attract to itself a frame that shall be "*without a single corporeal characteristic in it, yet not without the character of matter !*" Is not matter itself a " corporeal characteristic"? Was Weiss of Hibernian descent?

Is there not a lack of precision and consistency in an argument like this? Shutting his eyes to the facts of Spiritualism, how could he help being carried into these gross contradictions? For be it said, John Weiss, when he has truth on his side, as he often has, argues with a precision and force which places him high among the best and most original thinkers of the nineteenth century.

Against the phenomenon of form-manifestation, or the power of spirits to " materialize themselves into visibility," he brings this objection : " They already have a body of their own, and yet we are told they make another body out of some property of the medium. The spirit could not exist for an instant without its body, and yet it slips into one which the medium exhales."

There are two theories as to the mode of the presenta-

tion. One is, that the spirit does not really become in-
corporated in the visible body or member, but that he has
that power over the elements of matter that he can create,
independently of his own spirit-body, an animated simulacrum of his earthly body as it was at any period of its existence. The other theory is, that the spirit-body may
attract to itself from the atomic spheres of the medium and
others, or from the atmosphere, the ultimate particles, finer
than the effluvia of musk, which by condensation are made
to resemble any material object, according to the will of
the spirit, and that he can do this with the rapidity of
thought. The latter is the common theory, though the
former is perhaps more consistent with the fact that the
manifestations are often so fragmentary and imperfect.
The extemporization is then merely tentative ; the memory
of the " materialized " spirit is often at fault; and the
mind sometimes works as if it were in a mist.

It has been asked : " Do the spirits really extemporize
bodies possessing all the chemical constituents and organic
parts belonging to the corporeal forms which they occupied
during their rudimental life on earth ? " Obviously this is
a question which cannot as yet be answered. There is
good reason to believe that spirits economize their efforts,
and give no more than is necessary for the purpose in view.
If they can suggest identity by simply presenting a hand,
known by some peculiar malformation to be a fac-simile of
a hand once belonging to the earth-body of a relative or
friend, they may confine themselves to this one manifestation. Sometimes merely the facial part of a head is presented, while the back part is hollow or amorphous. Dr.
J. M. Gully, an educated physician, formerly at the head
of the well-known water-cure establishment at Great Malvern, has brought his powers of calm, philosophical investigation to our phenomena, and in one of his letters to me

he writes, July 20, 1874, in regard to the experiments with Florence Cook :

" That the power grows with use was curiously illustrated by the fact that, for some time only a face was producible, with occasionally arms and hands ; with no hair, and sometimes with no back to the skull at all — merely a mask, with movement, however, of eyes and mouth. *Gradually the whole form appears* — after, perhaps, some five months of séances, once or twice a week. This again becomes more and more rapidly formed, and changed, in hair, dress, and color of face, as we desired."

Mr. Tapp, of the Dalston (England) Association of Inquirers, relates that he was frequently permitted to scan the face and figure of the spirit form known as Katie, coming through Miss Cook, in a good light. Once she laid her right arm in his outstretched hands, and allowed him to examine it closely. It was plump and shapely, longer than that of the medium. The hands, too, were much larger, with beautifully shaped nails, unlike those of Miss Cook, who was in the bad habit of biting her nails. Holding the arm of the materialized form lightly in one hand, he passed the other hand along it from the shoulder. "The skin," he says, "was beautifully — I may say unnaturally — smooth, like wax or marble ; yet the temperature was that of the healthy human body. *There was, however, no bone in the wrist.* I lightly felt round the wrist again, and then told Katie that the bone was wanting. She laughed and said, 'Wait a bit ;' and after going about to the other sitters, she came round and placed her arm in my hand as before." This time Mr. Tapp was satisfied ; the bone was there. On another occasion he caught the spirit-form by the wrist, and he says : "Her wrist crumpled in my grasp like a piece of paper or thin card-board, my fingers meeting through it. I let go at once, and expressed my regret." Katie reassured him, and forgave the unintended rudeness, saying she could " avert any untoward consequence."

Facts like these may not yet be as scientifically demonstrable as the typical facts of my "basis," but they are credible and consistent. They show that these spirit-materializations may be often fractional and imperfect. At the same time, we have reason to suppose that all the parts of a human body, exterior or interior, including the blood and the viscera, may, *if wanted*, be either imitated or duplicated by spirit-power. The fact that parts are often omitted in the materialization is no argument against the power to produce a complete whole. The existence of untestable atoms is assumed by materialism as a reasonable hypothesis. May it not be that spirits can exercise over those atoms a power not easily conceivable by mortal intelligence, in composing and dissipating transient forms, just as they can do many other things, as to which we cannot as yet begin to explain the *modus operandi?*

My own experience confirms that of Dr. Gully. It is not to specialists in science, wholly unprepared for proofs of psychic power, that I address myself here. What I have to say will not, I am well aware, help my credit with many whose good opinion I would like to have. But I must make a clean breast of it. Of the fact that I have witnessed the attempt of a venerated relative, not of this world, to manifest to me objectively at a medial séance, her identity through her power over matter in producing a simulacrum of her earth-body, I have never had a doubt since the occurrence. At first the face presented was a mere disk, with hardly a feature prominent, reminding me of the face-like picture of the moon in story-books. I at once said : "This manifestation cannot be for me" (as it had claimed to be) ; "I do not recognize a single trait." There was a delay of half a minute at the aperture, and then the entranced medium said : "The spirit insists ; she says it is for you that she is waiting, and asks you to look again." I consented, went up again to the aperture, and at once, without any forethought or anticipation, exclaimed, 'Is it possible!' The recognition was instantaneous. I mentioned no name, asked no question. But the spirit, through the simulacrum, seemed to know at once that her attempt had been successful; and her familiar and peculiar demonstrations of delight and affection were even more convincing than words. Every little gesture, the dainty and playful putting up of two hands to pat me on the cheeks, the kiss on the forehead, were all reproductions of the old ways which characterized her, when during her last illness I used to enter her room to receive her good-night kiss. "Can you give me no message for L.?" I asked. Instantly she seemed to pull away at her cap-strings, tore off a strip of lace, and pressed it into my hand. There ended the interview, and I was convinced, not only from internal evidence, but from other indescribable circumstances, that it was no transfiguration of the medium, but an independent act of the spirit. I had, before the sitting, never once thought of her in connection with her possible manifestation; and that the medium knew nothing of the relationship, I have not the slightest reason to doubt. The facts cannot be described in a way to be scientifically presentable, but they are none the less facts confirmatory to the one mortal to whom they were given. I should add that the cap-string was recognized by L—— as a fac-simile of those which the individual used to make for herself out of lace. The strip was put in a box and placed in a drawer: in a few months it had disappeared, how we know not, as we have no reason to suppose the box was ever meddled with.

It has been asked, What becomes of the matter of these tangible simulacra, when they disappear? It has been said that a corpse ought to be left as evidence of the vacation of a body, whether extemporized or of gradual growth, by a spirit. Now until we know what matter is, and until we

can accurately gauge the power of a spirit, it is unwise to
assume that spirits cannot have the power of dissipating
extemporized matter, so that the atoms shall be just as
invisible as they were previous to the formation. The
amazing celerity with which they do this is no evidence
against either the fact of formation or of dissipation; for
we know that this spirit-power can exercise a superhuman
celerity in moving things, and in producing long written
messages. If superhuman power can be exercised in one
direction, why not in another? To give to this power the
bad name of *magical* does not alter the well-attested facts.
Everything that is inexplicable to us may be stigmatized
with the same epithet; and yet all finite causes and effects
may be strictly within the sphere of the natural. But here
I should add that there are investigators who testify to
having experienced a cadaverous odor at the dematerializa-
tion of these fugitive forms.

This theory that the spirit is simply exercising its power
over matter, and is not at all presenting itself as an embodied entity, entirely does away with the objections raised
by Weiss. What I may call his *contingent* objections to
the belief that the so-called spiritual manifestations are
from spirits, are thus summed up:

"If you owe your belief in immortality to the assumed
facts of a spiritual intercourse, your belief is at the mercy
of your assumption. It has not sprung from the vital
necessity of your own soul, it is not a craving which justifies and demands its future satisfaction, but it is merely an
opinion derived from a variety of phenomena; and when
those which attracted your attention, or when the tricks
which imposed upon your love of the marvellous, are explained away, your immortality is also explained away.
You did not derive it from a spiritual fact of your own
consciousness; you did not build it out of reasonable
judgments; you are at the mercy of what may prove to
be a delusion. Can a delusion import a spiritual truth
into the soul? Now, grant that eventually we shall dis-

cover that we are immortal, whether we believe it now or
not; grant that, in the meantime, it is human and proper
to wish to believe it and to know it, to see the horizon of
our life expand, lifting and ennobling all our thoughts,
justifying our love, and putting before our deeds a boundless career. *But we cannot derive a faith in personal immortality from occurrences which take place in darkened
rooms and cabinets.* Your opinion derived from them is
worth no more than the ordinary opinion which is based on
texts and dogmas. Withdraw the theology, and the truth
comes toppling down. Withdraw your phenomena, and,
for all you know, annihilation may have been the fate of
those you loved, and may be your own."

Here the pith of the whole argument is evolved from a
mistake. It proceeds from the premise that the facts of
Spiritualism are *assumed* by us, and not *known*. Now the
experienced Spiritualist *knows* that certain phenomena are
as much facts, proved by his senses and his common sense,
as the fact that the sun shines or the grass grows. He has
no more fear that certain phenomena can ever be proved to
be tricks, than he has a fear that life itself is a trick, imposed on us by some malignant Power. We need but
instance the phenomena of clairvoyance and of direct
writing. Any one, who has faithfully, practically, and
intelligently studied the subject, actually *knows* that these
take place under conditions which utterly exclude the possibility of trick, hallucination, or any abnormal state of
our consciousness.

It is not, then, in the least true that our " belief in immortality " is " at the mercy of an assumption; " for it is
a belief — nay, much more than a belief — founded on a
knowledge of actual facts, supersensual and preterhuman
in their nature. What if it has not sprung from " a craving which justifies and demands its future satisfaction"?
So long as the belief, or rather the conviction, confirms the
craving, are not both mutually strengthened? The intima-
tion that it is " a love of the marvellous," which leads the

serious and well-endowed mind — such minds as Whately, Fichte, Wallace, Chambers, Elizabeth Browning, and Franz Hoffman — to accept certain phenomena as giving evidence of spiritual power, is an unwarrantable accusation, which we need not answer.

When Weiss would narrow down our anticipations of immortality to "the vital necessity" of our own soul — to what he calls a "craving," — he leaves out of view the important fact that there are many excellent persons who do not feel that "vital necessity," or that "craving." William Humboldt, David F. Strauss, Harriet Martineau, and many other skeptics, did not feel it

The Spiritualist does not have to draw on those doubtful arguments for immortality which depend on the fact that the majority of men deduce it from the "emotions," or crave it as "a vital necessity." Such, as we have elsewhere shown, is not the true genesis of the wide-spread belief. The inherited "cravings" of the race may change. Those who agree with Strauss and Humboldt may become the majority. What, then, becomes of one of the great arguments for a future life, which are used by such reasoners as Weiss?

I do not regard such an event as possible — "thanks to the human heart by which we live!" Referring to materialistic atheism, Professor Tyndall says: "I have noticed during years of self-observation that it is not in hours of clearness and vigor that this doctrine commends itself to my mind; that in the presence of stronger and healthier thought it ever dissolves and disappears, as offering no solution of the mystery, in which we dwell, and of which we form a part." And Thomas Shorter, one of the clearest expounders of Spiritualism, tells us that G. L. Holyoake, the English founder of Secularism, which, like Positivism, denies or ignores God and a future life, in a passage of great tenderness and pathos, describing the death of his child, avows that even to *him* a pure and rational faith in immortality would be more congenial than the cold negations and dreary platitudes to which his life has been mainly devoted. Referring to his daughter, Holyoake says: "Yes, a future life, bringing with it the admission to such companionship, would be a noble joy to contemplate."

Thackeray, who was more than half a Spiritualist, and who caused an outcry against himself because he admitted into his magazine an article asserting the phenomena, says, writing about death: "I know one small philosopher"—meaning himself—"who is quite ready to give up these pleasures; quite content (after a pang or two of separation from dear friends here) to put his hand into that of the summoning angel, and say, 'Lead on, O Messenger of God our Father, to the next place whither the divine goodness calls us!' We must be blindfolded before we can pass, I know; but I have no fear about what is to come any more than my children need fear that the love of *their* father should fail them."

When Weiss says that immortality may be explained away as soon as the phenomena are explained away, he supposes a case which we do not admit as any more possible than that the soul's own faculties should be explained away. A fact like clairvoyance cannot be *explained away;* it can be explained only by the theory of the action of a spiritual faculty; and we may say the same of the fact of pneumatography. We know that in the nature of things they can never be proved to be tricks, any more than the genius of a Shakspeare or of a Mozart can be proved to be a trick. It is not true that facts like these are not as real as any external fact can be; or that they are not built "out of reasonable judgments;" or that we are "at the mercy of what may prove a delusion,"—unless we assume that human life itself is a delusion.

The climax of Weiss's course of reasoning is, that "we

cannot derive a faith in personal immortality from occurrences which take place in darkened rooms and cabinets." Here he shows the limitation of his acquaintance with the real facts. His supreme argument is made null and void by the simple truth. Had he bravely, and without being hampered by his preconceived notions, entered into an investigation of the actual phenomena, he would soon have learned that the most important of them may occur in broad daylight under conditions where fraud is actually impossible, and where the knowledge got can never be surrendered. Try to argue out of his convictions the true man, who, by many and long-continued experiments, has once satisfied himself as to the phenomena of clairvoyance and direct writing : — Can your *ignorance*, however subtle your arguments, be a match for his *knowledge?*

Until you can show him that you can read what is written on a tightly-folded, untouched pellet, and teach him how to do it himself, by a trick impenetrable to the vigilance of the most experienced juggler, you can make no impression. And this you cannot do, since it is impossible for you to read without eyes, unless helped by some supersensual faculty, as we suppose the medium to be.

" For as he thinketh in his heart so is he." Solomon's wisdom is also the wisdom of Spiritualism. Thought is the supreme factor in the universe. Thoughts are not mere evanescent nothings. They have an almost objective force. They build up and shape the fabric of our minds, as snowflakes make the avalanche. Even the thoughts of delirium, though we may not be responsible for them, leave their impress. All that we are is the result of what we have thought. ("If a man speaks or acts with an evil thought," says Buddha, "pain follows him as the wheel follows the foot of him who draws it. If a man speaks or acts with a pure thought, happiness follows him like a shadow that never leaves him." To drive out bad thoughts by good, error by truth, and to give our best, most unbiased thinking to the cause of truth, is the road to the gate of Heaven. This is the great admonition which we get from Spiritualism. Let us say, in the words of Zoroaster, "Come to me, ye high realities! Grant me your immortality, your duration of possession forever!"

The Spiritualist who has not in his own reason an umpire higher than that which any medium can bring, is badly provided, and for him Spiritualism may indeed be "a delusion and a snare." The late Pocasset horror, where a father slaughtered his helpless child in the fanatical notion of emulating the faith of Abraham, shows the dangers of *bibliolatry;* but the dangers of *demonolatry* are quite as great; and the incautious Spiritualist, accepting as infallible the message of a spirit, may be led into blunders hardly less tragical than that of poor Freeman.

Rightly studied, Spiritualism is the strongest possible safeguard against all such superstitions. But if we are to accept as gospel the impositions of any spiritual tramp who, under the name of St. Paul, Bacon, or Swedenborg, may wish to fool us, we had better go back at once to the old theology and rest in its bosom. Spiritualism, in this its inchoate state, is for clear heads and patient hearts and tranquil temperaments. To those who have surmounted the perplexities, abuses, misconstructions, and frauds, the *ennui* and the disaffections which beset one's way to it, and which are all accounted for by eternal laws operative both in the sensual and supersensual spheres, it is the summit of all earthly content. I may say of it, in the words of Sir Archibald Alison: "It is like the black mountain of Bender, in India; the higher you advance, the steeper is the ascent, the darker and more desolate the objects with which you are surrounded; but when you are at the summit, the heaven is above your head, and at your feet the kingdom of Cashmere."

CHAPTER VI.

PHENOMENAL PROOFS. — FORM-MANIFESTATIONS. — CARTESIAN
ERRORS. — THE PAULINE DOCTRINE OF A SPIRITUAL BODY.
— INTUITIONAL TESTIMONY.

ALL that is meant by the phrase spirit-materialization is,
that a spirit has such a power over the elements of matter,
that he can make animate and palpable the whole or a part
of a body resembling that which he had at any period of
his earth-life. Ever since 1848 these partial or full-form
manifestations have been common. In all ages of the world
they have been known, though the testimony in regard to
them has been rejected often by the inexperienced. At the
manifestations of the celebrated Davenport Brothers as far
back as 1850, a full spirit-form would not unfrequently
appear. Their father, Dr. Ira Davenport, whom I have
questioned on the subject, and of whose good faith no one
who knows him can doubt, assured me (1879) that the phenomenon was proved repeatedly in his own house, and
through the medial attraction of his own sons, under conditions where fraud or delusion was impossible. There
have been charges of fraud (by no means conclusive)
against the " brothers," but that genuine manifestations
were given by them cannot now be disputed.

The late Dr. H. F. Gardner, of Boston, informed me
that on one occasion, in broad daylight, D. D. Home being
the medium, he had grasped a detached human hand, which
melted away as if into impalpable, invisible vapor, and disappeared in his grasp.

Dr. John Garth Wilkinson, of London, describes a similar experiment with Home. Carrying out the idea of a spiritual body infolded within and controlling the physical, he says : " Could we behold an apparition of the nervous spirit, waving and sweeping through the nerves of the body, we should see that there are motions and mechanisms which transcend the mere external likeness and habitation of life, and should know by solemn experience that our organization is an imperishable truth that derides the grave of the body."

The formation of the spirit-hand has been watched under conditions scientific, though as yet limited to the experience of a few. In the *Banner of Light*, of August 3, 1878, Mr. Austin A. Burnham, of Chagrin Falls, Ohio, gives an account of eighteen sittings which he had in the summer of 1875 with the Bangs Sisters, one fifteen years old and the other eleven, at their home in Chicago. During the first four sittings no hands appeared, but musical instruments were played on, and there was slate-writing — all under the table. During the next six sittings beautifully formed white hands were thrust upward through the aperture of the table, showing that they were guided by an intelligent power. During the next eight sittings different-sized hands and arms of both whites and Indians were projected (often simultaneously) from the aperture.

An interesting feature was the gradual formation of a spirit-hand. A slender white cylinder, about three inches in length and one-eighth inch diameter, resembling a common wax lighting-taper, was thrust upward through the aperture. At the next sitting *two* cylinders were displayed, each the same size as the first. At the next sitting *three* cylinders were shown, about the diameter of an ordinary lead-pencil, at first perfectly rigid, and seeming to adhere one to another. These however soon became flexible, and on close inspection were found to be *spirit-fingers*, with perfect joints and tiny nails. On the next evening " a complete and finely-formed spirit-hand was presented, which had developed to maturity before our eyes from the little spindles of refined matter that our senses had first perceived. It was a demonstration that knowledge and power have been given to the spirit in its supermundane existence to exercise such control over the molecular forces of the universe as to arrange matter in harmonious forms, and endow the same with intellectual life."*

Dr. F. L. H. Willis, who was at one time a medium for physical manifestations, to which I have referred on page 142, writes, May, 1879, in regard to his own medial experiences: "It is twenty-three years ago that these materializations of hands occurred. Did they not occur under the great law of form-materialization that has been operative through all the ages from the days older than Abraham, who had three full form-materializations at one time in his tent upon the plains of Mamre, down to the materialization of Moses and Elias upon the mount in Judea? And if a hand, or even a finger, can be materialized, can the workings of the law be limited to that, so that it shall be pronounced impossible for the full form to stand out in the perfection of human proportions? Is not the one the sure prophecy of the other?"

Truly I see no way of answering this question except by admitting that the spirit-hand makes possible the full-form manifestation, appropriately clothed. Often these hands would show some deformity or defect by way of identifying the spirit manifesting ; and Dr. Willis says, referring to his own mediumship :

"On one occasion a gentleman present drew a knife from his pocket with a long, keen blade, and taking no one into his counsel, watching his opportunity, pierced with a vio-

---

* The author has himself both seen and felt the spirit-hand repeatedly under conditions that seemed to preclude both imposture and hallucination. He has also seen the hand write messages, indicating clairvoyant power.

lent blow one of the psychic hands. The medium uttered a shriek of pain. The sensation was precisely as if the knife had passed through his hand. The gentleman sprang to his feet exultant, thinking he had made a most triumphant *exposé* of trickery, and fully expected to find the medium's hand pierced and bleeding. To his utter chagrin and amazement there was no trace of a scratch even upon either hand of the medium; and yet to him the sensation was precisely as if the knife had passed through muscle and tendon, and the sensation of pain and soreness remained for hours.

"On another occasion a gentleman was present who, a year before, had lost, as he supposed forever, a beloved wife. He had no faith in immortality, and to him death was indeed the blackness of an endless night, and the grave an abyss that had swallowed forever his most precious treasure. A hand was formed and placed in his, and he started with the exclamation in thrilling tones of ' Oh, my God!' and burst into tears. He recognized the hand of his wife, and felt upon two of the fingers *fac-similes* of the betrothal and marriage rings he had placed thereon."

Augustine Calmet, author of the well-known " Dictionary of the Bible," was born near Commercy, in France, in 1672, and died in 1757, " greatly esteemed," says the *British National Cyclopœdia*, " both for his learning and moderation." Calmet well knew, what our modern phenomena have abundantly confirmed, namely, that spirits can take on objective forms of different degrees of materiality; some so attenuated as to be invisible to the normal sense of mortals; some, though still invisible, probably sufficiently near to the material to have caused, in our day, an impression on the photographer's sensitive plate, which it is well known will be impressed by objects not visible to the human sense; and some that can be seen only by persons in a state of high clairvoyance. The proof is in the following passage from Calmet:

" It is necessary to study and distinguish the apparitions during sleep from those that appear during your wakeful state ;— studying apart, also, those apparitions in solid bodies, that talk and walk and eat and drink, and the same with regard to those that appear as nebulous and airy."

Here it is evident that the great fact of materialization was known to the erudite author of " The Dictionary of the Bible ; " and he also justifies the belief of the lower races in " a filmy body " for the spirit, by showing that the spirit may regulate at will the degree of molecular attenuation in his assumed body.

Of the fact of materialization to such a degree of density that the spirit " can talk and walk and eat and drink," Calmet has evidently no doubt. It is all in strict conformity with our present facts, together with what is related of the reappearance of Jesus. In the common phenomenon of the spirit-hand, moved by intelligence, lie all the potencies of the full-form manifestations. Given the spirit-hand, and all the rest is made credible.

Should any one want testimony more remote than that of Calmet to the fact of a spiritual body, he may learn that in Egypt, two thousand years before our era, though the unknown God and Lord of life was worshipped under various names and attributes, the popular religion and household cultus had Spiritualism for its basis. In London, on the 15th of April, 1879, in a lecture at Steinway Hall, Mr. Le Page Renouf (not known as a Spiritualist) undertook to set forth the results of the latest and fullest researches into the civilization and religion of Ancient Egypt. These results, it must be observed, are no matter of surmise or inference from a few disputed passages or obscure texts. Five thousand years ago the Egyptians left their belief written at large in all conceivable forms, from royal edicts to private prayers and memoranda.

A principal and pervading tenet among them was the double nature of man. Every human being had his double, wraith, or astral spirit, as much a part of him as his fleshly frame—" *at times, and in certain conditions, independently visible and palpable.*" The Egyptian name for this was *Kàr*, a word exactly corresponding to the Latin *imago* and the Greek *εἰδωλον*. Through this mystic companion, separate individual existence was continued and carried on after the dissolution of earth-life, and the communication with it by survivors formed the greater part of that ancestral worship and reverence for the dead that so remarkably distinguished Egyptian social life. Possession and obsession were familiar and recognized phenomena, and scientifically dealt with. In the Ishtar tablets (B. C. 2250) there is a glimpse of materialization in the line: "The spirit of Heabani, like glass, transparent from the earth arose."

Among physicists the question *what is matter?* will be answered in different ways, according to their affinity with this or that school of thought. Strict materialists, like Büchner, Haeckel, and Vogt, prefer an expression which will not credit matter with any spiritual potency whatever. They would have it appear that mind is derived from the mechanical action of purely material atoms — not the soul-atoms of Democritus, nor the monad of Leibnitz, nor the mind-stuff of Professor W. K. Clifford — but something in which there is neither life nor the promise of life. The consideration that thinking cannot be a property of matter, unless the conception of matter be so enlarged that it no longer answers the purposes of the atheistic hypothesis, has no weight with these extremists.

To both classes of minds the crowning phenomenon of Spiritualism, the full-form manifestation of a human figure, with appropriate clothing, all improvised apparently out of nothingness, is a scandal and an impossibility; something too incredible for any amount of human testimony to verify. Equally incredible to them are the phenomena of levitation, pneumatography, and the independent movement of objects.

But all these phenomena, which to the average scientific conception are in direct violation of the laws of nature, are in truth attributable to the intervention of higher laws which do not at all contravene any natural law, but which, being unknown, assume in popular estimation the rank of magical miracles.

Thus the levitation, or lifting, of a human being, which I have often witnessed, though abundantly confirmed in Catholic annals, is pronounced absurd because it is a violation of the law of gravity. And when we reply, "Nay! it is in no sense a violation; an invisible, impalpable power is at work, and causes the lifting," we are told by the physicist, who trusts to his "deductive reasoning," that we are "the victim of a prepossession," or, as Carpenter expresses it, "have surrendered our common sense to a dominant idea."

Saint Theresa, a nun in a convent in Spain, was often raised into the air in the sight of all the sisterhood. Lord Orrery and Mr. Valentine Greatrak both informed Henry More and Joseph Glanvil that at Lord Cornway's house, at Ragley, in Ireland, a gentleman's butler, in their presence and in broad daylight, rose into the air and floated about the room above their heads. Butler, in his "Lives of the Saints," says that many such facts are related by persons of undoubted veracity, who testify that they themselves were eye-witnesses of them.

The Rev. Wm. Fishbough, of New York, a veteran in the cause of Spiritualism, writes (July, 1876,) : "To my own positive knowledge, based upon an actual occurrence, these materializations can take place without a cabinet, or any other medium than myself, and that, too in the private solitude of my own chamber."

Charles Bonnet (1720–1793) the great Swiss naturalist, believed that man's future body exists already with the body visible; and he believed that science would some day have instruments which would enable it to detect this body, formed as it probably is of the elements of ether or of light.

"Let us distrust," says Chaseray, "our imperfect senses, since there are so many substances which we can neither feel nor see. Let us not be precipitate in denying the duality of the human being because the scalpel of the anatomist cannot reveal to our sight a principle eminently subtile. Man is not driven to annihilation even under the hypothesis of materiality." Chaseray thinks that the spirit-body may some day be proved by science.

By its nature and in its normal state the spirit-body is invisible, and it has that property in common with many fluids which we know exist, and yet which we have never seen; but it can also, the same as other fluids, undergo modifications that render it perceptible to the sight, whether by a sort of condensation or by a change in the molecular disposition; it then appears to us under a vaporous form. By further condensation the spirit-body may acquire the properties of solidity and tangibility; but it can instantaneously resume its ethereal and invisible state.

We can understand this state by comparing it with that of invisible vapor, which can pass to a state of visible fog, then become liquid, then solid, and *vice versa*. These different states of the spirit-body are the result of the will of the spirit, and not an exterior physical cause, as in our gases.

"It is an extravagant conjecture of mine," says Locke, "that spirits can assume to themselves bodies of different bulk, figure, and conformation of parts." Locke's extravagant conjectures are sometimes better than the sober hypotheses of other philosophers.

Science has to hypothecate the intermediary ether to account for the passage of light, heat, electricity, magnetism, gravity, through space. Why may we not quite as reasonably hypothecate an intermediary, partaking both of matter and spirit, through which an Infinite Spirit may act in controlling the universe? The grounds for the latter hypothesis are quite as ample as those for the former; and if we fortify it by our admitted facts, we have a broader basis for the spiritual than for the accepted material hypothesis.

Dr. John W. Draper, of the University of New York, has been quoted by Professor Tyndall as good scientific authority. But in his "Human Physiology," referring to the human body, Draper remarks: "There animates the machine a self-conscious and immortal principle — the soul. . . . In the most enlarged acceptation, *it would fall under the province of physiology to treat of this immortal principle.*" Here Dr. Draper plainly intimates that there must be a psycho-physiological science.

Among modern German philosophers, Baader, Hoffman, Ulrici, Wirth, Wagner, Fechner, Beneke, Dressler teach, though in different ways, substantially the theory of a spiritual body. Ulrici believes in the non-atomic character of the soul's organism, describing it as "a fluid-like substance, undivided, continuous, simple, penetrating all parts of the body." Beneke teaches that the faculties are the elements of the substance of the soul itself; that they are not inherent in a substratum, distinct from themselves, inasmuch as a thing is only the sum of its own combined forces. Wagner believes in an "individual, permanent, psychical substance." Baader, Franz Hoffman, and I. H. Fichte are in harmony with the teachings of Spiritualism in regard to the spiritual body. As I have already shown, we may also claim the illustrious Kant as accepting the probabilities of an actual inter-communication between the spirit-world and ours, in the remark, "It may be proved yet that the human soul, even in this earthly life, is in indissolubly connected communion with all the immaterial existences of the spirit-world."

Our clairvoyants are unanimous in asserting this inner

fluidic organism. Mechanical science gives a reason for it.
Mr. Gillingham, an English manufacturer of artificial
limbs, in Chard, Somersetshire, argues, from the phenomena with which he has become acquainted in the way of his
profession, that there must be a spiritual body co-existing
with the physical. The sensations often felt where the
amputated limb ought to be, is one of the facts he adduces.
And Müller, in his *Handbuch der Physiologie*, remarks:
"Professor Valentine has observed that individuals who
are the subjects of congenital imperfection, or absence of
the extremities, have, nevertheless, the internal sensations
of such limbs in their perfect state."

"If," says Miss A. B. Blackwell, "we must call in the
action of a refined class or classes of matter to explain the
transmission of all the more rapid and subtle forms of energy, as electricity and gravity, then the supposition that
every mind may have a more permanent, ethereal body,
which mediates between it and its grosser organism, cannot
involve a shadow of scientific absurdity. It even becomes
highly probable."

"We are logically constrained," say Stewart and Tait,
in their "Unseen Universe," "if we regard the principle
of continuity and the doctrine of immortality as both true,
to admit the existence of some frame or organ not of this
earth, which survives dissolution"; and they add: "It is
possible that there have been, and that there are, occasional
manifestations of this spiritual nature." Not only occasional, but very frequent manifestations, it might be said.

"I could multiply citations to infinity," says Guizot,
"proving that in the first century of our era, the materiality
of the soul was an opinion not only permitted but dominant."

Pliny the younger, a born skeptic, admits, but with evident reluctance, that phantoms of the dead reappear to
man, and that events occur prophetic of an inevitable
doom, which wise men might sometimes interpret correctly.

Mr. T. P. Barkas, of Newcastle-on-Tyne, a scientific
investigator with whom I have had some correspondence,
writes, May 3, 1875 :

"I have experimented and investigated under every
kind of reasonable test that my ingenuity could devise ; in
my own private rooms, in the private rooms of personal
friends, in public rooms, and in the private rooms of mediums. I have examined the rooms with utmost care ;
have personally fitted up the recesses for the reception of
mediums ; have personally provided every thing connected
with the séances, and am certain that no arrangement for
trick was in the room. I have tied, sealed, nailed, and
held the mediums in almost every possible manner. I have
undressed the medium, and re-dressed him in clothes of my
own providing. And notwithstanding all tests and all
precautions, phenomena have taken place that are utterly
inexplicable by reference to any known physical or psychological law. All this I have done with the cold eye and
steady pulse of a scientist. I am prepared to give £100 to
any man or woman who by trick can produce similar phenomena under similar conditions."

Again he writes : "The phenomena appeal not to one
sense merely, but to all the senses. Sight, hearing, smell,
taste, and touch are all called into requisition during the
course of our séances. Mesmeric subjects can be placed
under illusion, but when relieved from the influence of the
operator they are conscious of the change ; such is not the
case at séances ; the sitters are not conscious of having
been under any influence whatever."

Mr. Barkas gives an account (May 14, 1875) of some
remarkable séances with the boy, William Petty, under
perfect test conditions. The boy stripped himself absolutely naked. He was then re-dressed in dark clothes
which Mr. Barkas had provided. Not a white or light
article of any kind was there on the lad's person. Mr.
Barkas had himself provided the cabinet ; excluding every
thing that had the appearance of whiteness. Under these

conditions, a figure draped in white, about four feet high, came out, moved about the room, and cut from its garments a piece, seven inches by two and an eighth, which was found to be very white lawn. There were present two ladies and seven gentlemen, who were willing, if required, to authenticate this statement.

In the London *Spiritualist* of March 7, 1879, will be found an account by Mr. John Mould, of Newcastle-on-Tyne, of the sawing of a piece of flooring deal, twenty inches long, six inches wide, and five-eighths of an inch thick. An ordinary hand-saw was used; Miss Wood was the medium, and, as she had been once charged with fraud, the conditions were made perfect, she being in full sight of the spectators and known not to have moved. After describing the success of the phenomena, Mr. Mould says: "I unhesitatingly affirm, after a persistent investigation of nearly six years, — which means attendance, on an average, of two sittings weekly at nearly six hundred *séances*, — that the statements I have just made are, in my judgment, statements of fact, however antecedently improbable they may appear." Mr. Mould considers the two theories in explanation of the problem: one that of the activity of a spirit external to the medium, and the other, of which he remarks: "Assuming the phenomena to be produced by the soul of the medium making a *sortie* out of its dark cottage, the fact of action at a distance is the unfoldment of a possibility making a future life at least more conceivable, and to that extent is a light, and therefore more likely to influence our ideas on a future life than if we had no light at all."

Dr. J. M. Gully, formerly of Great Malvern, England, a thoroughly experienced physician and a careful investigator, wrote me, under date of July 20, 1874: "To the special question which you put regarding my experiences of the materialization of the spirit-form with Miss Cook's mediumship, I must reply, that after two years' examination of the fact and numerous séances, I have not the smallest doubt, and have the strongest conviction, that such materialization takes place, and that not the slightest attempt at trick or deception is fairly attributable to any one who assisted at Miss Cook's séances."

From the facts here brought together, it may be inferred that the spirit-body is not a mere hypothesis : it is proved by the phenomena and the inductions of Spiritualism ; by the objective appearance of spirits themselves in extemporized bodies ; by the testimony of clairvoyants who can see spirits, and by the testimony of the spirits, who claim not only a super-ethereal organism, human in its form, but the power of assuming visible bodies like those which, at different stages of the earth-life, they had while here ; by the phenomena of somnambulism and clairvoyance giving evidence of spiritual senses, for as the bodily senses imply *their* object, so do the spiritual senses imply *theirs*, and are prophecies of an endless life ; by all the analogies which reason and experience supply ; and by the belief of men in all ages and climes — a belief founded on the actual reappearance of deceased relatives and friends.

Add to these considerations the facts of a manifold consciousness, pointing to a complex but unique organism ; also the marvels of memory, in which faculty impressions inhere and persist which are inexplicable under the theory of materialism, involving as it does a constant flux and removal of the molecules of the organs of thought. Only the existence of a spiritual body can account for these things ; though I am aware this has been denied.

The anthropological conception, for which I am indebted to the facts of spiritualism, is that of a trichotomy of physical body, spirit-body (or soul), and spirit, — a trinity of principles, physical, psycho-physiological, and spiritual, all proceeding from the Infinite Force, but the last, like

God himself, inscrutable. In this notion I am supported by the belief of the early Christians, as it appears in their writings up to the fourth century. I also have the concurrence of Lord Bacon, who says: "Two different emanations of souls are manifest in the first creation: the one (the rational soul, or the spirit,) proceeding from the breath of God; the other (the sensitive soul, or spirit-body,) from the elements." The spirit, he tells us, is scientifically incognizable; but the sensitive soul (spirit-body) whose " substance even," he tells us, " may be justly inquired into," must be allowed " a corporeal substance, attenuated by heat and rendered invisible, as a subtle breath, or aura, of a flamy and airy nature (electro-luminous), and diffused through the whole body." *

Such is not only the early Christian belief, but such, so far as relates to the spirit-body, is the so-called *animism* of the barbarous tribes. It is consistent also with the views of both Plato and Aristotle. In the progress of philosophical speculation this simple idea, explaining so many of the phenomena that have puzzled mataphysicians as to how an immaterial, unextended principle can act upon a physical body, was superseded by a doctrine which identified spirit-body and spirit in substance, and distinguished them only in function. Aquinas, and after him Calvin, pronounced in favor of this dualistic rendering; but it was chiefly through the influence of Descartes that the belief in a psychical organism or spirit-body, distinct from the physical, was ruled out of philosophy, literature, and religion. Then began to arise the clamor, still kept up, against the " gross materialism" of the Pauline doctrine of a spiritual body; and hence the scornful defamation of Spiritualism as being a worse materialism than that which it would displace.

---

* The passages in parenthesis here are not in Bacon's text.

14

The rejection by Descartes of the notion of two emanations of souls, a sensitive (spirit-body) and a rational (spirit), compelled him to confound the two principles; but this he could not do without making the only soul left an indefinable, abstract principle, having neither extension, form, nor conceivable substance. Thus he could give us no assurance of the continuous life of man; he destroyed the etymological signification of the word *immortal* (not dying); and he referred us to revelation alone for our grounds of belief in a future state. In all this he was a retrograde teacher; he reversed the wisdom of the past; he fortified the unscientific doctrine of a resurrection of the physical body; and he blinded theologians and philosophers generally to the import of the great fact announced by Paul, that there is not only a natural but a spiritual body.

The attempt to reconcile with the opinion that the soul pervades our whole physical organization, the Cartesian notion that there is no extended psychical entity, — that the mind (which Descartes makes the only soul) has no substratum for inherence, — has been the despair and confusion of philosophy up to this time. I have already instanced the eminent contemporary philosophers in Germany who have rejected or supplemented the Cartesian theory. They have postulated a continuity of life, made possible by the presence of a principle in the human organization, occult and impervious to the scalpel, but actual, like the potency of the chrysalis in the worm. Philosophers like Fichte and Hoffman were first attracted by Spiritualism because they had independently arrived by their own inductions and deductions at the fundamental doctrine it corroborates.

The Spencerian philosophy, as expounded by Mr. John Fiske, who gives to it the epithet *cosmic*, adheres to the Cartesian notion of the soul. Indeed, Mr. Spencer told

Professor Gunning that he rejected Spiritualism on *à priori* grounds, by which he doubtless meant that he regarded certain preconceptions of his own on the subject as having the force of axioms. But there are signs that the more scientific German philosophy is destined to reinstate the Pauline doctrine of a spiritual body.

I have before me an American volume * of recent date, in which the author, Dr. Walter, carrying out the views of I. H. Fichte and Ulrici, ably combats the religious and metaphysical objections to the doctrine of the soul's extension. In his language, let it be understood, *soul* covers the whole region of *mind*, and he at times uses the word indiscriminately. He makes no sign that he accepts the phenomena of Spiritualism. His arguments are mainly metaphysical, and not physiological. He says:

" The assertion that the soul is not extended is exactly balanced by the no more dogmatic assertion that the soul *is* extended. To conceive of the soul as coextensive, and in union, with the whole nervous system, is no more difficult than to conceive of it as unextended and confined, or not, to a particular part; and certainly much less difficult than to conceive of it as unextended and yet in immediate connection with all parts."

He tells us that to attribute extension to mind is indeed ascribing to Spirit a property of Body; but to have one property in common is not identity. Space is extended, and in that respect is like matter, and yet certainly is not matter. The two existences are still substantially different. If, then, between mental and material substances, both being considered as having extension, as great difference exists as between space and matter, why should the fastidious Cartesian be disturbed? The two may possess one common attribute, but it cannot make them the same. It

* " The Perception of Space and Matter, by Rev. John Estep Walter, Principal of the Classical and Scientific Institute, Mt. Pleasant, Pa. Boston: Estes & Lauriat, 1879."

neither materializes mind nor spiritualizes matter, but leaves them as radically distinct as could be desired.

There are a number of well-known facts pertaining to the growth and generation of the lower animals, which Dr. Walter instances as strongly corroborating this doctrine of psychical extension. If the polype or certain ring-worms be cut into pieces, each of the pieces will, in a brief time, develop into a complete organism like the original whole. This fact seems to put it beyond question that the sensitive principle of the original, undivided organism extends to all its parts.

Philosophers, who oppose the doctrine of psychical extension, at the same time make admissions which favor it. Sir William Hamilton tells us that "the first condition of the possibility of an immediate, intuitive, or real perception of external things, which our consciousness assures us that we possess, is the immediate connection of the cognitive principle with every part of the corporeal organism."

Mansel says of the soul that it "must be regarded as present in all the sensitive organs alike." He also has this remarkable sentence: "Sensation is not an affection of mind alone, nor of matter alone, *but of an animated organism*, i. e., of mind and matter united." What does such an utterance amount to, if not to a recognition of a spirit-body as a necessary *nexus* between spirit and earth-body? And yet Mansel is a Cartesian.

President Noah Porter affirms that the soul "occupies," "*pervades*," "animates," is "united with," and "connected with" the extended sensorium or organism; that "in sensation proper the soul knows itself as united with the extended sensorium."

"Thus it seems perfectly clear," says Dr. Walter (to whom I am indebted for these quotations), "that the Hamiltonian theory of the perception of the extended imperatively requires that the soul be extended; and that for its advocates to deny extension is to make their theory a superstructure without a foundation,—a puerile assumption. . . . Why they, or any thinkers, after they have explicitly taught that the mind pervades, or is in immediate connection with, all parts of the extended bodily organism, should find any difficulty in accepting the proposition that the soul is extended, is wholly incomprehensible."

The convictions of seers, mediums, and intuitionalists generally, in favor of a spiritual organism involving the universal presence of the mind in the physical body, may be fairly accepted as confirming the philosophical views of Ulrici, Walter, Hoffman, and others on this particular subject, and are an earnest that the Cartesian dogma has had its day, and must soon give way to the re-establishment of the old Pauline doctrine, as affirmed by Spiritualism. Thus does the most advanced philosophical analysis come to the support of the great generalization from our facts, that there is in man a psychical organism, released from the physical by death, and carrying the guaranty not only of his continuous life, but of his unimpaired individuality in all its essentials.

"Even here in this life," says Cudworth, "our body is, as it were, twofold, interior and exterior; we having, besides the grossly tangible bulk of our outward body, another interior spiritual body, which latter is not put into the grave with the other."

"The soul," says Lavater, "on leaving its earthly frame is immediately clothed in a spiritual frame withdrawn from the material. The soul itself, during its earth-life, perfects the faculties of the spiritual body by means of which it will apprehend, feel, and act in its new existence."

CHAPTER VII.

MESMERISM. — INDUCED SOMNAMBULISM. — COGNATE PHE-
NOMENA. — MRS. MOWATT. — MISS FANCHER. — MISS REY-
NOLDS. — PREVISION. — PROOFS OF SPIRITUAL POWER.

THE facts of mesmerism are too well known to require
recapitulation. Introduced by Mesmer to the Parisian
world in 1778, they were extended in 1784 by Puysegur,
who was the first in modern times to report the fact of mesmeric somnambulism and clairvoyance. In 1825 the French
Academy of Medicine appointed a commission, of which
Magendie, Fouquier, Leroux, Husson, and seven other
eminent physicians were members, to investigate and report on the facts. They occupied more than five years in
their labors. Their report, presented in 1831, gives a clear
account of their experiments. They were well guarded
against charlatanism and fraud, for they say that "it is only
by a most attentive examination, the severest care, and by
numerous and varied trials, that one can escape illusion."

They admit the most important of the phenomena, and
say in regard to clairvoyance : "We saw two somnambules
who distinguished, their eyes being closed, the objects
placed before them : they have designated without touching
them, the color and value of cards ; they have read written words, also several lines of books. This phenomenon
took place even when the opening of the eyelids was kept
exactly closed by the fingers."

Cuvier, the great naturalist, admitted the phenomena (in
his "*Anatomie Comparie*" vol. 2, p. 117) ; so did La-
place (in his "*Traité Analytique du Calcul des Probabilités*").

Gall, Spurzheim, Hahnemann, Hufeland, Sir Wm. Hamilton, and a long list of eminent men of science, were also believers in the mesmeric phenomena. Lacordaire, the famous French theologian (1802–1861), says: "The somnambule appears to know things which he was ignorant of before his sleep, and which he forgets on the instant of awaking."

The compound word *somnambulism* (sleep-walking) is an inapt one to designate the various phenomena that come under it; but our present science has to use it in the absence of a better term. As the phenomena are indicative of supersensual powers in the human subject, they properly come in to illustrate and confirm the theory of Spiritualism. My first acquaintance with the facts of induced somnambulism dates back to the year 1836. Dr. Collyer, a young English physician, happened to be in Boston, and gave some public experiments in mesmerism at the Masonic Temple. I saw enough to convince me that they were not wholly illusory. Subsequently I witnessed the experiments of Mr. Peale, at his Museum in Broadway, New York. In both the subjects I had seen, the lucidity had not advanced to that degree of high consciousness which seems to be a rise upon that of the normal state. Still it was evident that the somnambulists in both cases were sensitive to the unexpressed will of the mesmerizer, and many curious phenomena, indicating a faculty that could not be explained by materialism, were developed.

In 1840 I became acquainted with Mrs. A. C. Mowatt (1820–1869), who afterwards won distinction on the stage, wrote novels and plays, and "The Autobiography of an Actress," and, some years after her first husband's death, married Mr. Ritchie, of Richmond, Va. Dr. Channing, a bachelor physician, in whose house on Broadway, New York, I had taken rooms, attended her professionally for an affection which finally resulted in congestion of the brain. He tried the effect of mesmerism upon her, and gradually she developed into quite a remarkable somnambule. One day when she and her husband were at Dr. C.'s rooms I happened to be present. He began to read to her from one of his addresses. I sat near, and hiding my face with a pamphlet, as if to shelter it from the light, thought I would test the mesmeric theory of the operation of the will without contact. The effect upon Mrs. Mowatt was almost instantaneous. The balls of her eyes rolled up, and her eyelids drooped; whereupon I suspended the action of my will and she was herself again. I tried this several times till I satisfied myself there was a positive effect from my volition, unaided by any sign, look, or movement visible to the subject. At last Dr. C., looking up from his reading, detected from the appearance of her eyes what was going on, and charged me with it. I had to plead guilty.

Some weeks afterwards, as Mrs. Mowatt grew worse, and he was obliged to leave the city, he urged me to take his place in treating her mesmerically. With reluctance I accepted the responsibility, supposing it would last only a few days. Then there commenced a series of experiences which to me were new and interesting. By a few passes of my hand without contact I could throw her into what seemed a profound state of coma, rarely lasting more than a minute, from which she would emerge in a state of consciousness, which, though it commanded all the contents of her normal state, was evidently distinct and superior. Her eyeballs were rolled up and the lids drooped loosely, though when she became animated in conversation the lids would close tightly, and her countenance become more expressive than the open eyes could have made it.

That the subject, through some psychologizing power independent of the mesmerizer, might have produced this state is highly probable. We see, in the case of trance-mediums, that by a sort of self-magnetization they may pass into a state of consciousness of which they carry no recollection back into the normal state. But the process of mesmerization by a second person is to some subjects, according to their idiosyncrasies, an important prerequisite. They may at the same time be so constituted as to exercise a volition quite independent of the mesmerizer should he attempt an influence to which they might object. Mrs. Mowatt was always the dictator in her lucid state; she would predict crises in her disease with wonderful accuracy, and take all responsibility both from mesmerizer and physician as to prescribing for her case. Indeed the physician's office soon became a sinecure. She, in her abnormal state, was always her own physician, and her own despotic ruler, showing absolute confidence in all her prescriptions.

Still she seemed acutely sensitive to the mesmerizer's unexpressed will, especially in her normal state. While somnambulic she wished me to give her the power of passing from her abnormal to her normal state, and to effect this, directed me to magnetize her ring, so that in my absence she could, by pulling it off, pass into her usual condition.

Braid's theory that the phenomena in mesmerism depend on the physical and psychical condition of the patient, and not at all on the volition or passes of the operator throwing out a magnetic fluid, or exciting into activity some mystical universal fluid or medium, may be true in much that it asserts, but it is wrong in much that it denies. The sensitiveness of the patient to the undemonstrated volition of the operator (a fact I have repeatedly tested) is a proof that there is an actual communication of will-force producing objective effects. This cannot be denied by any experienced student. Mr. Braid found that he could develop the mesmeric phenomena by causing a person to sit still, and simply directing his attention, by means of the eyesight, to some particular object, as a lancet-case or a cork; but he leaves out of consideration entirely the question how far his own unexpressed will may have been a factor in producing the result which he was expecting and unconsciously helping on.

As for the assertions of Dr. Hammond and Dr. Beard that the phenomena can all be accounted for by their theories of epilepsy, hallucination, &c., the studies and experiences of more than forty years have convinced me that they are wrong. Their explanations are wholly inapplicable to a case like that of Mrs. Mowatt. In her abnormal state there was that perfect self-poise, intelligence, and self-control, which made the idea of a merely morbid development ridiculous. She seemed to look down upon all the contents of her normal memory as from a superior position.

If I put anything hot or cold in my mouth she would at once recognize it, unless her attention was directed to something else at the moment. There was a quick sympathy with all my moods and physical conditions, and yet she was supremely and independently conscious all the time, and would reason upon the phenomena, describe them, philosophize upon them, and oppose my own opinions with an ability far transcending that which she exhibited in her normal state.

For two years I had an opportunity of studying the phenomena in her case, almost daily, in all their variety. Never was there the slightest symptom in all that time of any attempt at deception. Invariably, in her abnormal state, the appearance of the eyes alone was a sufficient proof of the peculiarity of the condition. Never would any occurrence startling or unusual cause the eyes, when she was somnambulic, to assume their normal aspect. Always the eyelids hung loose, with the balls rolled up, or else would be tightly closed. Her husband was her constant attendant, and took an intelligent interest in the phenomena. But the state of his health did not allow him to exert the mesmeric influence himself.

On one occasion, by her own direction when somnambulic, she was kept so two weeks, without returning once to her normal state. As we resided quite near each other on Broadway, I had frequent opportunities of visiting her. Her last recollections in her normal state were of seeing Broadway heaped with snow; while a rose-bush on a stand in her parlor had on it a bud yet green. When, a fortnight afterwards, I suddenly removed the mesmeric influence, brought her back to her natural state, and led her, first to the window, so that she saw that the piles of snow had disappeared, and then to the rose-bush, so that she saw the bud had become a flower, she — having no consciousness whatever of the lapse of time, supposing that she had been " asleep " not more than an hour or two — became wildly agitated and almost frantic. I saw that I had made a mistake in not preparing her for the change. This I could easily have done by giving her what she called an " ordination " to carry the remembrance of the experiences of the last fourteen days into her waking state. My only resource was to put my hands on her head and force her back into her abnormal state. This I accomplished at last, after much opposition on her part and much effort of volition on my own. After a somewhat prolonged state of profound coma, the well-known change in her countenance and the unconscious, child-like smile, admonitory of the coming of her second and higher self, to whom while somnambulic she had given the name of the " gipsy," appeared, and, after a breath of relief, she took my hand and said, " You should have known better than to wake her so suddenly. You should have guessed that the changes to which you were to introduce her would bewilder and astound her. Now put your hands on her head and ordain that she shall be reconciled to the change, and take it as a matter of course." I obeyed the direction, and the "simpleton," as the normal self was called, returned and accepted the situation as if nothing remarkable had occurred.

In her abnormal state Mrs. Mowatt would always refer to her waking self in the third person. She would be agitated by the touch of any one except her husband or her mesmerizer, unless the person touching her was previously put *en rapport* with her, or "in communication," as she termed it, by the mesmerizer. Without this precaution a foreign touch would produce a painful shuddering. She would take no notice of persons in the room until they had been put *en rapport* with her.

By making a few passes over the arm or hand I could paralyze the muscles of voluntary motion and render the limb cataleptic. In this state it was utterly insensible to perforation or incision. In complete catalepsy, as medical science tells us, there is an absolute suspension of the functions of the animal life, while the processes of the organic life go on with comparatively little change. On the return of consciousness no memory is retained of anything that may have passed during the paroxysm, the very same train of ideas returning when consciousness is restored as was present at the instant it ceased.

Quite analogous with this phenomenon was one I have experienced hundreds of times in the case of Mrs. Mowatt. While she would be in animated conversation and in the midst of a sentence in her abnormal state, I would suddenly wake her. She would look around for a moment with a dazed expression, and then resume the ordinary tenor of her waking occupations. On again inducing the abnormal state — it might be hours or days afterwards — before quite regaining the clear state of complete somnambulic consciousness, she would go on and finish the sentence in the utterance of which she had been interrupted long before. I never knew this experiment to fail. There could be no better evidence than this of the separation between the two states of consciousness. The opinions she held in the two states were often widely different. Persons she liked and trusted when awake, she would shrink from when somnambulic, and *vice versa*. Her religious notions were greatly modified by the somnambulic impressions which she was allowed to carry into her waking state.

In her highest state of consciousness — for there were different degrees — she would claim to see and talk with spirits; but finding me incredulous on the subject, she did not urge it. She spoke always of that circle of the spirit-world proximate to this world as containing beings subject to the same laws of progress that we find here.

Why should not this be true? Consider the great discoveries of the last few centuries; the advance in general culture. Can we suppose that our spirit friends and predecessors have been idle all this time; that they have lost that divine thirst for knowledge, those incentives to diligence and activity, which were necessary for their happiness while on earth? Is it probable that they enter at once into the same state of enlightenment which may distinguish those who left this life thousands of years before them? It may be that advancement will depend more on our moral status than on our intellectual attainments; but from all we can learn the correspondence with our present moral and mental activities will be much closer than we are apt to imagine. Life will still be progress, and progress through the voluntary exercise of our own powers, our own earnestness in the pursuit of truth.

That there will still be new changes and expansions of being to look forward to, as wonderful and inexplicable to us as the transition of death is to us while here, is rationally to be expected. Man may develop a complex, triune nature in the next life as well as in this. There will always be a new goal for us to look forward to and strive

for.   There will still be an horizon for our orderly limitation.   Therefore the objection made by David A. Strauss
that the prospect of an endless being strikes him with dismay, springs from a wholly chimerical anticipation.   "As
our day our strength will be."   This good mother nature
will not desert us, even in the next stage of being.   All
will be adapted to the soul's inherent energies and needs.

The developments now going on for facilitating the intercourse between the two spheres of being, are a proof that
our spirit brethren are not inactive; that among them are
operative the same laws of progress that make the moral
and mental life of mankind on this planet.

Among the persons I remember to have introduced to
Mrs. Mowatt while she was somnambulic, were N. P. Willis, Dr. Mott, and Dr. William E. Channing, the great
Unitarian divine.   Willis, whom Goethe would have classed
among his "demoniac men," was deeply interested, and
kept up an animated conversation for an hour or more with
the somnambule.

Dr. Valentine Mott, the eminent New York surgeon
(1785–1865), had been a pupil of Sir Astley Cooper, who
said of him, "He has performed more of the great operations than any man living, or that ever did live."   Mott
told me that he was present, April 8, 1829, at the operation
mentioned in the Report of the French Academy of Medicine, 1831, in which Cloquet, the French surgeon in Paris,
removed an ulcerated tumor from the breast of Madame
Plantin while she was in a state of partial catalepsy induced
by mesmerism.   In her waking state she had manifested
the greatest horror at having the operation performed.
Somnambulic, she spoke of it with perfect calmness, and
while the operation was going on, which consumed more
than nine minutes, conversed tranquilly with the operator,
and did not exhibit the slightest sign. of sensibility.   No
movement of the limbs or of the features, no change in

the perspiration nor in the voice, no emotion, not even in the pulse, was manifested.

Learning that I had induced somnambulism in Mrs. Mowatt, whom he had known well from a child, Mott sought an opportunity of testing the fact of physical insensibility in her case. This he did to his entire satisfaction. I made a few passes over her arm, causing rigidity. With his lancet he probed the flesh, and tested her in various ways. She talked and smiled, giving not the slightest indication of physical feeling.

The wonderful fact of discrete degrees of consciousness is fully proved in somnambulism. This consciousness may be above that of the normal state or below it. The case is on record of a pious clergyman who, when somnambulic, would manifest kleptomania. He would steal and secrete articles without any rational purpose. The somnambulists who walk on the roofs of houses, or jump out of windows, have a certain consciousness, though it may be disordered by delusion. Dr. Pritchard says, "A somnambulator is nothing but a dreamer who is able to act his dreams." Insensible to external phenomena, his functions are still obedient to an inward consciousness. But as there are many degrees of somnambulic consciousness, Pritchard's definition is a very limited and misleading one.

In Mrs. Mowatt's case the state was in every respect a superior one, intellectually, morally, and, I may add, physically, for her powers of enduring fatigue were greatly increased. Frequently with her husband we would cross the river to Hoboken, and pass hours strolling through the beautiful grounds. She would be in the somnambulic state all the time, wearing a veil to conceal the peculiar expression of her eyes from passers-by. Her spirits were always exalted in this state, and she was full of vivacity and glee. Awake she would scream if a caterpillar got on her dress. Somnambulic she would manifest the greatest tenderness for every living thing, taking up even a wounded snake from the road, and placing it where it would be safe from passing wheels.

I have letters that were written by her in utter darkness, and the chirography is a great improvement on that of her waking state. She would embroider and do all sorts of fancy work in the dark. She would predict crises in her disease, and in one instance I knew her to predict a severe hemorrhage of the lungs six months before it occurred, naming the very day and hour. Those who discredit these phenomena will say there was deception. I cannot look back to the most trifling incident that would justify the suspicion; and yet I was so unduly skeptical that I was always on the lookout for something that might raise a question of the reality of what I witnessed.

I met her and her husband at Lenox, Mass., in the summer of 1842. In the same house with us was the Rev. Dr. William Ellery Channing (1780–1842), who took a deep interest in her case. Both in her normal and abnormal state she had several conversations with him. They discussed Swedenborg and other topics, and while somnambulic she answered with rare acuteness some of his objections to the great seer's " memorable relations." At Channing's request I mesmerized her for a dental operation ; and I well remember his getting down on his knees to watch the expression of her face while she sat in the chair, and the dentist extracted with his instrument one of her firmly fixed molars. Channing was amply satisfied that there was insensibility to pain in her case.*

---

* Mrs. Mowatt, though of a remarkably sensitive constitution, and not weighing a hundred pounds when I first knew her, was much benefited by the treatment she prescribed for herself while somnambulic, and attained a weight of one hundred and fifty pounds. She died at Twickenham, on the Thames, in 1869. I saw her two days before her death, and never did I witness such perfect, cheerful tranquillity as she manifested. In that supreme moment, when death seemed to have his hand on her, her thoughts and conversation were all

The phenomena presented by Miss Fancher resemble many of those through Mrs. Mowatt; but Miss Fancher is independent of any mesmeric aid, and her state of consciousness would seem to be uniform and normal, or else producible at will. Two well-known physicians of New York, — William A. Hammond and George M. Beard, "experts in nervous diseases," — have attempted to throw discredit upon the testimony in her case. Both are very absolute in their repudiation of the thoroughly well-established fact of clairvoyance. Dr. Hammond declares that "no one has ever read unknown writing through a closed envelope;" and Dr. Beard says, in regard to the same subject, "It is capable *of absolute proof* that no phenomena of this kind have ever appeared in the world in any human creature, in trance or out of trance." It is generally the fate of error to be betrayed by the very terms in which it expresses itself. What is this "absolute proof" offered us by Dr. Beard? It is simply his own individual deduction from certain facts as construed, or denied, by his own *à priori* intuitions. And we are seriously called upon to accept this as a scientific argument, while in extravagance it transcends all the claims of all the trance-mediums themselves.

So far is it from being true that experts are the persons best qualified to pronounce upon phenomena contradicting their own confirmed theories, experience shows that the preconceptions of the expert are often a decided hindrance to the proper appreciation of the truth. Physicians of the highest standing were those who most opposed Harvey, the discoverer of the circulation of the blood. Experienced navigators and geographers were those who opposed

---

of others, not once of herself. It was not faith or hope, but actual certainty which she felt in regard to the future. "The invisible world with her had sympathized." Mary Howitt wrote of her, "How excellent in character, how energetic, unselfish, devoted, is this interesting woman!"

Columbus. It was Bacon who repudiated the Copernican system. Those persons most conversant with the post-office were the last to approve of the plan of uniform penny postage. Chemists and physicists were the experts who said it was impossible to light cities with gas. Eminent men of science were those who disbelieved in the practicability of ocean steam-navigation.

The greater any one's skill and experience in his own special department, the more competent he may be to judge of admitted facts, and of details not foreign to his professional routine; but the more unlikely will he be to give a fair hearing to any fact or phenomenon introducing a radical change in his notions upon a subject of which he imagines he has a full mastery.

Dr. Hammond declares that " no one has ever read unknown writing through a closed envelope." But here comes a whole avalanche of testimony — not from Spiritualists, oh, no ! — but from some of the most eminent physicians, clergymen, and men of culture in Brooklyn and New York, testifying that Miss Mary J. Fancher, the phenomena in whose case have been going on now for some fifteen years, has repeatedly read " unknown writing through a closed envelope."

Miss Fancher was born in Attleborough, Mass., August 16, 1848, and was educated at the Brooklyn Heights Seminary, under the care of Mr. Charles E. West. In her eighteenth year she fell from a horse, and had several ribs broken. Soon afterwards, as she was alighting from a horse-car, the conductor rang the bell too hastily, her dress caught on the step, and she was dragged for a block over the pavement. Her spine was badly injured, and her body and head were so frightfully bruised, that she went into convulsions. This was in 1865.

She soon underwent astonishing physical changes, and has been bed-ridden ever since. In succession she was bereft of vision, speech, and hearing. For thirteen years the amount of food she took was hardly so much as a hearty man could eat in forty-eight hours. Eventually all efforts to make her take nourishment were abandoned by Drs. Speir and Ormiston. Her physical condition changed. One day all her senses, except that of touch, seemed to be paralyzed; the next, she could hear, and taste, and talk. But her eyes did not open for nine years. She was very sensitive to heat. In midwinter her only covering would be a single sheet, while the window would be kept partly open. She has successively lost and regained several of the senses. Mr. West writes:

"For many days together she has been to all appearances dead. The slightest pulse could not be detected: there was no evidence of respiration. Her limbs were as cold as ice, and had there not been some warmth about her heart, she would have been buried. When I first saw her she had but one sense — that of touch. By running her fingers over the printed page, she could read with equal facility in light or darkness. The most delicate work is done by her in the night. . . . Her power of clairvoyance, or second sight, is marvellously developed. Distance imposes no barriers. Without the slightest error she dictates the contents of sealed letters which have never been in her hands. She discriminates in darkness the most delicate shades of color. She writes with extraordinary rapidity."

Mr. Henry M. Parkhurst, the astronomer, of 173 Gates Avenue, Brooklyn, N. Y., testifies as follows:

"From the waste-basket of a New York gentleman acquaintance he fished an unimportant business letter, without reading it, tore it into ribbons, and tore the ribbons into squares. He shook the pieces well together, put them into an envelope, and sealed it. This he subsequently handed to Miss Fancher. The blind girl took the envelope in her hand, passed her hand over it several times, called for paper and pencil, and wrote the letter *verbatim*. The seal of the envelope had not been broken. Mr. Parkhurst himself opened it, pasted the contents together, and com pared the two. Miss Fancher's was a literal copy of the original."

Dr. C. L. Mitchell, of 129, and Dr. R. F. Speir, of 162, Montague Street, Brooklyn, both testify to Miss Fancher's clairvoyance. Dr. R. Ormiston is convinced there is no deception in her case. The Rev. J. T. Duryea says: "The child cannot deceive. How does she arrange and decipher the contents of a letter that has been cut into pieces and sealed within an envelope — a letter of the contents of which those who gave it to her had not the slightest notion?"

I present not a tithe of the testimony in this remarkable case. Though blind and in darkness, Miss Fancher has been known to distinguish the nicest shades of color in worsted before they were taken out of the packets in which they were enclosed. There is nothing in the facts foreign to those of Spiritualism; but as having occurred in the presence of non-Spiritualists they have a high confirmatory value.

In his book Dr. Hammond says : " In the fact that the spinal cord and sympathetic ganglia are *not devoid of mental power*, we find an explanation of some of the most striking phenomena of what is called Spiritualism." As well might he say, that in the fact that the violin is *not devoid of musical power*, we have an explanation of the musical genius manifested by a Paganini or a Vieuxtemps. Not only the spinal cord and the ganglia, but other parts of the body besides the brain, have been made *apparently* instrumental as conductors of mental force ; but what does this prove if not that the mind, in abnormal states of the system, may act independently of the brain, thus showing that the materialist's theory, which regards the brain as " the organ that secretes thought," and the only one, does not cover the phenomena? Does not sight without physical eyes imply thought without a physical brain?

In a tract entitled, " The Scientific Lesson of the Mollie Fancher Case," Dr. George M. Beard remarks :

" Unsought-for evidence has been brought to me from various quarters — from physicians and from clergymen as honorable and able as any whose names have appeared in connection with this case — that Mollie Fancher intentionally deceives ; that she lives on the fat of the land ; that the fancy articles she professes to make are made for her ; that her reading without eyes is done by trickery ; but all this, like the evidence on the opposite side, is of a non-expert character, and can, in science, receive no consideration."

Could Mrs. Candor herself have done it better in this attempt to slay a reputation? Sheridan's lady limited her scandalous remarks to the drawing-room ; the doctor sends his broadcast over the land in a published tract.

It is not surprising that he should be disturbed by the strong and respectable testimony in regard to phenomena similar to those which he has been denouncing lustily for years as impostures or delusions. He is committed to a theory which would dismiss all supersensual facts as impossibilities. He claims to be qualified as an expert to decide this question of clairvoyance, but, when we come to inquire into his qualifications, we find that they are mostly of the negative order, and based, not on his acquaintance with inductive facts, but on his estimate of his own remarkable cleverness at " deductive reasoning." So that when he wishes to prove Miss Fancher an impostor, he drops from physics into metaphysics.

Why is clairvoyance untrue? And he gives us to understand that it is untrue, because "absolutely disproved by deductive reasoning," (that is, by reasoning from *à priori*, *intuitive* assumptions,) — and because the " special sciences " to which its claims must be referred know them " to be false without any examination " !

" Studying the subject through the reason," he says,

" we know deductively by the law of biology that no member of the human species can have any quality different in kind from those that belong to the race."

" A quality different in kind!" No such chimerical claim as that which Dr. Beard imagines, is set up for any clairvoyant. There are some persons born with no ear for music ; but here is Mozart, who at five years of age shows wonderful genius both as a composer and performer.

Some persons are very dull at figures ; but here are the boys, Colburn, Bidder, and others, who perform in a few seconds what even an accomplished accountant would find it hard to do in a day. When asked how he did it, Bidder replied, " I do not do it, I see it."

It is estimated that ten per cent. of the children born into the world are color-blind. Do we therefore argue that they are destitute of a faculty which the rest of the human race possess? Far from it. We conclude that the faculty in them is undeveloped or perverted, either through lack of attention, or because of some derangement of the visual organs.

So it is in respect to clairvoyance. The theory is not, as Dr. Beard blindly supposes, that one person has what the rest of the race are deprived of. The real expert in psychology learns by his inductive facts, as well as by his deductive reasoning, that clairvoyance is a faculty common to every human being, though developed only under peculiar conditions. This is proved in dreaming and other phenomena. It is a spiritual endowment which, though latent, undeveloped, or working in secret, in this life, is yet the foregleam of an extra sense, which we may have in the next ; for, as Professor Pierce, of Cambridge, remarks, " There is no reason why our senses should not be multiplied through the possibilities of the electro-luminous body which will be disengaged from the physical at death."

So much for Dr. Beard's wild assertion that he can absolutely prove that there never was a case of clairvoyance, in trance or out of trance, in the history of the world! His deductive reasoning in the case is founded in a gross misconception, not on an axiomatic truth, and has no scientific force. Clairvoyance is a proof that our spiritual or transcendent faculties co-exist with the normal, even in the earth-life.

Induction, according to Watts, is reasoning from particulars to generals, and deduction is reasoning from generals to particulars. But in the process of induction there may be a deductive or intuitional element, as when we devise an hypothesis, and bring facts to justify the inference of an alleged law. To assume that deductive reasoning is infallible is absurd. History is full of the blunders of eminent men, who allowed their deductive reason to discredit real facts.

Dr. Beard divides the universe into the known, the unknown, and the supernatural; and he tells us that " in the realm of the supernatural all things are possible, and all things are undemonstrable." Would it not be a little less unscientific to say that no objective phenomena can be supernatural; that what seems to us such may be merely the natural, unrecognized or misunderstood? What possible reason has a man, claiming to be a man of science, for saying that " in the realm of the supernatural all things are possible," when he does not even know of the existence of the supernatural?

The rotundity of the earth would not have been proved to this day, if men of science had been " experts " of the type of Dr. Beard, and maintained that facts cannot be demonstrated as well as propositions, or that they can be annihilated by " deductive reasoning." It is demonstrative evidence only that is in the true sense scientific; and how, out of his purely negative notions, is he going to give us any demonstrable proof of his negations? In his claim to

judge of scientific possibilities by his " deductive reasoning," he is simply an idealist or an intuitionalist.

The late E. W. Cox, serjeant-at-law and President of
the Psychological Society of Great Britain, but not at the
time a Spiritualist, says : " I do not shrink from the avowal
of more than of mere faith — of a firm conviction, induced
by positive evidence derived · from this examination of the
mechanism of man at rest and in action — that soul is a
part of this mechanism ; that man is in fact a soul clothed
with a body; that for this soul there is a future, and, in
this future, God."

A party of experts, of whom Serjeant Cox was one, was
planned to test Alexis Didier, of whom I have already
given some account. A word was written by a friend in a
distant town and enclosed in an envelope, without any of
the party knowing what the word was. This envelope was
enclosed in six others of thick brown paper, each sealed.
The packet was handed to Alexis, who placed it on his
forehead, and in three minutes and a half wrote the contents correctly, imitating the very handwriting. See "What
am I?" by Serjeant Cox; vol. ii. p. 167.

" Fear of experts," says Dr. Beard, referring to Miss
Fancher's case, " is one of the symptoms almost pathogno-
monic." But the real motive that makes the sensitive subject shy of experimenters who, with their incredulity,
bring the predetermination not to be convinced, is not a
fear of genuine experts, but a sense of the folly of attempting to convince those who are wilfully committed
against the fact, and who, unconsciously perhaps, try to
prevent what they might not wish to find true.

Dr. Hammond proposed to test Miss Fancher by placing
in an envelope a check for over one thousand dollars, and
having her tell, under prescribed conditions, the number,
amount, &c. Such offers have been repeatedly made, and
declined for a reason, which is this: You might as well

expect the needle to point true while you are agitating the compass, as expect to elicit clairvoyance under the stress and excitement of an anxious motive, or under the disturbance produced by the simple presence of an uncongenial person, aggressively disposed.

Clairvoyance is a phenomenon as delicate and uncertain as that manifested in the caprices — the sudden flashes and sudden eclipses — of memory. A subject's lucidity is always impaired or spoiled by anything that excites anxiety or irritation, or appeals to cupidity. Nay, the very presence of a person convinced that there is imposture, and eagerly bent on detecting it, would, without any external manifestation, be felt by a *sensitive* as readily as she might feel, in her normal state, a freezing current of air.

Every patient investigator knows all this; and it was the reason why such physicians as Dr. Gregory and Dr. Haddock, having the command of clairvoyants, always refused to subject them to the money test. Such negative proofs of indisposition to act under conditions that would introduce all these adverse influences, do not reach the real truth, for, as Mr. Wallace remarks, "How can any number of individual failures affect the question of the comparatively rare successes? As well deny that any rifleman can hit the bull's-eye at one thousand yards because none can be sure of hitting it always and at a moment's notice."

There is no great subject in regard to which investigation has been so barren of results, as in that of *discrete states of consciousness*. With the exception of a few students of mesmerism, who among the philosophers has treated it intelligently? who has penetrated to the actual significance of the phenomenon?

In certain abnormal states, in trance and somnambulism, a consciousness is revealed which is not that of the individual when he is awake or not "under influence." The somnambulic consciousness may comprehend the normal, but the normal may know nothing of what is peculiar to the somnambulic; of facts and persons familiar to the somnambulist, the same subject may be wholly ignorant in his normal state, and in that state he may entertain opinions diametrically opposed to those he holds in his higher and more lucid state.

Townshend, in his "Facts in Mesmerism," relates the case of his subject, E. A., in whom good talents and a good disposition had been warped by an unfortunate education. Young as he was, he had imbibed infidel opinions at Paris, and had no belief either in God or a future state. In somnambulism, all this was changed. His ideas of the mind were correct, and singularly opposed to the materialistic views he took of all questions when in the waking state. "Is there a future punishment for evil-doers?" Townshend once asked of him when somnambulic. "Undoubtedly, a great one." "In what will it consist?" "In seeing themselves as they are, and God as he is." The theory that E. A., while somnambulic, merely reflected the opinions of his mesmerizer, will not serve; for on many subjects he would maintain independent opinions, and argue with great acuteness.

Instances in which a great change of character has been manifested in somnambulism could be quoted without number. Such changes are often produced by disease. "Sometimes," says Hahnemann, "a man who is patient while in the enjoyment of health becomes passionate, violent, capricious, and unbearable, or impatient and despairing while he is ill; or those formerly chaste and modest often become lascivious and shameless. It is frequently the case that a sensible man becomes stupid in sickness, whereas a weak mind is rendered stronger, and a man of slow temperament acquires great presence of mind and resolution."

"These physical defects," says Dr. Gorton, "are frequently observed in adult life, in the progress of chronic maladies. The vicious become amiable, and the amiable vicious; the irritable and combative become kind and obliging; the weak-minded become strong-minded, and the strong-minded weak-minded. . . . Sometimes the psychical symptoms are more clearly characteristic of the malady than are the so-called physical symptoms."

One of the most remarkable instances of a change of consciousness is that of Mary Reynolds, one of an English family that settled near Meadville, Pa., early in this century. A full and remarkably well-authenticated history of her case was published in *Harper's Magazine* for May, 1860, from the pen of the Rev. William S. Plummer. In 1811, when nineteen years of age, Mary fell into a state of insensibility. From this she recovered, but subsequently, for fifteen years, presented the phenomenon of a duplex consciousness. In her abnormal *second* state, however, there was a peculiarity distinguishing it from all other cases (with one exception) that I have known of; for, instead of having in her *second* state the memories of her *first*, all the knowledge she had ever acquired seemed to have passed away from her. She knew neither father nor mother, brother nor sisters; she had not the slightest consciousness that she had ever existed before. She would play with a rattlesnake she met in her path, wholly ignorant of the danger. She was quick to learn, however, and made rapid acquisitions. In her thirty-fifth year, the alternations from one state to the other ceased, *leaving her permanently in her second state.* In this state she was a very different person in character from what she was in her *first* state. Sedate, melancholy, slow of thought, and unimaginative in her *first* state, she was gay, social, jocular, and fond of poetry in her *second* state. Her handwriting, too, was very different from that of number One.

" The phenomena," says Dr. Plummer, " were as if her

body was the house of two souls, not occupied by both at the same time, but alternately, first by one, and then by the other. That the case was a genuine one admits not of a doubt. The two lives were entirely separate. The thoughts and feelings, the knowledge and experience, the joys and sorrows, the likes and dislikes of the one state did not in any way influence or modify those of the other.

"The leading facts are authenticated by a chain of testimony of unimpeachable character, covering the whole period. Mary Reynolds had no motive for practising imposture; and her mental and moral character forbids the supposition that she had either the disposition or ability to plan and carry out such a fraud; and had she done so, she could not have avoided detection in the course of the fifteen years during which the pretended changes alternated, and the subsequent quarter of a century, which she professed to pass wholly in her second state." The Rev. Dr. Wayland, in the last edition of his "Intellectual Philosophy," refers to this case as "more remarkable than any that he had met with elsewhere."

It is indeed a curious case. Which was the accountable being, number One or number Two? If, as Locke tells us, personality consists in identity of consciousness, was Mary Reynolds a person? In physical form she was the same in the two states, but in mind, disposition, and memory, she was wholly different. What became finally of number One? Was she rubbed out, as one rubs out an unsatisfactory drawing? Was number Two a distinct spiritual entity? If the two were one in essence, but manifesting two distinct consciousnesses, then why should there not be for all of us a distinct consciousness, stowed away somewhere in our complex organism, into which we may emerge at death? But if we lose our familiar consciousness, and become radically changed in character and memory, do we not lose our identity? Can we be said to be the same being we were in this life? Are we not in a sense annihilated?

Our solution of the puzzle is this: There was only one Mary Reynolds, and only one consciousness; but of that consciousness there were what Swedenborg calls *discrete degrees*. If in one state she did not have the memories of the other, it was not because any mental possession was obliterated, but because in the revolution a new phase, a distinct degree, was arrived at. The memories and the suspended consciousness were all in the soul, like a faculty unexercised or superseded. The soul, rising in this life or the next, to a consciousness as high above the *second* as the *second* was above the *first*, would comprehend all that was in both degrees; appropriating to itself what was best in each — the memories remaining unimpaired forever.

A case somewhat analogous to that which I have described in my own experience, as illustrating the fact of a distinct somnambulic consciousness, may be found related in *La Revue Scientifique* of May 20, 1876, edited by Germer Baillière, Paris. It is that of Felida X., born at Bordeaux, in 1843, of healthy parents. At fourteen and a half years old, she presented the curious phenomenon of "a double personality." Dr. Azam, of the Public Insane Asylum, investigated and described the case. Passing through a state of cataleptic prostration, Felida would emerge into a state where she was no longer the same person. Sullen and sad in her normal state, the Ego Number Two would be gay, vivacious, and active. She would now remember all that took place during previous similar states, as well as during her normal life; but when she relapsed into her normal state she would have no remembrance of what had happened during these attacks. In this second life there were no hallucinations; she seemed in the full possession of all her faculties; there was no physical pain; it was a superior life in every way. The phenomena seem to have been similar to those in the case of Mrs. Mowatt; only Felida was independent of mesmeric influence.

An illustration of that interior or psychical cónscious-ness, the reality of which is verified by our phenomena, is contained in an incident originally communicated to me by my sister, Mrs. Henry B. Hoffman, of Davenport, Iowa, in a private letter, which was published by me in the Boston *Evening Transcript* of October 2, 1874. Bishop Lee, of the American Episcopal Church, died September 26, 1874. My sister's letter, dated Davenport, September 28, 1874, is as follows :

"We have been very anxious the last two weeks over the illness of Bishop Lee, which terminated in his death on Saturday morning. Some two months ago he got up in the night and took a bath, and on returning to his room he made a mis-step, slipped down a long flight of stairs, and landed at the foot with a tremendous crash, as he was very heavy, weighing over two hundred pounds. It aroused the whole family; Mrs. Lee and Carrie sprang from their beds, and lighting each a candle, went to see what had happened, and found the bishop lying on the floor of the entry. He got up, however, without aid, and seemed to have received no injury except a few slight bruises, though his right hand was a little lamed.

"Mr. Hoffman and myself called on him two days after, and while telling us the circumstance of the fall, he mentioned this coincidence : He had a letter in his hand, which he had just received from his son Henry, living at Kansas City. His son wrote : 'Are you well? For last night I had a dream that troubles me. I heard a crash, and standing up, said to my wife, *Did you hear that crash? I dreamed that father had a fall, and was dead.* I got up and looked at my watch, and it was two o'clock. I could not sleep again, so vivid was the dream.' And it made him anxious to hear from home.

"The bishop said he was not superstitious, but he thought it remarkable that Henry should have had the dream *at the very hour of the same night that the accident occurred.* The difference in the time there and here (Kansas City and Davenport) is just fifteen minutes, and it was a quarter past two by his watch, *making it at the same moment.* It was as if Henry had actually heard the fall. And the fall finally caused the bishop's death. His hand became intensely painful, and gangrene set in, which, after two weeks of suffering, terminated his life. We are none of us Spiritualists, as you know, but surely facts like this must go far to make us realize that there is a basis of truth for the hypothesis of spiritual faculties resident in man. How did Henry Lee become cognizant of the accident to his father?"

How, indeed? Was his whole mental and psychical region in a state of insensibility and unconsciousness? Surely not; for in that case there would have been no faculty in a state to receive a supersensual impression. Was there a spiritual faculty, sufficiently awake to be in a state of receptivity, while the physical senses were locked in slumber, and the phase of cerebral consciousness was eclipsed? Yes; it was through his spiritual consciousness that he, while his physical body was hundreds of miles away, heard the fall, and received the impression that his father had been mortally hurt. And such was the shock that it was communicated to his normal (cerebral) consciousness, and sleep was dispelled.

A merchant of New Orleans, while in Paris, was awakened from sleep by hearing in a vivid dream, as it seemed, his son, who was in America, utter the words, " Father, I'm dying." So impressed by it was the merchant, that he rose from bed, struck a light, and recorded the dream and its date in his memorandum-book. On arriving in New Orleans, a month afterwards, the first acquaintance he met told him that his son was dead, and that his last words had been, " Father, I'm dying," — the date of the death corresponding perfectly with that of the dream. This incident I published at the time in a Boston newspaper, as I found it related, with names, in a New Orleans journal. It is adopted by Justinus Kerner, in his published Memorabilia.

The Pacific Hotel, in St. Louis, was destroyed by fire, February, 1858. A little brother of Mr. Henry Rochester, living at home with his parents near Avon, N. Y., woke screaming from sleep the night of the fire, and declared that his brother Henry was burning to death in an hotel. Such was the boy's horror and alarm that it was with difficulty he could be pacified. This was about midnight. Twelve hours afterwards the parents received a telegram from St. Louis, confirming the boy's vision in every particular.

In almost every family, whose traditions have been carefully kept, there is some incident to parallel these. They point to the great and significant fact of a spiritual consciousness, independent of the cerebral. Some finer organism than the physical and external is needed to receive subtile impressions remitted on the instant from Kansas City to Davenport, from Ems to Boston, from Paris to New Orleans, and from Avon to St. Louis. The external senses are not used in these communications. Only the theory of spiritual senses, transcendent in their nature, will account for them. Multiplied as these phenomena have been within the last thirty years, they cannot be reasonably explained away as coincidences. They are made credible by the now familiar facts of Spiritualism.

In the harbor of Norwalk, Conn., June 7, 1873, a little row-boat, containing nine boys, members of Mr. Selleck's school, under the charge of Mr. Farnham, their teacher, was struck and overturned by the rudder of a steamer, which had suddenly backed in consequence of an accident on board. Three young and noble boys — Eddie Morris, Willie Crane, and Charley Bostwick — were drowned by the collision. From the *Norwalk Gazette* of June 10, 1873, I quote the following particulars of a dream which preceded the accident:

" A curious circumstance of a dream has gained some notoriety, and though all parties disclaim all inclination to be superstitious, yet it is so singular that we have been at the pains of getting the facts. Last Friday (the day before the accident), Dr. Hays, an assistant teacher, and a man of medical attainments, remarked to a fellow-teacher, ' I have dreamed, two nights in succession, that three of our boys were drowned. It is very foolish to speak of it, but somehow it haunts me, and please have a care to the boys when on the water.' Saturday morning, he remarked to Mr. Farnham, who was to head the party to Peach Island, ' Farnham, look out for the boys, for somehow I can't rid myself of that presentiment.' When Charley White — the first boy who reached the house Saturday night — came in, drenched with water, the doctor exclaimed, ' How bad is it? Who is drowned?' and fainted, and fell into White's arms."

Wishing to authenticate this remarkable statement, I wrote to the *Norwalk Gazette*, and in a few days received this reply :

"NORWALK, June 5, 1870.

" DEAR SIR : Yours of May 27th was duly received. We have delayed answering for several days in hopes of finding a copy of the *Gazette* containing the dream alluded to. We have finally found one copy, which we forward to your address by this mail. You will find a full report of the accident, &c. The dream was personally related to us at the time, as much pains was taken to obtain all facts and incidents of interest. Yours truly,

" A. H. BYINGTON & Co."

Here is not only clairvoyance, but prevision through a dream. It is in perfect accord with the testimony of Aristotle, Hippocrates, Galen, Cicero, Plutarch, and thousands of other eminent men of ancient times to similar occurrences. Indeed, the number of well-attested cases in our own day is overwhelming.

Does divination require the aid of independent spirits? The question, as I have already shown, is discussed by

16

Plutarch, and he concludes, with Cicero, that there may be two kinds of divination, one from the gods (spirits), and one from the godlike powers of the human soul. This fully accords with the theory, that a class of spiritual phenomena may, under conditions, be produced by spirits in the flesh, as well as by those out of the flesh.

On the subject of human testimony, La Place, the great mathematician, remarks (in his *Essai sur les Probabilités*), that " any case, however apparently incredible, if it is a recurrent case, is as much entitled to a fair valuation, under the laws of induction, as if it had been more probable beforehand." How opposed to this rule is the demeanor of physicists generally towards spiritual phenomena !

" Orthodox science," says Edward Maitland, " has three defects : First, it assumes that it knows, in advance of experience, both what are the limits of natural fact, and what are the limits of the natural faculties by which the fact is to be judged. Secondly, it assumes that there are no facts which are not expressible *in terms belonging to a single plane of consciousness;* that is, it assumes the reality of all that is perceived by the senses on one plane, namely, the physical, and it attempts to explain, in terms derived from that plane, phenomena which pertain to other planes ; and failing to find such explanation, it rejects all insoluble phenomena as fraud." . . . .

Thus any super-physical fact is, in the estimation of the pseudo-science that would identify mind and matter, non-existent. And yet, in many ways, it asserts, or hypothecates, doctrines for which experience cannot vouch.

CHAPTER VIII.

ADVENT OF MODERN SPIRITUALISM. — SPIRIT—COMMUNICA-
TIONS. — TRY THE SPIRITS. — INCONSISTENCIES OF TRANCE-
MEDIUMSHIP. — MORE OBJECTIONS ANSWERED. — MORE
PHENOMENA.

COLERIDGE once said of mesmerism, that "it might be the refraction of a great truth, still below the horizon." This seems much like a premonition of the advent of modern Spiritualism.

Andrew Jackson Davis, in " Nature's Divine Revelations," written as far back as the year 1845, remarked in regard to the intercommunication of the spirit-world and ours : "This truth will ere long present itself in the form of a living demonstration." The words were uttered two years before the manifestations at Hydesville. Parts of the book were read in manuscript to the Rev. George Bush, the eminent Hebrew scholar, and myself, as far back as the year 1845.

The following passage from a communication got medially through the little gyrating tripod called a planchette, is a fair specimen of the better sort of writings purporting to come from spirits :

" Hitherto science has been almost wholly materialistic in its tendencies, having nothing to do with spiritual things, but ignoring or casting doubt upon them ; while spiritual matters, on the other hand, have been regarded by the Church wholly as matters of faith with which science has nothing to do. But through these modern manifestations God is providentially furnishing to the world *all the ele-ments of a spiritual science which, when established and recognized, will be the standpoint from which all physical science will be viewed.* It will then be more distinctly known that all external and visible forms and motions originate from invisible, spiritual, and ultimately divine causes ; that between cause and effect there is always a necessary and intimate correspondence ; and hence that the whole outer universe is but the symbol and sure index of an invisible and vastly more real universe within."

All this is directly at variance with the declaration of Mrs. Richmond's " controls," that there can be no scientific basis for Spiritualism.

Phenomena outside of all scientific verification offer a field for abject superstition and for medial or spiritual despotism ; for credulous submission on the one side and arrogant assumption on the other. Every sincere truth-seeker will desire to have a purely rational and scientific co-ordination of our facts. He will submit to no imperious " Thus saith the Lord," as to their interpretation, whether it come from a spirit or from a medial seer claiming inspiration.

The editor of a leading scientific journal tells us that the man of science may logically reply to the Spiritualist as follows :

" I cannot waste time in listening to you. I am limited to nature ; you take your stand outside of it, and there is no common ground between us. You come to me denying that which I find demonstrated everywhere. Between your Spiritualism and my materialism there is a fundamental antagonism ; your position is radically anti-scientific, and so let us keep clear of each other."

Science takes cognizance of phenomena, objective and subjective. I have shown by overwhelming testimony that Spiritualism has its objective, though conditional, phenomena, which are just as much addressed to the senses as the phenomenon of opening flowers in spring. The physicist may affect to rule out Spiritualism from the domain of science ; but this he cannot do without a violation of his own principle of loyalty to the experimental method. So far as it deals in such demonstrable phenomena as pneumatography, so far is Spiritualism scientific, and if our materialistic opponents do not realize this, it is because they persist in ignoring facts now experimentally known to intelligent millions. The pretence that these facts are contrary to nature has been amply answered in preceding pages. No reasonable man will deny that the testimony of a hundred competent observers to a constantly recurring fact is sufficient to neutralize the speculations of all the philosophers and all the physicists. The assumption that there cannot be such an occurrence as a manifestation by spirit-power is as grossly unscientific as was the assumption of those who rejected the theory of the rotundity of the earth. And yet it is upon this mere assumption that our editor would justify his refusal to listen to our facts and our reasons.

Science is not a mere knowledge of facts; it is also a fit method of construing them. It has been said that " the common knowledge of people is imperfect because they find it easier to invent fanciful explanations of things than to discover the real ones; that for thousands of years the knowledge of nature was rude and stationary because the habits of thought were so defective." All this is true; but the following is also true:

" The first step to a scientific view of things was one of self-assertion, implying *that degree of mental independence which led men to think for themselves.* They learned to make their own observations and to trust them against authority. It was found, as a first and indispensable condition of gaining clear ideas, that *the mind must be occupied directly with the subject to be investigated.* In this way scientific inquiry at length grew into a method of forming judgments which were characterized by the most vigilant and disciplined precautions against error. The scientific method is applicable to all subjects whatever that involve constancy of relations, causes and effects, and conform to the operation of law. It is applicable wherever evidence is to be weighed, error got rid of, facts determined, and principles established."

Do our specialists in science, who pretend to decide upon our facts, observe this first great requisite, namely, to " occupy the mind directly with the subject to be investigated"? On the contrary, they dispose of it by the *à priori* method: it is all wrong because it conflicts with their preconceptions as to the order of nature. Well and wisely is it remarked by C. C. Massey: " To the present writer, at least, so-called Spiritualism represents no religious craze or sectarian belief, but an aggregation (not yet to be called a system) of proven facts of incalculable importance to science and speculation. Those who so regard the subject would be unmoved in their convictions of its truth and importance, though it were proved that every medium was a rogue, and that many Spiritualists were their willing dupes. Much of the evidence on which we rely *has proceeded on that very assumption, and on the precautions which were accordingly taken.*"

Huxley objects to the low character of the communications; and so do we all object, when these can be fairly characterized as low. The claim of a class of mediums that they are writing or speaking under the control of some spirit, once eminent in the earth-life as poet, philosopher, or seer, has been too freely admitted by uncritical Spiritualists. It cannot be too emphatically enjoined upon the inexperienced that one of the most difficult things to be satisfied of is the identity of a spirit. That cases of identification do occur, I am well aware. From my own experience I can believe that identifications by the materialization process are not unfrequent. My friend, the Rev. Samuel Watson, of Memphis, tells me he has repeatedly had such experiences in his own library, where the conditions were perfect. The following relation, which I find in a discourse delivered in Brooklyn, N. Y., by Mrs. F. O. Hyzer, June 12, 1880, is similar to many that I have heard from credible witnesses. In this case Mrs. Hyzer and her sister were wholly unknown to the medium:

"At length a female form presented itself, and in answer to our inquiries claimed to be my mother, who passed from earth fifteen years ago. Although her height, and size, and general appearance corresponded perfectly with the form of my mother, — having something resembling a pointed paper cap covering the head and upper portion of the face, (as they informed us, to shield their faces from the de-materializing effects of the light,) — I could not assure myself of her identity, and so my sister and myself ad-mitted to each other. In a moment, as though in response to our remarks, she raised her hand — the hand which in earth-life had become so deformed with paralysis as to have brought the middle joints of the fingers down upon the wrist — a position reached only through the intensest tor-ture, prolonged for three years. As she reached to us this distorted hand, we exclaimed, in one breath, 'Oh, that is indeed mother's hand!' She bowed, and then again held it towards us. We then said, 'Mother's hand is not de-formed in spirit-life, is it?' She instantly extended it again, in a fair and beautiful outline."

The late Luther Park, of Boston, informed me that on one occasion, D. D. Home being the medium, a spirit, claiming to be Mr. Park's father, presented a proof of his identity by showing his hand, in which there was a peculiar malformation of the thumb.

But how are we to explain the contradictions and incon-sistencies in the declarations of trance-mediums as to their "controls," if we take the ground that their claim is to be accepted without question? A medium in New York, claiming to speak under the control of Parker, may directly contradict a medium in Chicago, making the same claim. How shall we decide as to which is right? By the internal evidence? Undoubtedly. But then we might not decide in favor of either. The two may be equally honest and capable; but one of them must be in error. I believe that both may be in error, and both sincere.

"How so?" it is asked. "The medium, by the hypothesis, is honest. Why, then, does his spirit, in the state of unconscious trance, present itself as Parker or Franklin? Truthful in the normal state, why is it guilty of a falsehood in the abnormal? Is it the body that keeps it straight? When freed from its control, does it act a part, or play the fool, or take pleasure in deceit?"

To all this it would be sufficient to reply, We merely give the fact; the explanation of it may be difficult, but the fact itself is not affected thereby. Which of the mediums is right in regard to identity of control? Obviously we are thrown back on our human reason for a decision. Forever apt and true, therefore, is that injunction from the evangelist John, "Beloved, believe not every spirit, but try the spirits whether they are of God; because many false prophets are gone out into the world."

I am aware that some mediums, honestly claiming to get their inspiration from the spirit-world, reject Christ's doctrine of the existence of malevolent spirits. That such spirits are kept in check by natural laws, I do not doubt; that they exist is, I fear, too true. Mrs. Maria M. King, one of the ablest of our American intuitionalists, says: "The medium who is susceptible to the influence of a beneficent spirit sufficiently to become his subject, is safe from the influence of malignant spirits, from several causes." All this may be true, and Mrs. King would here seem to admit that there are such things as malignant, or, as she elsewhere calls them, "undeveloped" spirits. That these may interfere in the affairs of mortals, and do some mischief, she also admits. So that, after all, there is but a slight shade of difference — that conveyed in the words *evil* and *undeveloped* — in our views. That I may do justice to her opinions, I quote her words:

"What is claimed in the philosophy I have been instrumental in giving is, that civilization in the spiritual state does what civilization in the material state aims to do. Being spiritual and higher in the strictest sense, it can do more than has yet been done on earth in dealing with elements of evil and ignorance. Superior methods of dealing with the lowly have been developed in that life, where nothing can be concealed from those whose duty it is to oversee society there. Men disrobed of materiality come more readily under the control of spirits of strong psychological power, and this power is used for good to all in earth and spirit life, as a safe and wise policy dictates."

I do not accept the theory, sometimes advanced, that our evil dispositions are not carried with us into the spirit-world; that with the loss of our physical appetites, we lose all those inducements to evil by which we have been beset in the earth-life. Be not deceived. Between the earth-life and the proximate spirit-life there is a correspondence of all things, whether good or evil; and the evil we have not put under subjection to the higher faculties in this life will go with us as a part of our incumbrances into the next, there to be got rid of only by our own efforts and the energy of our own volition.

Still I admit that man is a complex being, and that he may be interiorly much better or much worse than he appears to be, to himself and others, in his normal state. Some saints may find themselves sinners, and some sinners saints, in the life where all disguises will be stripped off.

In the mystery of this hidden, interior state may lie involved one of the solutions of the question, Why can we not trust the assertions of trance-mediums as to their "controls"? There are mental phenomena in abundance which will analogically justify us in the assumption that the medium himself may be innocently the subject of a self-imposed delusion as to identity. And then the high probability that there are unscrupulous spirits, who, to win attention, will assume the name of some great man, must not be left out of the account. If a human mesmerizer can create delusions in the mind of his subject, why may not a spirit-mesmerizer be able to do as much? That he has this power is made more than probable by a multitude of well-known facts.

There are higher and lower grades of consciousness, or states of mental activity, than the normal, as somnambulism and mesmerism have proved; and these grades, though in certain moments of psychical illumination they may be fused into a unity, may be quite distinct from our habitual state of mental activity. That we have psychical powers of which we have ordinarily no conception, is a truth which Plato, Leibnitz, and Schelling have all taught. Our modern phenomena confirm it.

"How is it," we are asked, "that an uneducated woman can, when medially impressed, give forth utterances far transcending all that she knows or is capable of in her normal state?" The answer is: She may have got much from her own psychometric appropriations, practised independently of her normal consciousness; or she may, in some instances, be influenced by a spirit, either truthful or deceptive.

One of the daughters of my valued correspondent, the late William Howitt, a well-known English author, was a mesmeric sensitive. Howitt told Professor W. D. Gunning, whose words (slightly abridged) I here use, that, on one occasion, his daughter, being entranced, wrote a communication signed with the name of her brother, supposed to be in Australia. The import was, that he had been drowned a few days before in a lake. Dates and details were given. The parents could only wait, as there was then no trans-oceanic telegraph. Months passed, and at last a letter came from a nephew in Melbourne, bearing the tidings that their son had been drowned on such a day, in such a lake, under such and such circumstances. Date, place, and all the essential details were the same as those given months before through the daughter. Howitt believed that the freed spirit of his son influenced the sister to write; and I know of no explanation more rational than this.

Plutarch, born about 50 A. D., discusses the subject of spirit-identity. In one of his dialogues an interlocutor says: "Why should we seek to deprive these souls that are still in the body (human beings) of that power by which the former (freed spirits) know future events, and are able to announce them? Is it not probable that the soul gains a new power of prophecy after separation from the body, and which it did not possess before? We may rather conclude that it had all its powers, though in a lesser perfection, during its union with the body."

Again Plutarch says: "If the demons, being human spirits disembodied, may foresee and foretell human events, why may not human spirits, embodied, possess a similar power? Our souls indeed *are* interiorly endowed with this power." At the same time, as I have already shown, he takes the ground, that the medium may not unfrequently be impressed by spirits to utter their thoughts, if not their exact language.

Porphyry (born 233 A. D.) tells how the "demon" (spirit) sometimes speaks through the mouth of the "recipient" (medium) who is entranced; sometimes presents himself in an immaterial or even material form. The trance state is mixed with "exhausting agitation or struggle." Right choice of time and circumstances for inducing the trance state, and obtaining oracular replies, is, he says, most important, for a Pythian priestess (medium), compelled to prophesy (speak in trance) while under control of an alien spirit, died; and under unfavorable conditions, "the spirit would warn the auditors that he could not give information, or even that he would certainly tell falsehoods on that particular occasion." "On descending into our atmosphere the spirits become subject to the laws and influences that rule mankind . . . and then a confusion occurs; therefore, in such cases, the prudent inquirer should defer his researches: a rule with which inexperienced investigators fail to comply."

Given a favorable day and a "guiltless intermediary" (a true medium), "some confined space would then be selected, so that the influence should not be too widely diffused." This place was sometimes made dark, and the spirit was invoked with "yells and singing." During this singing the medium "falls into an abnormal slumber, which extinguishes for the time his own identity and allows the spirit to speak through his lips," or, in the exact words of Porphyry, "to contrive a voice for himself through a mortal instrument." *

Anaxagoras, who lived 500 years before Christ, and who maintained that pure mind, free from all material concretions, governs the universe, teaches that the human soul has powers of divination in its own right, and independent of what it may get from spirits no longer earth-bound. Pythagoras held a like belief.

"To the question *Cui bono* morally, it is but a hollow answer that Spiritualism returns," says one of our reverend assailants. To call upon us to explain *what's the use of it*, in regard to any fact of nature, is not a philosophical but a childish objection. Nature does not need our human apologies. If our facts occur, they must be as justifiable morally as the facts of humanity itself. To say that they return a hollow answer to the question *Cui bono?* is simply to make human deafness or blindness the measure of Infinite wisdom.

These questions, *What good has it done?* or, *Has not its*

* For these passages from Porphyry I am indebted to Mr. F. W. H. Myers's able essay on "The Greek Oracles."

influence been evil? are impertinent, since the only scientific question is at present, *Is it true?* The notion that it may be true, and yet something very bad, seems to spring from a distrust that the cosmos is not rightly named; that it has no divine Orderer; or that He allows things to take place not at all consistent with clerical notions of spiritual propriety.

Perhaps with the advance of our own intelligence the *Cui bono* question will be answered. Perhaps Spiritualism comes fraught with divine instruction to our favored age, and if we fail to listen to its lesson, the loss will be our own. It is surprising how persistently men otherwise sensible bring up this *Cui bono* objection. Referring to certain spiritual phenomena an editor remarks: "Their existence as a class once being granted, we fail to discover among the facts a single one possessing either esthetic beauty, intellectual originality, or material usefulness." To all which the obvious reply is: If the facts are admitted, as you grant, then your complaint of their nonconformity with your esthetic sensibilities should be addressed to the Author of Nature, and not to the recorder of the facts.

In a discourse before the "Concord School of Philosophy" (1880), the Rev. Dr. F. D. Hedge remarked of Spiritualism: "Science has examined its pretensions and pronounced them groundless." I am unwilling to suppose that Dr. Hedge would wilfully misrepresent a fact, but the reverse of what he here affirms is the truth. Eminent men of science are every day contradicting his assertion; and I am confident that Dr. Hedge cannot name one man of high scientific authority who has ever carefully investigated Spiritualism and pronounced it "groundless." Dr. G. Bloede, a well-known German investigator, resident in Brooklyn, N. Y., writes me that his correspondent, Zöllner, Professor of Physics and Astronomy in the University of Leipzig, describes the state of Spiritualism in Germany (August,

1880) as being such as to interest the best scientific minds; and I learn that "the young men have caught the infection, and are experimenting for themselves."

The so-called "investigations" of Huxley and Tyndall were, if we may credit their own accounts, farcically superficial. The *de haut en bas* air with which these and other specialists, really knowing nothing of our facts, affect to look down on them, widely attested as they are, seems to partake at once of arrogance and alarm. The German Schopenhauer says: "The gentlemen of the crucible and the retort must bring it home to themselves that mere chemistry may enable a man to be an apothecary, but that it does not make him a philosopher. Certain kindred spirits among the naturalists, too, should understand that a man may be a consummate zoölogist, have the sixty sorts of apes strung together in perfect order, yet, knowing nothing besides, be on the whole an ignorant man, merely one of the vulgar."

In reply to a complaint that spiritual communications are not to be trusted, my friend Thomas Shorter wisely remarked: "Well, perhaps that is the very lesson they were chiefly designed to teach you." An intelligence claiming to be spiritual gave the following through a planchette:

"It is one of the important providential designs of these manifestations to teach mankind that spirits in general maintain the characters that they formed to themselves during their earthly life — that, indeed, they are the identical persons they were while dwelling in the flesh — hence, that while there are just, truthful, wise, and Christian spirits, there are also spirits addicted to lying, profanity, obscenity, mischief, and violence, and spirits who deny God and religion, just as they did while in your world. It has become very necessary for mankind to know all this; it certainly could in no other way be so effectually made known as by an actual manifestation of it; and it is just as necessary that you should see the *dark* side as the *bright* side of the picture."

That there are some medial communications not un-worthy the powers of what we might suppose to be an advanced spirit, is a fact which any candid person of good literary judgment will, on examination, have to admit.

The utterances of trance-mediums at times carry with them, by the force of internal evidence, the conviction of the identity of the communicating spirit. Circumstances foreign to the medium's knowledge, and not only unknown to the sitter, but contrary to his own belief, are brought up, and subsequently found by him to be true. Mrs. Brown (formerly Mrs. Fish), when in New York, in 1852, used to give messages which bore the stamp of genuineness. One evening while Mr. E. W. Capron, author of "Modern Spiritualism, its Facts and Fanaticisms" (1855), was visiting her, two young men from Tennessee came in. One of them asked if a spirit could communicate with him, and was answered in the affirmative. "What spirit is it?" "Your father." The young man then wrote down on a piece of paper the following question : "By what means did you die?" Immediately the alphabet was called for, and the word *poisoned* spelled out. The young man started with evident astonishment, for he did not anticipate so prompt and correct a reply. He then asked if his father had anything to communicate to him, and received the following :

"My son, lift your thoughts to God and remember your wrongs no more. To dwell upon the past will retard your progress and blight your future prospects. Your path leads on to glory ; then labor to overcome evil with good, and a crown of righteousness will be yours in time and eternity.
Your affectionate father,
HENRY CHAMPION."

The young man then said that his father was murdered by poison administered by a brother, who had escaped the penalty of the law. The son declared that he had been for years determined on avenging his father's death. Unlike Hamlet's spirit-father, this one advised his son to dispel all vindictive feelings, and the son declared that from that hour his schemes of revenge would be given up. Here we have all the elements of a genuine communication: remarkable clairvoyance, noble, christian advice, forgiveness of an injury, good plain English, and marks of affection.

A little girl was present with her father, both unknown to Mrs. Brown. The little girl's hand was moved, and she gave signs of being a *sensitive* for writing. The following kind admonition was then spelled out to the father through Mrs. Brown:

"I feel deeply interested in your little daughter. I want you, therefore, to be led according to your own good judgment and reason in regard to taking her into promiscuous parties. She should not always be led by advice which she thinks comes from pure and elevated spirits. My dear David, I will give you a rule by which you and Mary shall always be guided, as you are responsible for the protection and elevation of your children. When a spirit assumes *author-ity* in giving directions, follow not such direction. God made you a free man, and he has given you light and liberty to act accordingly. When a spirit speaks unreasonable things, be kind to him, but maintain your own ground, and gently lead him along in the paths of progression."

In this case, the names of "David" and "Mary" were entirely unknown to the medium, or to any of the company present except the ones to whom the message was delivered. Instances like these are not so rare as many may suppose. The intent is good, the advice excellent, and the language unexceptionable. The clairvoyance implied in the knowledge of the names of father and daughter is another reason why the communication might be safely accepted as genuine. The internal evidence in both these cases is very strong, and would justify the parties receiving the messages in having faith in their supposed origin.

Before me is a pamphlet of communications compiled by my friend, Thomas R. Hazard, of Rhode Island, from the utterances of the late John C. Grinnell, of Newport, R. I., while apparently in an unconscious state. Let us see if they are utterly devoid of sense and purpose:

" . . . The soul-body that is born with the child has a greater effect on its destiny in the spirit-world than its education on earth has, although it carries its earthly proclivities with it. These causes and effects should be understood, in order to understand the laws of progression. . . .

" Thus the soul and spirit unite and constitute an individual immortal being. If the spirit did not unite with and take the soul with it, there would be no individuality for the spirit to communicate through, but it would be a mere essence floating about, as it were, a thing of life without consciousness. *Thus the soul is the spirit-body* not only in earth-life, but in immortal life through eternity. . . .

" Everything in existence is continually revolving and drawn onward to higher conditions of finer and finer qualities of spirit magnetism, leaving the grosser to assist in advancing states of being still more gross. There can be no stillness or cessation to the action of the soul, nor can there be to the inspiration of the spirit within the soul. For the spirit must, by divine love, ever vibrate and strive within the soul, to qualify it for its immortal condition. . . .

" The spirit constitutes the light and life within, whilst the individual soul has the power to give itself any direction, whether for good or evil, it chooses. . . . . He who accepts his soul's inspiration is a free man, but not otherwise, as he has to conform to other personalities that go to make up that which he might call his own, through the ingrafting of their ideas on his individuality or soul memory. . . . When man is thus individualized, the simplicity and divine harmony of his nature become a fountain of joy, whence ever flows the expression, *I am free! I am free!* Whilst to those whose souls have become darkened and shackled, as it were, by the acceptance of the personal teachings or ideas of their fellow-mortals, life becomes the enjoyment of a dream rather than a reality. . . .

" The spirit is the entire life of the soul and the body, and without it nothing whatever can be uttered. But, al-

17

though the dictates of the spirit are always truthful, still the same power that is conferred on the soul to accept and give forth the truth, may be, and is in countless instances, directed through the promptings of its coarser desires into false channels of expression and communication, and thus used for sinister purposes and ends. In striving to express the truth through the soul organization, we thus see that spirit has many counteracting influences to contend with, which cause many unreliable communications both in the material and spirit world. . . .

"The kingdom of God is without and within. As *existence* expresses everything that is individual, so does *spirit* everything that is infinite and divine. As we could have no life without the Divine Spirit, so we could have no conscious existence without the individual soul. Thus spirit and existence make up the great divine attribute of the Supreme Being. . . .

"As the life and the spirit are imparted to existence, so each soul or individuality has a separate self-existence, but all under the control of the Divine Spirit. But all quality of soul is not all the same, as it depends upon the amount of inspiration that each individual soul has received and accepted of the spirit, — a portion of which is given to all, and which in itself is always the same pure and undefiled essence, as is the great Fountain of all spirit whence it is derived. . . .

"Throughout all existence it is the spirit that makes the shape or form of the thing that exists, whether it be a grain of sand or a living being.* As all existence is but an expression of the divine will, so should each individual existence that has a larger share of the divine expression within itself, impart of its abundance to those who have less. None should be turned away. . . .

"We are all independent, both in the structure of our individual being and in our individual progress, and con-

---

* G. F. Fechner, the eminent German physicist and philosopher, who, as the *N. Y. Nation* says, "scandalized German society by entering the ranks of the Spiritualists," in 1877, teaches "that every diamond, every crystal, every plant and star, has its own individual soul, besides man and the animals; that there is a hierarchy of souls from the lowest forms of matter up to the world-soul; and that the spirits of the departed hold psychic communication with souls that are still connected with a human body."

sequently we must ever become the architect of our soul's unfoldment and progress. . . . As we have the power to seclude and darken the spirit in the cloud of our individual selfishness, so too we have the power to shut ourselves out from a higher and more celestial spirit-knowledge. So it depends upon ourselves to choose what we shall be."

The thought here is clearly conveyed, and could have come from no ordinary mind. Of the medium, Mr. Hazard tells us: "He was from a child among the poorest of the poor, and almost wholly uneducated, never having been to school six months in his life. He had but little mental ability of any kind." The psychological theory, of which this illiterate individual was the utterer, would seem to be like that of Paul, who, in his first epistle to the Thessalonians (v. 23), writes: "And the very God of peace sanctify you wholly; and I pray God your *whole spirit and soul and body* be preserved blameless unto the coming of our Lord Jesus Christ." Here we have the trichotomy of (1) *spirit* (divinely influent, primary, life-giving) ; (2) *soul* or *spirit-body* (psycho-physical, organic, intermediary, essentially immortal, but potentially mutable in its corporeal relations) ; (3) *earth-body* (physical, ultimate, chemical, and transitory in its parts, but indestructible as to its dissipated atomic constituents). Thus the action of the spiritual upon the material, or the non-atomic upon the atomic, becomes intelligible by virtue of the intervening link, and the puzzle of the metaphysicians, who marvel how mind can rule matter, is solved.

I am indebted to my esteemed friend, the Rev. Samuel Watson, of Memphis, Tenn., formerly of the Methodist Episcopal Church, for calling my attention to the following remarkable passage in the writings of John Wesley, who, commenting on the verse I have quoted from Paul, enumerating *spirit, soul, and body* as a trinity, says:

" Is not the body that portion of organized matter which every man receives in the womb — with which he is born into the world, and which he carries with him to the grave? At present it is connected with flesh and blood, but these are not the body — they are only the temporary clothing, which it wholly puts off at the grave. *The soul seems to be the immediate clothing of the spirit*, the vehicle with which it is connected from its first existence, and which is never separated from it either in life or in death. Probably it consists of ethereal or electric, the purest of all matter. It does not seem to be affected by the death of the body, but envelops the separate as it does the embodied spirit."

Critically analyzed, the word *to*, in the third line, should be *beyond*, as it contradicts the plain meaning of the whole. Wesley, as the reader already knows, had the spiritual phenomena in his own family, and declared that " with his latest breath " he should " protest against giving up to infidels these proofs of the soul's immortality." *

This, then, is the summing up : — (1) It does not require the theory of independent spirits to explain a large majority of the phenomena we get through mediums for writing by their own hands or for so-called trance-speaking. (2) That mediums may be impressed by spirits to personate them, or to utter their thoughts, or to write their words, is however distinctly admitted. (3) Man being a spirit, even while fettered to matter, has spiritual faculties, which, in certain abnormal states, may be manifested. (4) A trance-medium, in a state of limited consciousness, may utter thoughts generated or appropriated by himself in another

---

* In February, 1771, Swedenborg wrote to Wesley: " I have been informed in the world of spirits that you have a strong desire to converse with me. I shall be happy to see you, if you will favor me with a visit." Wesley confessed he had wished to see Swedenborg, but had mentioned his wish to no one. He wrote that his engagements were such he could not be in London for six months. Swedenborg replied that a visit would then be too late, as he should be in the spirit-world March 29th, never more to return. Wesley could not break his other engagements, and so they never met. Swedenborg died the day he had named.

and discrete state of consciousness; and he may himself originate the impression that he is uttering the thoughts of some spirit, once eminent in the earth-life. It is not denied, however, that the false impression may be insinuated by some independent spirit; nor is it denied that the " control " may, in rare instances, be the individual he medially claims to be. (5) The phenomena of distinct states of consciousness must be studied for more light upon all these questions.

In an article in *Scribner's Magazine*, charging Spiritualists with accepting " as a fact that which only has its lying semblance," Dr. Holland, the editor, a believer in the Bible, tells us that he does not regard our facts as *à priori* improbable. He says :

" In both the Old and the New Testament we have multiplied records of the communications of spiritual existences with men and women in the flesh. The doctrine of demoniacal possession is taught with great distinctness. The ministry of angels, the return to the earth of those long dead, familiar intercourse with Christ after his resurrection, are all in the line of phenomena claimed as genuine by modern Spiritualists. It is, or would seem to be, easy for a Christian to believe that visitants from the unseen world are about him, influencing his mind, and endeavoring to make themselves known. That is precisely what they used to do in the olden time. Why should they not do it now as well as they did it then? "

This question of his own putting Dr. Holland makes no attempt to answer. Thus it will be seen that he is quite willing to receive from David, Ezekiel, Matthew, Mark, Luke, and John, accounts of phenomena that happened centuries ago ; but similar phenomena, vouched for by many of the principal scientific men of our own day, he rejects as " lying semblances." That a writing came to Jehoram from Elijah, the prophet, in the spirit-world, is quite credible ; but that independent writing came through Guldenstubbé, Watkins, Powell, Phillips, Mrs. Simpson, Mrs. Mosser, and Slade, must be rejected as a delusion.

It has been seen that some of the leading German physicists admit our phenomena. Zöllner testifies to the spirit-hand. He says in his "Transcendental Physics," as translated by Charles Carleton Massey, of London, a philosophic student and a close observer of our phenomena:

"Slade sat at his usual place; at his right Frau von Hoffman, I next, and Herr von Hoffman at my right. We had already laid our hands, linked together, on the table, when I remarked it was a pity we had forgotten to place a small hand-bell on the table. At the same moment it began ringing in the corner of the room at my right front, at least two metres from the middle of the table; and the room being faintly illuminated by gaslight from the street, we saw a small hand-bell slowly hover down from the stand on which it stood, lay itself down on the carpet of the floor, and move itself forward by jerks, till it got under our table. Here immediately it began ringing in the most lively manner, and while we kept our hands joined together as above described on the table, a hand suddenly appeared through an opening in the middle of the curtain with the bell, which it placed on the middle of the table in front of us. I hereupon expressed the wish to be allowed to hold that hand once firmly in my own. I had scarcely said this, when the hand appeared again out of the opening, and now, while with the palm of my left hand I covered and held fast both Slade's hands, with my right I seized the hand protruded from the opening, and thus shook hands with a friend from the other world. It had quite a living warmth, and returned my pressure heartily."

From St. Petersburg we get the testimony of Boutlerof, Wagner, and Aksakow to similar phenomena. Aksakow, Imperial Privy Counsellor, testifies to the slate-writing phenomenon, as got by the Grand Duke Constantine. He says: "I can, as a witness, testify that the writing was produced upon a slate which the Grand Duke *alone* held under and close to the table, while Slade's hands were on the table." This corresponds to my experiment with Watkins, only I held the slate unconditionally open to the light in my left hand, the medium standing four feet off, and not touching the slate.

Here is what William Crookes, F.R.S., has to say (1874) in regard to his experience with the so-called spirit-hand :

"Under the strictest test conditions, I have more than once had a solid, self-luminous, crystalline body placed in my hand *by a hand which did not belong to any person in the room*. In the light I have seen a luminous cloud hover over a heliotrope on a side-table, break a sprig off, and carry the sprig to a lady ; and on some occasions I have seen a similar luminous cloud visibly condense to the form of a hand, and carry small objects about."

The testimony in regard to this phenomenon of the materialized hand is so ample that I should be justified in including it as part of a scientific basis. For the past twenty-five years I have repeatedly seen or felt the materialized hand under test conditions.

(The full fruits of these revelations of spirit power, with the philosophy that must grow out of them, under the fearless auspices of modern science, unchecked by the superstitious fears which paralyzed investigation in ancient and mediæval times, must be the result of many conflicts with unbelief and of a long lapse of time. The misconceptions and follies which attend the science in its inchoate stage, are the unavoidable accompaniments of its transitional development. They must give way eventually to an anthropology based on accepted facts, and comprehending, in its synthesis, the spiritual, psychical, and physical nature of man.

Thus far the assailants of spiritualism have done nothing but call it hard names. They have confounded with the great subject itself the human abuses, follies, and errors attending it, but have not solved or made less credible one of our facts; have not accounted for the simplest of our phenomena; and yet they think to put a stop to investigation by telling us of its evils and dangers.

" The danger from Spiritualism," says the editor of *Sunday Afternoon*, " consists chiefly in the *ungirtness* it induces in all thought and conduct; the evil it has wrought in this direction is immense." Which, being interpreted, means: Spiritualism, like every great emancipating truth, is an iconoclast and a revolutionist. It frees men from old shackles of doctrine, and makes them, what they ought to be, *free-thinkers*, in the large and good sense. In the casting off of shackles, some undisciplined minds may be mischievously affected; just as in a wholesome national revolution mischief may be wrought by bringing the scum to the top, and tempting thieves and demagogues with opportunities which they might not have had under a despotism. And so when the editor last quoted says that Spiritualism has wrought immense evil, all the significance of the declaration is in its analogy with the assertion that the American revolution, or the Lutheran reformation, did the same. If Spiritualism in this sense has done harm, the good it has done, and is likely to do, may preponderate.

All this short-sighted antagonism is unphilosophical and unjust. Spiritualism is a synthesis of facts, and every investigator of those facts is at liberty to put upon them what construction he pleases. My own inference is, that they conclusively prove that natural phenomena or material existences are the raiment or visible appearance of some inner invisible power; that when we see a material hand, replete with life, and obedient to will, created in the void air, without tricks or illusions of any kind, we have reason to infer that there is a real form and a real intelligence interior to or ruling the outward material member, in such a case; that the matter used is transient, fleeting, adjective, to the underlying, substantive hand of the spirit; or else that the spirit, in its power over matter, can independently present a simulacrum of the mortal hand, and make it indicative of mind and life.

In a communication to the Royal Society (1879) William Crookes gives a condensed summary of the evidence in proof of the existence of a fourth state of matter. In conclusion he says:

"That which we call matter is nothing more than the effect upon our senses of the movements of molecules. The space covered by the motion of molecules has no more right to be called matter than the air traversed by a rifle-bullet has to be called lead. From this point of view, then, matter is but a mode of motion; at the absolute zero of temperature the inter-molecular movement would stop, and, although *something* retaining the properties of inertia and weight would remain, *matter*, as we know it, would cease to exist."

These considerations help us to a nearer comprehension of the fact that to spirit-power matter is a thing very different from what it is to our earth-bound faculties.

Some persons who admit our phenomena are disposed to refer them wholly to the action of evil spirits. The Catholic doctors do this very generally, though they make an exception when the manifestations favor their own religious views. Christ was more liberal. That he believed intensely in the action of evil spirits is manifest. He said, "Simon, Simon, Satan hath desired to have thee, that he may sift thee as wheat; but I have prayed for thee that thy faith fail not." Again: "Get thee behind me, Satan." Again: "This is your hour and that of the powers of darkness." And so Paul: "We are not wrestling with flesh and blood, but with principalities and powers, and the leaders of the darkness of this world, and against wicked spirits in high places."

* M. Camille Flammarion, the eminent French astronomer, writes (1880): "It is by the study of Spiritualism that Mr. Crookes has been led to his magnificent discoveries."

But that Christ and his apostles also believed in a counteracting force of good spirits is apparent from many passages. To Nathaniel he said: "Thou shalt see greater things than these. Hereafter ye shall see heaven open, and angels of God ascending and descending on the Son of man." Recall also the passage where he says of children: "Despise not one of these little ones; for I say unto you, that in heaven their angels (guardian spirits) do always behold the face of my Father." When he was transfigured on the mount, Moses and Elijah appeared to him. In the garden, an angel (spirit — see Rev. xxii. 9) appeared and ministered to him. Thus it will be seen that those priests who hold that all the spirits communicating with the laity must needs be evil, can hardly make it appear that they have Christ's authority on their side.

The Rev. Joseph Cook has drawn down upon himself the attacks of some of his evangelical brethren because he and his friends had the candor and the courage to testify to certain objective phenomena which they witnessed in my library. Upon these they are at liberty to put what construction they please; to explain them by an undiscovered psychic force, or by the co-operation of evil spirits, or by nothing in particular. It is enough for Spiritualism that they have not ignored or misrepresented what actually occurred.

That Mr. Cook, accepting the Bible as infallible, is justified in his fears, as to the ill effects of Spiritualism, by the cautions against necromancy which he finds in the Old Testament, no one will deny. I think that we Spiritualists can afford to be denounced as meddling with forbidden keys, so long as he has had the honesty and the intrepidity to testify to occurrences the very mention of which is an offence to many, and the admission of which he knew might lead to unjust aspersions upon his motives. These, I cannot doubt, were the promptings of an earnest and disinterested truth-seeker, not stopping to weigh adverse consequences, and not hesitating to proclaim what he had witnessed. I shall not grudge him the exercise of the same fearlessness in construing the phenomena, which he has shown in testifying to them, however widely I may differ from his interpretations.

Are there no cases in the Church, differing from that of Mr. Cook only in the fact that the recipients of the truth keep it to themselves? Yes, there are many such. I have myself been present at *séances* with two eminent Unitarian clergymen, now deceased, — one the Rev. Dr. Hall, of Dorchester, Mass., the other the Rev. Dr. George Putnam, of Roxbury, — both of whom admitted to me that they accepted the phenomena as genuine, beyond all possibility of collusion or trick. Miss Jennie Lord, now Mrs. Webb, was the medium, and, though it was a dark circle, the evidences of a preterhuman power at work that could see in the dark as well as in the light, were conclusive. The tangible spirit-hand, the playing on instruments, the placing of a full tumbler of water at the lips of the different sitters, so that not a drop was spilled, the violent, repeated dashing of the tambourine on the table, and then on the floor, with inconceivable swiftness, without touching one of the hands placed on the table, — and all this in the dark, and while the medium was held, — were phenomena that must have impressed the most apathetic as preterhuman. Both these reverend doctors, while admitting the genuineness of what transpired, excused themselves from saying anything about it publicly, on the ground that it would involve them in controversy; that it was too " big a subject " for them to take up at their age; that they could not investigate further without giving to it more time than they could spare from their parochial duties, &c. Both were noble, sincere men, and if they had been as young and as daring as Mr. Cook, they would doubtless not have allowed the phenomena to remain sterile in their minds.

I also took the well-known Edinburgh author and publisher, the late Robert Chambers, then in America, to witness the manifestations in Miss Lord's presence. But he was already a Spiritualist, and had no hesitation in recognizing them as among the most convincing he had ever experienced. His views and arguments in regard to the phenomena are clearly set forth in his Introduction to the second volume of the Life of D. D. Home, the celebrated medium.

I subsequently tested the phenomena through Miss Lord several times in my own library, when only my own family and a single friend were present. There was no conceivable chance for an abettor. Under test conditions, and while the medium's hands and feet were held, a large bassviol was taken from the corner of the room and played on vigorously and well. Several familiar psalm tunes, among them "Coronation," were accurately given. That it was a preterhuman performance (judging human capacity solely by what science admits) I absolutely *know*. The spirit operator first touched us all on the head with the viol-bow. The spirit-hand, twice as large as that of the medium, proved its tangibility by being placed repeatedly on our heads; it took down the hair of two ladies present, and carefully put it up again, and indicated in various ways the intelligence guiding it — and all this while the medium was held.

If any other witness from the Church is wanted besides Mr. Cook, I could refer the curious to the estimable Episcopal bishop of Rhode Island, Mr. Clark. Towards "interviewers" he may be reticent; but to those in his confidence he may narrate experiences far transcending those to which Mr. Cook has testified — experiences which, if accepted, make credible the re-appearance of Christ in the room with closed doors.

Bishop Clark preaches openly the Pauline doctrine of a spiritual body; thus rejecting or superseding the unscientific notion of a re-composition of the material remains. His extreme spiritualistic views and his long entertained convictions are well known to his brethren; and there has been question occasionally of a convocation to consider the heresy in his case; but he has not yet been summoned to the bar for examination, and I hardly think the indiscretion will ever be attempted. In England not a few clergymen of the established church are avowed Spiritualists. But if the elasticity of that church prevents its touching Bishop Colenso, it may well spare the recipient of the simple belief in continuous life, as justified by the demonstrated facts of Spiritualism.

An unprofessional medium testifies that the following words came to him from a spirit: " The spiritual body is made up by deposits of human thought even as the human material body is sustained by food. Hence the thoughts and affections of the heart go to construct the spirit-body, enter into it, become it. I warn you how you indulge in thoughts that are evil. The spiritual body does not change as easily as you imagine."

Edmund Spenser, one of the most medially gifted of poets, and who tells us that " all that's good is beautiful and fair," plainly inculcates this notion of a spirit-body, made fair or foul by the habitual character of our thoughts. He says:

> " So every spirit, as it is more pure,
>   And hath in it the more of heavenly light,
>   So it the fairer body doth procure
>   To habit in, and it more fairly dight
>   With cheerful grace and amiable sight;
>   For of the soul the body form doth take;
>   For soul is form, and doth the body make."

CHAPTER IX.

DISCRETE MENTAL STATES. — THE FACT ADMITTED BY MEDI-
CAL SCIENCE. — INFERENCES FROM THE PHENOMENON.—
SPIRIT-ANALOGIES. — HARTMANN'S THEORY OF THE UN-
CONSCIOUS.

THE facts already recorded show that the human mind
is so constituted that it may manifest discrete, or entirely
separate, states of consciousness. I have illustrated this
in the cases of Mrs. Mowatt, Miss Reynolds, and others.
In the case of Mrs. Mowatt, the superior consciousness included the lower; in that of Miss Reynolds, the consciousness of each state was entirely distinct from the other.
Even medical science admits the phenomenon of discrete
states in catalepsy and other affections; so the question of
its reality has been settled. Indeed the phenomena of our
daily natural sleep confirm it.

But as the subject from my standpoint introduces views
not yet admitted by philosophy, in regard to the nature of
consciousness, a somewhat more extended survey will be
necessary before I formally draw my inference, which is
briefly this: — An analogous fact of discrete mental states
as they affect communicating spirits, may be fairly postulated as accounting for many of the shortcomings, contradictions, and stupidities on the part of supposed spirits,
which have so mystified and baffled investigators.

That mental phenomena and changes take place in the
utter absence of consciousness, and that we may even think
without it, seems to be now the doctrine generally taught

and accepted. My purpose is to show that this doctrine must be dismissed as not proven ; that some degree of consciousness attends all mental operations, even those which go on in sleep ; — that there is no such phenomenon as "unconscious cerebration," but that all intelligence involves the exercise of a conscious discrimination, more or less active.

By the law or maxim of *parcimony*, we must not multiply substances or entities unnecessarily ; and my further conclusion under that rule is, that the theosophic theory of a partition of the spirit, under which a *geist*, or shadow-man, independent of the spirit, is left behind to manifest itself to mortals, and play many unaccountable antics, is wholly superfluous, since the doctrine of discrete states, applied to spirits as well as to mortals, is a sufficient explanation.

Locke's assertion that *self* is not determined by identity or diversity of substance, but only by identity of consciousness, requires qualification.

Hartmann, of Berlin, the pessimist, whose "Philosophy of the Unconscious" has been more widely circulated than any recent philosophical work in Germany, has undertaken to treat the subject exhaustively, and he seems to agree with Locke ; for he assumes that belief in a double consciousness in the human subject is equivalent to belief in a double personality. As the issue of Hartmann's inductive philosophy, based as it is more on physiological facts than on metaphysical abstractions, is that the Supreme Power in the universe has intelligence and will, but is destitute of consciousness, and therefore unworthy of adoration, — it will be seen that if it can be proved that consciousness is merely the equivalent of active intelligence, all Hartmann's excellent scientific arguments, proving the operation of mind and purpose throughout all animated nature, fall to the service of theism, and his atheism, or pantheism, whichever it may be, is annulled. I defer for the present my notice of what he has to say of Spiritualism, the facts of which he admits on testimony.

The Ego is not a product of memory, but memory is a product of the Ego. Those who believe in a double or even in a manifold consciousness, need not believe in the constant incommunicability of the different states. On the contrary, the facts all tend to prove that there is a supreme consciousness, even in the human complex, which includes and colligates all that is subordinate, thus reducing the manifold to unity.

If unconsciousness is the suspension of all sensation and all mental operations, then consciousness must be our mental activity in any of its modes. Consciousness is not a distinct faculty, at one moment active and the next inert; it is the mind active and cognizant of the forms of its activity in some of its multiplex states, whether in sleeping or waking.

We wind up a watch, and the next moment cannot recollect that we did it. We say we must have wound it up automatically. But our forgetfulness of the fact of the consciousness is no proof that it did not exist, however transiently. In cases of absence of mind like that of the German Professor, — who called at his own house one evening, and on being told that the Professor was not at home, walked away, forgetful that he himself was the Professor, — self-consciousness is merely diverted from its operation by a consciousness directed to other thoughts than that of self.

When we are walking, immersed in thought, two independent consciousnesses may be at work, one regulating our bodily motions, the other busy with our thinking. The fact that soldiers on a march, or persons walking for a wager, have been known to sleep while walking, does not affect our inference: a certain consciousness may accompany their acts even in sleep.

A man of ordinary self-control rarely oversleeps himself when it is important that he should wake and rise three or four hours earlier than usual. The anxious mother wakes at the slightest motion from her suffering child. What is it but consciousness that produces the waking in such cases? A person stunned will pick up his hat, walk home, undress, and go to bed, though his consciousness may seem to be annihilated, and he may have no recollection of what he has been doing when he comes to his senses. That there was an obscure consciousness regulating his movements is the explanation.

The case is related of a woodman who, while in the midst of uttering a sentence, was felled insensible to the earth by a blow on the head from a falling tree. He remained for months in a semi-comatose state, and was at last trepanned for the accident. The minute the crushed fragment of bone was lifted, he went on finishing the sentence he had begun several months before. Compare this with the analogous facts I have related in the case of Mrs. Mowatt.

Epileptics have been known to finish, in a new paroxysm of their complaint, a sentence begun in an attack which had occurred days or weeks before. Combe relates that an Edinburgh porter, who while drunk left a package at the wrong house, could not when sober summon any recollection of where he had left it; but on being drunk again at once recalled the place and got back the package.

Facts like these show that trains of thought, carried on in one state of consciousness, may be interrupted by the access of another state, but resumed when the former suspended state returns. The phenomenon is one which every experienced student of somnambulism will admit. Indeed, as I have already stated, medical science admits it as common in catalepsy.

Similar facts could be multiplied indefinitely. Maudsley, whose authority will be readily accepted by materialists, relates the case of a groom who was kicked on the head by his mare Dolly, and made insensible. When, after three hours, a portion of bone pressing on the brain was removed, the patient cried out with great energy, " Whoa, Dolly ! " The words he had just been going to utter had been locked up, as they might have been in the phonograph, to be let go the moment the obstructing pressure was removed. The incident is quoted as a proof that by pressing on the brain we can stop a thought or a volition. This may be true ; but it does not prove that the mind remains vacant of thought, or that every degree of consciousness is suspended. One mental state has been superseded by another less demonstrative — that is all.

" Persons have lived for years," says Dr. Wm. Gregory, of Edinburgh, " in an alternation of two consciousnesses, in the one of which they forget all they have ever learned in the other."   Even Huxley admits the implied fact. In his Address, Aug. 25, 1874, before the British Association at Belfast, he describes a case in which two separate lives, a normal and abnormal one, seemed to be lived at intervals by the same individual.

" The more we examine the mechanism of thought," says Dr. O. W. Holmes, " the more we shall see that the automatic, unconscious action of the mind enters largely into all its processes. . . . We all have a *double*, who is wiser and better than we are, and who puts thoughts into our heads and words into our mouths."   With a little qualification this is good spiritual doctrine, since there are undoubtedly spiritual faculties within us transcending those of our normal state (as clairvoyance proves) ; but can our " wiser and better double " be destitute of consciousness? On the contrary, he is as superior in that respect as in others.   Do we not regard it as a detraction from the character of the Supreme Being to deny Him the attribute of consciousness? Hartmann gives his God intelligence and will, but represents Him as unconscious; and it is this defect, the philosopher tells us, that makes deity unworthy of human adoration.

The late Professor Clifford, of England, who, had he not died young, would probably have outgrown his wild theories, hypothecated what he called " mind-stuff" to account for life and mind on materialistic and Sadducean principles. He entirely overlooked the consideration that when he annihilated what extreme materialists understand by *matter*, by identifying it, in ever so limited a degree, with *mind*, he surrendered his whole atheistic argument, and became a simple idealist.

Much more rational and consistent is the theory of Dr. Heinrich Tiedemann (1877), who argues that the original matter, imperceptible to the senses, which constituted the entire universe, must have been heterogeneous, and not homogeneous, as Herbert Spencer would have it; and this heterogeneous matter must have been composed of physical, psychological, and psychical elements ; so that all which we see before us — minerals, plants, animals, and man — had their origin in the mutual acting on one another of the qualities of this heterogeneous matter. Tiedemann says that Materialism, in declaring that matter must be perceptible to the senses, or that things which cannot be recognized and investigated with the limited sensual organs and their adjuncts, have no existence, or are mere transient phenomena, has started from false premises, and hence all its inferences therefrom must also be erroneous. He says:

" All that we perceive has originated from something that existed before ; it must have been so at all times and everywhere. Atoms, molecules, and monads, therefore, are conceptions which must all have originated from something that existed previously, as the eternal past is no more limited than the eternal future. But with the adoption of original atoms, molecules, or monads, we should limit our deduction into the indefinite past, and the moment we arrive at them, we should be compelled to assume a stationary condition of them in the indefinite past, and thus everything would have a beginning, and must have been created : — by *whom*, where, *how*, and of *what?*"

Thus it will be seen that Tiedemann leaves room for the theistic theory, — indeed, finds it inevitable. From a sincere Materialist he became, through free investigation, a sincere Spiritualist. He argues that the atoms, &c., must have originated from something before them, since a state of rest extending back into the eternal past is an impossibility; such a state of rest would be motionless death, which cannot be proved to have existed anywhere, or at any time in the universe. If motion had ever *commenced*, that which moves must previously have been without motion, which is simply impossible.

The monistic doctrine, which teaches that only one matter, physical matter, constituted the universe, is ably combated by Tiedemann. Nobody, he says, will deny that physiological essence and matter predominate in plants, while in animals and man there is a psychic essence, which must necessarily be combined with psychic matter, and manifest itself through corresponding phenomena. A psychic force, he argues, without a corresponding psychic matter, is the phantom of an unsound speculation. Hence, in his trinity of grades of matter, soul-stuff must have a place.* Of the materialization phenomena, Tiedemann says :

" It seems as if the higher developed spirits possess the faculty to mould the omnipresent physiological and physical elements into such objects as were known to them during their earthly existence, which is generally called *materialization*, though this must be regarded as a misnomer, because it admits of the supposition that immaterial ele-

---

* Dr. E. D. Babbitt, in his elaborate work entitled "Principles of Light and Color" (1878), assumes the existence of the "radiant or ultra-gaseous matter," afterwards proved by the experiments of William Crookes.

ments ·are wrought into material forms, a thing which occurs nowhere in nature, not even in the spirit-world, which cannot extend beyond the limits of infinite nature.

"In the same manner some spirit-bodies, inhabitants of the universe, have the power to use the surrounding elements, which they seem partly to borrow from a medium, for the purpose of appearing in such a condition that they become visible, and even tangible, to certain favorably organized persons ; — adopting once more the corporeal form in which they were known to men, and in which alone they can be recognized as the beings they pretend to be." *

Since all mental activity, all thought, implies consciousness in some form or degree, the fact that we may not be conscious at one time of having been conscious at a previous time, is no proof whatever that consciousness was not then present. To know and to be conscious of knowing are one and the same thing. The whole of consciousness is not included in a special act of attention or discrimination. I may be conscious of knowing that the whole is greater than a part, even when I am not attending to the fact. Indeed, this sub-consciousness must influence many of my acts. The thought that flashes to a conclusion, or solves a problem without apparent effort, may have been nothing less than the product of the conscious mind in one of its discrete states.

Mind may work in one state with a velocity wholly inconceivable to mind in a lower state. The mental phenomena of drowning confirm this. See the letter addressed by Admiral Beaufort to Dr. W. H. Wollaston, originally published in the Life of Sir John Barrow, who remarks of the letter :

"It proves that the spirit of man may retain its full activity when freed from the trammels of the flesh ; at least when all the functions of the body are deprived of animal

* See " Four Essays concerning Spiritism." By Heinrich Tiedemann, M. D., Philadelphia. Chicago: Religio-Philosophical Publishing House.

power, and the spirit has become something like the type and shadow of that which we are taught to believe concerning the immortality of the soul."

Admiral Beaufort, when a youth, fell overboard from a boat, and not being able to swim, sank before relief could be had, but was in the water less than two minutes. He says:

"Though the senses were thus deadened, not so the mind; its activity seemed to be invigorated in a ratio which defies all description, for thought rose after thought with a rapidity of succession that is not only indescribable but probably inconceivable by any one who has not himself been in a similar situation. . . . Travelling backwards, every past incident of my life seemed to glance across my recollection in retrograde succession; not, however, in mere outline, as here stated, but the picture filled up with every minute and collateral feature. Indeed, many trifling events which had been long forgotten then crowded into my imagination, and with the character of recent familiarity. . . . The innumerable ideas which flashed into my mind were all retrospective. . . . Not a single thought wandered into the future."

The mind is not only a unity, but a multiplex unity, and one that in its historical evolution is ever growing more multiplex. It has capabilities beyond all that can be imagined as coming from the mere exercise of the known senses. Its supersensual powers and achievements have been amply demonstrated in the facts of Spiritualism.

Mr. G. H. Lewes tells us that thinking, being a seriation, and involving time, the notion of ultimate unity and simplicity cannot be applied to a Thinking Principle. But this assertion has no scientific value in view of certain well-known mental phenomena. In drowning and the near prospect of death, the mind, we have seen, may act with miraculous celerity. Time is annihilated, and seriation is superseded. Indeed, clairvoyance proves this; and it is spiritually and objectively proved in the seeming supersedure of all time in the instantaneous production of long messages, written independently of any human agency. The events of a life-time may be presented to consciousness in a flash. I can only compare the effect to that photographic process by which all the minute details of a large picture may be compressed into a mere dot, and made visible only through the microscope.

The frequent absurdity of our thoughts in dreams is no proof of unconsciousness. It merely shows that while the reasoning faculty is inert, consciousness may accept the fanciful or superinduced for the real. Nor is the profound sleep from which we bring no recollection when we wake any proof of mental insensibility. When our sleep is deepest, the mind may be most active. Abercrombie relates that in the case of persons talking in their sleep, and thus indicating the subject of their dreams, it constantly happens that, when interrogated as to their dreams the next morning, they deny having had any; and even if the subject of their sleep-talking be suggested to them, it awakens no train of memory. If consciousness, then, be mental activity, how are we to prove utter unconsciousness? External signs are not to be trusted here for a solution of the mystery. The Rev. Mr. Tennant lay in a state of apparent insensibility for some thirty hours, but was conscious of what was going on around him, and also of certain spiritual experiences which he underwent.

The facts of idiocy are often quoted by Materialists as helping their theory. But the most advanced science on the subject gives them no comfort. Dr. Bateman, consulting physician to the Eastern Counties Asylum for Idiots, England, gives it as his experience that the results of idiot training furnish a forcible demonstration of the dualistic theory of matter and mind. Thought is not a mere function of brain protoplasm. The varied phenomena of nature are something more than mere molecular changes of matter. This is proved in the facts adduced by Hartmann. Volition and consciousness spring from something beyond nerve-centres and purely physical motions. The intellectual and moral faculties are not absent from the idiot. There is an independent spiritual consciousness which reveals itself by flashes at times. A celebrated German authority, Herr Seager, of Berlin, has stated that in his establishment he had indubitable cases of idiocy, in which the head was small and malformed, yet in which the results of education were so triumphant that his patients were ultimately able to mix with the world without being recognized as idiots. Further, he tells us that in one instance a young man underwent confirmation, without the priest's suspecting that he had been rescued from idiocy. Dr. Bateman says:

"Undoubtedly the idiot of the lowest class has the *germ* of intellectual activity and of moral responsibility; and this germ, cherished and nourished by the genial warmth of human kindness, fenced round and protected from the blasts and buffetings of the world by the cords of true philanthropy, watered by the dew of human sympathy, although possibly only permitted to bud here, is destined hereafter to expand into a perfect flower, and flourish perennially in another and a better state of being."

Agassiz, reaffirming the views of Dr. Brown-Sequard, says: "There are two sets, or a double set of mental powers in the human organism, essentially different from each other. The one may be designated as our ordinary conscious intelligence, the other as a superior power, which controls our better nature; . . . acting through us without conscious action of our own." Here the "superior power" to which Agassiz refers may be simply a discrete mental state, or a high spiritual consciousness. In the Supplement to Chauncey Hare Townshend's "Facts in Mesmerism" (London, 1844) will be found a letter from Agassiz, giving an account of the manner in which he himself was affected by mesmerism at Neufchatel, February 22, 1839.

J. Balfour Brown, in his " Medical Jurisprudence," says :
" In cases of pure somnambulism the waking consciousness
of the individual knows nothing of the sleeping consciousness.   It is as if there were two memories."   This is true ;
only it should have been added that the " sleeping " may
include the waking consciousness.

Abercrombie relates the case of a boy who was trepanned
for a fracture of the skull at the age of four.   He was
at the time in complete stupor, and after his recovery retained no recollection of the operation.   At the age of
fifteen, during the delirium of a fever, he gave a correct
description of the operation and of the persons that were
present at it, with their dress and other minute particulars.
He had never been heard to allude to it before, and no
means were known by which he could have become acquainted with the circumstances he mentioned.

Only the theory of a discrete mental state is applicable
here.   Is it likely that a boy four years old, while in a state
of stupor, took cognizance of things and persons about
him, and kept it all in his memory, unless there had been
a psychical consciousness at work?   May not Swedenborg
throw some light on the question?   He says :

" Whatever things a man hears, sees, and is affected
with, these are insinuated, as to ideas and ends, into his
interior memory, without his being aware of it, and in that
they remain, so that not anything perishes ; although the
same things are obliterated in the exterior memory.   The
interior memory, therefore, is such, that there are inscribed
in it all the particular things, yea, the most particular,
which man has at any time thought, spoken, and done, yea,
which have appeared to him as a shadow, with the most
minute circumstances, *from his earliest infancy* to extreme
old age."

Inconceivable as this may appear, it is in harmony with
innumerable facts.   " Our intuitions," says J. Le Conte,
" are in the nature of spiritual senses, by which we attain

knowledge directly by processes which transcend the power of our analysis."   Swedenborg says:

"Every man has an inferior or exterior mind, and a mind superior or interior. . . . These two minds are so distinct, that man so long as he lives in the world does not know what is performing with himself in his superior mind, and when he becomes a spirit, which is immediately after death, he does not know what is performing in his inferior mind."

Maudsley tells us that "consciousness is not coextensive with mind;" that "a mental power is being organized before the supervention of consciousness;" and that "the preconscious action of the mind, and the unconscious, are facts of which self-consciousness can give no account." But how do we know that consciousness is not "coextensive with mind"?   How *can* we know it, since facts prove that we may be wholly ignorant, in our normal state, of our higher or lower developments of consciousness?

To those mental operations of which our ordinary consciousness takes no note, Carpenter has given the not felicitous name of "unconscious cerebration."   Other phrases used to designate the phenomenon are, "obscure perceptions," "reflex action of the brain," and "automatic brainwork."   But we cannot think without knowing it, since thought without a knowledge of it is merely potential thought.   "Take away consciousness from an intellectual act," says Paul Janet, "and what will remain but an empty dead concept?"

But in cases of insanity, or where a sensitive is biologized, and seems to be subject to the will of the mesmerizer, is there not an absence of consciousness?   Nay, it is to identify consciousness with reason to instance such cases as any proof of the utter absence of the former.

The legitimate inference, then, from our facts is, that there is a psychical or inner consciousness distinct from the cerebral and outer, and that between the two there are

discrete degrees. Sometimes there may be an intromission
of thought from one to the other; and in highly sensitive
subjects this is not uncommon. Thoughts that come to us,
we know not how or whence, may come from higher grades
of consciousness; sometimes, perhaps, from lower; for
the essence of feeling, as well as of thought, is consciousness.

The "intuitive cognition" of Jacobi, the "intellectual
intuition" of Schelling, the "secret power" of Agassiz
and Dr. Brown-Sequard, the "ecstasy" of Plotinus, and
the "unconscious cerebration" of Dr. Carpenter, do not
suggest the whole truth; for the thought generated in the
state thus variously designated is not the product of mental
passivity, but the equivalent of an inner and at times a
superior consciousness.

Schelling's assertion that there is a capacity of knowledge above or behind consciousness, and higher than the
understanding, is merely another form of saying that there
is a distinct spiritual consciousness; and this I hold to be
the truth. Fully consistent with it is the theory that there
are spirits who, as Shakspeare says, "tend on mortal
thoughts," and perhaps impart much that we regard as
purely our own. In our highest, deepest, most intimate
consciousness we must be aware of our spiritual existence
and environments. Since all ultimate and absolutely simple facts are facts of consciousness, the logical basis of all
our knowledge must be consciousness, and without it there
can be no thinking.

The German word for consciousness (*Bewusstsein*, con-
scious-being) would seem to involve in its meaning the
identity of knowing and being, and to comprehend the
great fact of discrete mental states.

Lessing, an earnest, independent thinker, has this remark: "It belongs to human prejudices that we regard
thought as the first and chief thing, and wish to derive

everything from it; whereas, in fact, everything, ideas included, depends upon higher principles." All which may be reduced to this: There may be a divine ground of thought and consciousness, to which thought, as manifested by man, is an inferior force. This can be readily admitted, since in reply to the assertion, "There is nothing greater than thought," it may be replied, "Except the mind itself." Our interior psychical faculties, involving as they do clairvoyance, must transcend those of the external, speculative intellect.

The fact of those inner states, in the which our inner man is and thinks, before our normal consciousness perceives itself as existing and thinking in them, is clearly conceded by I. G. Fichte and by Schelling. But they do not seem to take it into the account that those inner states instead of being passive, may be also states of consciousness. Thus in the case of "intuitions," or results of "unconscious cerebration," our consciousness, according to these philosophers, perceives a defect within itself, a negation of its individual self-activity. But this negation is founded on illusion, and loses its force when we admit the great fact of discrete degrees.

Dr. Carpenter says: "Mental changes, of whose results we subsequently become conscious, may go on below the plane of consciousness, either during profound sleep, or whilst attention is wholly engrossed by some entirely different train of thought." This is a fair statement of the view now generally taken. But consciousness is not a "plane," a simple surface. It has its elevations and its depressions, its sunlight and its shade, in short, its discrete states. From one point its horizon is expanded; from another it is contracted. If there are mental changes in sleep, then there is consciousness in that sleep, though we may not know it when we wake. If, while our attention is engrossed by a certain train of thought, other thoughts are going on, they too may pertain to consciousness, whose very essence is thought. Can two consciousnesses coexist? Why not? That we are not conscious of a consciousness is no proof that it may not have existed and been active.

All degrees of consciousness may, like the three fundamental colors, red, yellow, and blue, be dissolved into a unity of white light; and so there may be — and my own experience in somnambulism affirms it — a supreme consciousness, in which all others may be blended.

May not these analogies of discrete states of the mind apply to spirits in their attempt to manifest themselves to mortals? In this attempt the spirit may not be in the exercise of his high spiritual consciousness, any more than in his materialized manifestation he is exhibiting his real spirit-form. In the last-named act his object is to extemporize a form in order to make himself recognized; and this form he tries to make like that which he had at some period of his earth-life. The experiment, accordingly, may involve a descent from a higher to a lower condition, one limited and obscured, and it is consequently a changed and partial consciousness which he brings. Thus his accounts of life in the spirit-world may be confused or contradictory; and his predictions and replies, though sometimes accurate, may be often fallacious. He may be powerless to say or do what in an ampler state of consciousness he might desire. We must not take it for granted that a spirit submitting to material conditions can manifest the same consciousness which he may have in a superior state.

The reticence, the mistakes, the lapses of memory, and the frivolous excuses or postponements, to which these manifesting spirits at times resort, and which occur even in the case of well-identified "materializations," may be explained by this theory of a change or limitation of consciousness. It is in harmony with the mental phenomena shown in the facts of this chapter. The materialized spirit-form does not adequately embody the consciousness of the spirit; since that form is as foreign to it as the molecules making up the body of the child are foreign to the same being when an adult.

That which physicists and philosophers have regarded as " unconscious operations of the mind," must, then, be referred simply to a discrete mental state. The fundamental truth lies in the words of Job: " There is a spirit in man, and the inspiration of the Almighty giveth them understanding."

Mark the force here of the relative *them*. It is to man and the spirit of man that the Almighty giveth understanding. Why this distinction? Is it not a distinction between the cerebral or normal consciousness, and that which is the property of the inner spiritual nature? If there are two " understandings," may there not be a dual consciousness?

Edward von Hartmann, author of " The Philosophy of the Unconscious," was ill at the time of the Berlin experiments with Slade, and could not witness them; but he accepts Zöllner's account of their occurrence, and attempts to reconcile the phenomena with his Sadducean philosophy, which may be summed up thus: There is no future for man, and the cosmos had better not have been.

Nominally Hartmann is atheistic; but as he argues in favor of an Intelligence and a Will, proved in the processes of nature, his system is not wholly antagonistic to Theism. He concludes that there is omnipresent in nature one Will and Intellect, acting unconsciously, in inseparable union with each other, through whose agency all the phenomena of the universe, including those of Spiritualism, may be accounted for.

He tells us that consciousness is not a fixed state, but a process, a perpetual becoming; that its antecedents are impenetrable to itself, and we can only hope to resolve

the problem indirectly. This he attempts to do. He first
distinguishes consciousness from self-consciousness, regarding the former as the prior of the two. Will and
Intellect he regards as belonging to the domain of the Unconscious ; a power operating on all unconscious functions,
human, animal, and vegetable. It is the one absolute
Subject. In other words, it is a union of Intellect and
Will, which we may call God if we choose, but which to
Hartmann has none of the qualities that command adoration.*

This unconscious Power, immanent in the universe, has
its phenomenal manifestation in a multitude of individuals ;
and consciousness first emerges from the cerebral organism
of man ; all belief in whose immortality, however, is a
delusion. For this attempt to evolve consciousness from
organism, Hartmann does not claim originality. Long ago
Schelling remarked, It is not thought itself, but the consciousness of it, which depends on organic modifications.
Thus by cerebral consciousness Hartmann means our normal state ; since any other consciousness of which we may
have experience is, in his system, merely a development
of the imparted activity of the Unconscious, and does not
fairly belong to the human individual.

The essence of consciousness, he tells us — and here let
the reader prepare to enter on very obscure ground — consists in the rupture of the companionship between Will and
Intellect. This divorce is effected by forcing upon the mind
a novel perception, which is not a purpose of its own volition, and therefore exists in opposition to the will. He
celebrates the birth of consciousness in these words :

" The grand revolution is now consummated ; the first
step is taken towards the world's enfranchisement. The
Idea is emancipated from the Will ; hereafter it will be

* See Professor Francis Bowen's excellent " Modern Philosophy " for a full
and fair account of Hartmann and his system.

able, as an independent Power, to oppose itself to the Will, and to subject it to its own laws, after having been hitherto its slave. The astonishment of the Will at this revolt against its authority, which up to this time has been recognized ; the sensation caused by the apparition of the Idea in the bosom of the Unconscious — that is consciousness."

Few readers, it is probable, will experience much of a clearing-up in their notions on the subject from this epitomized statement ; which, however, is quite as intelligible as the ampler details. Hartmann adopts the inductive method of the physical sciences, and professes to found his theories on observed facts ; and where he has mastered the facts of a subject his speculations are often sagacious. But in his remarks on somnambulism, the bearings of which on consciousness are all-important, he shows that his experience has been limited and his knowledge partial. Hence he overlooks the real significance of the phenomena. The tendency of the facts I have presented is to show that consciousness is the necessary accompaniment of all intelligence, divine as well as human.

How of that intelligence which, under the Spiritual theory, is imparted (we being unconscious of the influence) by spirits ? " Every grand thought," says Goethe, " which bears fruit and has a sequel, is no man's property, but has a spiritual origin. The higher a man stands the more is he standing under the influence of the demons (spirits). Everything is influence, so far as we are not it ourselves. In poetry there is decidedly something demoniac, and particularly in the unconscious, in which intellect and reason all fall short, and which therefore acts beyond all conception."

Here Goethe, corroborating Plato, is undoubtedly right in what he says of spirit influence. But when he gives us to suppose that the influence is unconsciously received, he omits an important qualification: he should have said,

unconsciously to our normal and subordinate apprehension.
The thought must fall on utterly barren soil if there is no
conscious receptivity, however occult, for its germination.

It is only by a resort to highly metaphysical subtleties
that Hartmann can make a show of defending his thesis.
The weak point in his system has been ably exposed by
Kirchmann, who says:

"Hartmann's idea of the unconscious includes all the
characteristics which impart to human knowledge the quality *conscious.* The form of conscious knowledge depends
on the following conditions: (1) Its contents are given
under the form of knowledge; (2) this knowledge knows
this form, or, in other words, the knowledge, besides its
contents, knows itself as knowledge (is self-conscious);
(3) the knowledge can reassemble the numerous elements,
one after the other, and co-ordinate them according to their
relations; (4) the knowledge, in spite of the rich diversity
of its contents, and the successive appearance of its ideas,
as separated in time, seizes on the idea of itself as a unity.
Of these determinations, proper to the form of knowledge,
the Unconscious Thought possesses incontestably the first,
the second, and even the fourth, according to Hartmann's
own showing. The Unconscious Thought, in effect, possesses reason, and manifests it moreover, because it joins
particular ideas, one to the other, by the tie of means to
end; and here comes in the third attribute, while the fourth
results sufficiently from the universal unity accorded to the
Unconscious."

To these affirmations Hartmann replies that "the Unconscious Thought does not recognize a separation between
the form and the contents of the knowledge, the subject
and the object, in the act of thinking; that it is just here
that the subject and the object are intimately identical, or
rather that nothing distinguishes them absolutely, since
they are not yet risen out of their state of original indifference."

This mere theory that the knower does not know that he
knows, is fairly offset, if not annulled, by the counter
19

theory that knowledge is not knowledge without a consciousness of it. The whole drift of my facts has been to show that Mind active is the equivalent of consciousness.

Clairvoyance is sometimes manifested in a state of ordinary consciousness. Schopenhauer testifies to this in his own case. Zschokke does the same. I have frequently known Charles H. Foster, the medium, while normally conscious, read what was written on a tightly folded pellet.

According to Hartmann, clairvoyance is merely "a finite Manifestation of the infinite prevision of the Unconscious, in which the seer and the seen are identical." Let us see what this theory involves in the case of the conscious clairvoyant. The Unconscious Infinite discerns what is wanted by the Conscious Finite, answers the want, prompts him to detect among a dozen folded pellets the right one, and to read what is written on it, — and does all this blindly and without a purpose. Only by robbing intelligence of all its human analogies, and making it something distinct from any human experience, can such a theory be maintained. Is there any conceivable reason why the intelligence credited to the Unconscious is not as distinctly conscious as any human act of discernment, discrimination, and communication can be?

Hartmann is a *monist* — that is, a believer in the Oneness of all things. Haeckel, also a monist, ridicules the manifestations through Slade, and sneers at Hartmann for believing in Zöllner's experiments confirming the fact of independent writing and other phenomena. It is from his *à priori* assumptions that Haeckel passes judgment on those facts of experience which he presumes to deny: and yet he would have the world think that he is faithful to the experimental method. It would seem that when his theory is interfered with, a great physicist may fall back on his "intuitions" as confidently as any seer.

Admitting the facts of Spiritualism, Hartmann does not

abandon the hope of making them fit into his Sadducean and pessimistic system. His objections to the spiritual theory are expressed in a letter to my friend, Dr. G. Bloede, of Brooklyn, N. Y., one of the most intelligent investigators of the supersensual phenomena. Hartmann writes:

(1) "If the spirits are unable to act without a living medium — if they have need of its unconscious will for their mediation — we may as well content ourselves with this unconscious will as a cause."

(2) "If we have to presume the spirits to be deceased persons, we would acknowledge thereby that *men* possess faculties of which they are unconscious as long as they live."

(3) "If this be so, then living men, too, could use those faculties unconsciously."

(4) "The contents of the communications often, indeed, surpass the intelligence of the media, but never that of the persons present (sitters), and are, in the average, proportioned to the latter."

Let us take up Hartmann's objections in their order. (1) He assumes that spirits are unable to act without a living medium. But this is far from being an admitted fact. The phenomena of haunted houses, the apparitions seen by persons not medially gifted, and when no medium is present, the stone-throwing occurrences, the instances on record in which coffins have been displaced without medial aid, all show that there may be independent spirit action.

It is not true that the spirit always operates through the "unconscious will" of the medium, and here the pith of Hartmann's objection is taken away. I have already mentioned the instances in which clairvoyance has been practised by Foster and others while normally conscious. In the case of Mrs. Andrews, of Moravia, N. Y., through whom remarkable materializations have taken place, the medium is unentranced and wholly conscious. The will may be passive; it is not unconscious. And from facts already given it has been seen that even where the medium is *apparently* unconscious (so far as we can judge by our external senses), he may at the same time be in the exercise of a superior consciousness. Thus the facts show that Hartmann's objection that the spirits require "the medium's unconscious will" is founded in ignorance on his part.

In regard to the materialization phenomena, the theory that man can act as a spirit, produce any number of form-manifestations, and other phenomena, while he is yet tethered to the earth-body, surely justifies the theory that he may do as much, and more, when wholly detached from that body. He may then command those higher grades of matter, of the phenomena,— proving one of which, the fourth state, or "radiant matter,"—Wm.Crookes remarks : "These phenomena differ so greatly from those presented by gas in its ordinary tension, that we are in the presence of a fourth condition of matter, which is as far removed from the gaseous condition as gas is from the liquid condition." That there is an increase of energy as matter becomes more sublimated and refined, is also clearly proved by Crookes's experiments.

(2) The supposition that there are spirits of deceased persons, Hartmann tells us, involves the acknowledgment that men possess faculties of which they are unconscious as long as they live. And this is just the great fact that I have been contending for — that men do indeed possess such faculties. Hartmann's objection, which he would present as a dilemma, is therefore accepted as a confirmation, when coupled with the supplementary fact of discrete mental states, of the spiritual theory. How are we to account for the phenomena in the case of Laura Bridgman, whose only medium of communication with the world of intelligence was by the sense of touch, except on the theory of the

existence of spiritual senses, which, while the physical were shut up, made possible the mental development to which she attained?

(3) "But," objects Hartmann, "if this be so," (*i. e.* if men have spiritual faculties,) "then living men, too, could use those faculties unconsciously." And, as I have already claimed, it is consistent with the spiritual theory that certain high spiritual faculties, like prevision and divination, should be sometimes exercised by man in the flesh, and he have no consciousness of it in his normal state. I have shown that in sleep, in the .act of drowning, and sometimes irrespectively of any abnormal conditions, faculties may be developed, of which we have no consciousness in our normal state. That this was the belief of some of the ancient sages, from Pythagoras to Plutarch, I have also shown.

Schelling distinguishes the "nature-element" of the Deity from his higher conscious intelligence; and there may be a great truth in this, if man is truly made in the divine image. If philosophical science can come so near to the borders of Theism as to admit a Divine Intelligence and Will, it is but taking one step more, and a very short one, into an ampler and higher generalization, to admit a Divine consciousness.

(4) Hartmann's fourth and last objection is an additional proof of his lack of acquaintance with the phenomenon. I have shown that the entranced medium's discourse may be often proportioned to his own intelligence and that of the persons present. But there are instances without number where the intelligence medially manifested is superior to that of the medium and of all the sitters, and can be accounted for only as coming, mediately or immediately, from an independent spirit.

Dr. Bloede, who shows the insufficiency of this fourth objection to support the conclusions which Hartmann would base upon it, remarks : " The trouble with these German philosophers, who, though claiming the privilege of calling their researches preëminently ' scientific,' are constantly constructing the world from the depths of their metaphysical vagaries, is their almost total ignorance of the overwhelming mass of spiritualistic facts, and their aversion to observing such when an occasion is offered them."

Hartmann contends that consciousness does not belong to the essence, but only to the phenomenal form, or manifestation, of individual being. On the contrary, our spiritual facts impress it upon us that mind, conscious of an object, is the very essence of being. Extinguish consciousness of every kind, finite and infinite, and the universe becomes meaningless and objectless. There can be no knowledge without a knower ; and, in order to know, we must be conscious of knowing. The very phrase *unconscious knowledge* is logically indefensible.

The phenomena classed under the generalization of " consciousness " have baffled the penetration of the profoundest thinkers. The subject is still in dispute between the materialistic philosophers and those who believe in a psychical element in man. Spiritualism, in its proofs of a spiritual organism, and of discrete mental states, throws a light on the question which must bring the philosophy of the future into accord with the unquestionable facts.

CHAPTER X.

MORE ANSWERS TO OBJECTIONS. — SUPERSENSUAL PROOFS. —
MESSRS. MERCER AND SWING ON SPIRITUALISM. — KANT'S
REMARKABLE PREDICTION. — SHELLEY INTUITIVELY A SPIR-
ITUALIST. — THE COMTIAN OBJECTIONS.

UNDISCRIMINATING opponents have tried to make Spiritualism responsible for much more than belongs to it. Rightly
defined, it is simply belief in the spiritual nature and continuous life of man, and in the power of freed spirits to
communicate in some way, subjectively or objectively, with
individuals still in the earth-life.

The attempt to identify Spiritualism proper with any other
doctrines, collateral and independent, whether they come
from freed spirits or from mortal seers, is the source of
much misapprehension and injustice. The various opinions
which so-called Spiritualists may hold upon subjects religious, moral, social, or political, will therefore be dismissed
by the candid philosopher as foreign to the one question —
Has Spiritualism an actual basis of facts?

As the same sun which ripens fruit may quicken corruption, so Spiritualism may have a good or bad effect, according to the state of the recipient. To charge upon it the
demerits of its professors is as gross an injustice as it
would be to charge moral delinquencies upon the moral
law. The arts of printing, of photography, of distillation,
may all be used to subserve foul purposes as well as good.
The art of writing makes possible the crime of forgery.
Obvious as these considerations are, they are repeatedly

overlooked by our assailants. Spiritualism does not *make* characters, it finds them made. To the good it is an aid, like all divine truth, to further good. By the bad its very good may be made the means of evil. The tendency to criminate Spiritualism itself because the unwise or the unprincipled may adopt it, or because the unthinking may misconstrue it, or the incautious be misled by it, is as contrary to reason as it would be to decry religion because intemperate Christian preachers may seem to have driven sensitive minds to insanity.

The clergy, one would think, would welcome our facts as giving the most cogent objective proofs of the continuity of our individuality, unimpaired beyond the tomb. But some of them have raised objections which a little more reflection would have checked. The Rev. David Swing, of Chicago, says, " In modern Spiritualism the mind falls into a trance, and is eloquent without labor, wise without study, clairvoyant without eyes, artistic without study or taste ; " mediums become " geographers without travels, readers of the strata of the earth without sinking a shaft." Hence, he argues, Spiritualism is " a new effort to leap over the great mediatorial laws " by which individual effort, skill, and labor "must be used for the accomplishment of an object."

It would be a sufficient reply to this to say : The facts persist, notwithstanding your disapproval of them. Instead of taking the trouble to verify them experimentally, the critic sits in his closet and evolves his objections from his own *à priori* speculations. So Melancthon and other great men, instead of qualifying themselves by study to pass an opinion on the Copernican system, raised futile objections out of their limited knowledge.

The boy Bidder being asked how he did certain wonderful computations, replied, " I don't do it, I see it." When the son of Bishop Lee, at a distance of some three hundred miles, was waked by the shock of his father's fall, was he not "a geographer without travelling"? When Captain Yount, as the Rev. Horace Bushnell narrates, saw in a dream a company of emigrants in the Carson-valley Pass, a hundred and fifty miles off, perishing in the snow, and in his simplicity, all on the faith of a dream, sent a party of men to their relief, and thus saved many lives, — was not he too "a geographer without travelling"?

When, as Richelieu relates, the prévost of the city of Pithiviers, in France, while playing cards in his house, suddenly hesitated, fell into deep musing, and then, turning to those present, solemnly said, "The king has just been murdered," and it proved true that on that same evening, at the same hour of 4 P. M., Henry IV. had really been assassinated, — was not the French officer "eloquent without labor, wise without study, clairvoyant without eyes"?

When Foster, Watkins, and other sensitives tell me what is written on tightly folded pellets, without once touching them, where is the physical organ through the employment of which can be explained the evidence of such a power?

Since the objections which Mr. Swing raises are annulled by constantly recurring facts, would it not be the better plan to investigate the phenomena experimentally before wasting time in constructing card-houses of imaginary disproofs?

The rapid production of messages in a handwriting where the letters are reversed as they would be in setting script type for printing, and where we have to read them from a reflection in a mirror, is a common medial phenomenon — the medium in his normal state being wholly unskilled in executing such writing. Does not this show by analogy that he may indeed be "artistic without study"?

But there is another consideration which Mr. Swing, a theologian and a biblical expounder, should not have overlooked. When he objects to the fact of abnormal intelligence through " minds that fall into a trance," how can he justify himself in preaching every week from texts involving the very phenomenon he would discredit? Read the account of Balaam's " falling into a trance, but having his eyes open," and being constrained to utter things opposed to his own wishes. See John's Revelation. Read Acts, 9th and 10th; and Paul's account of his entrancement (Acts xxii.); and again 2d Corinthians xii. 2–4. The very theory of the Bible's authority rests on the assumption that it came through the mediation of persons inspired, under influence, " eloquent without labor."

Is Mr. Swing prepared to throw discredit on the biblical record, or will he take refuge behind the indolent and unscientific assumption that entrancement was limited to " Bible times," and that human beings in our day are never subject to a similar influence? When an uneducated youth displays an inexplicable facility of arithmetical computation, like Colburn and Bidder, or an amazing musical proficiency, like the child Mozart, where do we find the proofs of study and labor, as preparatory to the display of such powers? Mozart said of his musical ideas, " *Whence* and *how* they come, I know not, nor can I force them. Those ideas that please me I retain in my memory." Here the theory of a discrete mental state, where the mind may be in communication with some influencing spirit, is not inapplicable.

My friend, William White, of London, author of the most liberal, independent, and interesting Life of Swedenborg yet published, and containing facts given in no other biography of the great Swedish seer, remarks:

" Our affections, thoughts, and dreams are spiritual manifestations; our good thoughts arise from the presence of celestial comrades, and our evil thoughts are due to our infernal acquaintance. We are, therefore, one and all, mediums; and a disciple of Swedenborg would maintain that spiritual manifestations are co-extensive with human activity. What is specially new in Spiritualism over Swedenborg, is the action of spirits *external* to the human medium — a possibility of which I incline to think Swedenborg was ignorant."

In a discourse delivered in Chicago in 1878, the Rev. L. P. Mercer, a Swedenborgian, remarks:

"Is it any wonder that the streams of tendency run to a materialism which denies any life hereafter, an epicureanism which cares nothing about it, and a Spiritualism which is only separated one remove from either, without any necessary belief in God or inspiration of righteousness?"

Truly, I would have my belief in God voluntary and not necessary, except in the sense of that divine constraint of universal reason which compels us to admit that the whole is greater than a part. Belief in human immortality may, as we all know, be entertained independently of any belief in God. That it may be so entertained logically and rationally, is a wholly separate question, into the discussion of which I do not propose now to enter.

To the patient thinker an all-embracing theism may seem as clear a deduction from the laws of reason and of Spiritualism, as it can be from the assumption that Swedenborg is infallible, and that what he says of God must be accepted in every particular. Spiritualism does not say to us, "There is one God, and Spiritualism is his prophet," but it points us to facts, by the faithful study of which we may arrive at the august conviction of a Supreme Spirit.

Now what is the theism which Mr. Mercer would commend to us as his "necessary belief" in God, in place of that which all the facts of universal nature, incalculably corroborated by our proofs of immortality, offer to the reverent and earnest seeker after truth? The former is a theism which would have us believe that in the year 1745, in the city of London, as one Emanuel Swedenborg sat in his room in his boarding-house, after dinner, the Lord God, in the form and dress of a man, came to him and said, " Eat not too much ; " and afterwards added, " I am God the Lord, the Creator and Redeemer of this world."

The construction which Spiritualists put on this extraordinary claim is, that Swedenborg, whom we all reverence and regard affectionately as a great and good man, subject to medial impressions, was, at the time referred to, either under a hallucination, partly produced by eating too much, or was under the influence of some psychologizing spirit, who claimed to be the Hebrew Jehovah and the infinite God.

One of the great benefits which the Spiritualism of our day is imparting to civilization is the evidence it brings that spirits may be as fallible as mortals ; that the wisest seer may mix error with truth ; that we must try both spirit and seer, even though they may preface their utterances with a " Thus saith the Lord."

Our stupendous facts are not vouchsafed to save us the trouble of doing our own thinking ; they are given to widen the sphere of thought and impart the stimulus of immortal motives. Those persons who would throw off individual responsibility, scrutiny, and labor are always liable to be misled by the impostures of communicating spirits, or the dictations of professing seers and trance orators.

It may be true, as Mr. Mercer says, that there is a Spiritualism only separated one remove from " a materialism which denies any life hereafter ; " or that there is a Spiritualism only one remove from " an epicureanism which cares nothing about any life hereafter."

The intuitive desire for continuous life is largely a matter of temperament. I have a friend, a Spiritualist by study and experience, who tells me : " It is a matter of indifference to me — I have no desire to live again ; but I know

I shall have to face it." My old acquaintance, Harriet Martineau, repudiating as nonsense all belief in a future life, said, some time during the last decade of her earth-life, "I see no particular reason why Harriet Martineau should be continued." My friend and correspondent, Professor Francis W. Newman, of England, not a Spiritualist but a devout theist, confesses that the desire for another life is in him "very weak." William Humboldt, David A. Strauss, and others, have expressed similar sentiments. And so, many persons, neither thoughtful nor reverent, may believe in Spiritualism, and not realize or care for its ineffable significance and its transcendent contents. Such apathy or such worldly indifference is no more to be credited to Spiritualism than moral blindness is to Christianity.

Are we likely to be any the less devout believers in God than the Swedenborgians, because we refuse to accept any diagram, whether from seer or saint, from priest or philosopher, of that inscrutable Being, of whom it was said by St. Denis, "It is when we acknowledge that we do not know God, that we know him best"?

In proving to us the reality of an undying spiritual principle in finite man, Spiritualism helps us to rise to the sublime realization of a supreme Spiritual Principle, behind and beyond all that may seem partial disorder in the universe; and from the summit of that principle Faith may look up through the veiling atmosphere to an Infinite Spirit, transcendently conscious, and in that sense personal and super-personal, in whom inheres all that there is of order, of life, of mind, and beauty, in the cosmos and in the soul of man.

The Rev. Mr. Swing tells his hearers that ours is "a more material kind of Spiritualism" than that of Swedenborg, inasmuch as we hold that there is "an actual exchange of language and sentiment between those who once lived and those who live now." But this is precisely what

Swedenborg also held. The Queen of Sweden said to him, "Is it true you can converse with the dead?" And his reply was, "Yes." "Is it a science that can be communicated to others?" she asked. "No." "What is it, then?" "A gift of the Lord." And a higher than Swedenborg manifested the same gift. John the Revelator declares that he conversed with an angel, who, when John fell down to worship before his feet, said to him, "See thou do it not; for I am thy fellow-servant, and of thy brethren the prophets." In this "exchange of language and sentiment," the angel gives us distinctly to understand that he is an ex-human being, and that he is exchanging "language and sentiment" with an individual still alive in the flesh. Other biblical passages could be quoted to show that by an angel was meant a spirit-man.

Will Mr. Swing, with his admirable powers of acute analysis, please explain to us how it is that what is expressly taught in the New Testament and in the writings of Swedenborg, is any less "material" than the same fact revealed in the phenomena of Spiritualism? Does he reject the testimony of John the Revelator as to the appearance and conversation of a human spirit or angel?

Mr. Swing further tells his hearers that the attempts of Spiritualists to rule out spurious phenomena, is an evidence that they are not yet perfectly assured that "the voices and forms and music might not be all of an earthly nature and origin."

This objection is much as if one should say that the passage of laws against counterfeiting is a proof that legislators disbelieve in genuine money. The faith of the experienced investigator in the genuine is not affected one jot or tittle by encountering frauds, even should these come from a medium in good repute. Our admitted phenomena are placed far beyond all danger from that source. Facts like pneumatography and clairvoyance do not depend on the veracity of a medium, and would not be affected by his repudiation of them.

Mr. Swing says: "God has thus far kept some door closed against returning feet. No man has yet *thrown back the bolts.*" Then what of the religion mainly founded on the tradition that the man Jesus came back from the dead? The Bible contradicts Mr. Swing on almost every page: does he repudiate all such passages as wholly mythical? So does not the modern Spiritualist.

"One may well wish," he says, "that Spiritualism might, in its highest form, be true." But why should it not be true in all its forms, high and low, if the spirit-world is peopled from this, as he teaches? He does not hold that sinners will be at once transformed into saints, or fools into sages. Why should he not rationally expect that if the fools and sinners form the majority here, they may form the majority in the vestibule of the spirit-world?

Spiritualism, like every other great fact of nature, is full of what to our short-sightedness is obscure, contradictory, baffling, and, to use Mr. Swing's alarming word, "undignified." And why not? It but introduces us to the rudiments of the great volume of creation.

One grand truth, at least, has modern Spiritualism extorted from this reticent Nature: the truth, namely, that the heart's premonitions, — that the intuitions and previsions of saints, seers, mediums, and little children, in all times, and among all races of men, — were not founded in delusion, but that they really presignified the veritable, objective fact that our departed ones still live, and move, and have their being.

Kant was as remarkable for his intuitional as for his reasoning powers. It was a rare combination. I have quoted elsewhere a brief extract from his remarks on the probability of a spirit-world. I here give them more at length, as quoted by Zöllner, and translated by Massey, premising that in his use of the word *immaterial*, Kant does not mean *unsubstantial*. That he was dissatisfied with the Cartesian, "hypothetical" notion of spirit is obvious :

"I confess I am much inclined to assert the existence of immaterial beings in this world, and to class my soul itself in the category of these beings."

"We can imagine the possibility of the existence of immaterial beings without the fear of being refuted, though, at the same time, without the hope of being able to demonstrate their existence by reason. Such spiritual beings would exist in space, and the latter notwithstanding would remain penetrable for material beings, because their presence would imply an acting power in space, but not a *filling* of it, *i. e.*, a resistance causing solidity."

"It is, therefore, as good as demonstrated, or it could be easily proved if we were to enter into it at some length ; or, better still, *it will be proved in the future — I do not know where and when — that also in this life the human soul stands in an indissoluble communion with all the immaterial beings of the spiritual world; that it produces effects in them, and in exchange receives impressions from them, without, however, becoming conscious of them, so long as all stands well.*"

"It would be a blessing if such a systematic constitution of the spiritual world, as conceived by us, had not merely to be inferred from the *too hypothetical* conception of the spiritual nature generally, but would be inferred, or at least conjectured *as probable, from some real and generally acknowledged observation.*"

This is remarkable language, and well worthy of the reader's profound consideration. Kant, among philosophers, ranks with Plato, Aristotle, and Leibnitz. He tells us substantially — and this was more than a century ago — that the fact of a communion of the human soul, even in this life, with the beings of the spiritual world, will be proved in the future. Is not that future at hand? Has it not already come? Our facts fully verify his prediction.

He goes further. Dissatisfied with the "too hypothetical conception of the spiritual nature generally" (the Cartesian conception was then dominant), he declares that it would be a "blessing" if the fact of the intercommunion of the two worlds, which he clearly anticipates, could be inferred, or at least conjectured as probable, from "some real and generally acknowledged observation" (Kant's Works, vol. vii. p. 32).

That "observation," which the great intellect of Kant looked forward to as something so desirable, is just what those investigators, who are now bringing the scientific method to bear upon Spiritualism, are desirous of prosecuting; and it is just what so many men of partial science are trying to discourage and prevent, since, if Kant's anticipation is proved true, — as it has been beyond all peradventure to millions, — it scatters the theories of materialism to the four winds.

Was Kant in error in supposing that the verification of an intercommunion between this and the spirit-world would be a *blessing?* Never has he indicated a higher sagacity than in putting this interpretation on the momentous desideratum. The present life will assume a new value and interest when men are brought up not merely in the vacillating and questionable *belief*, but in the settled, indubitable *conviction*, that this life is really but one of the stages in an endless career, and that the thoughts we think and the deeds we do here will certainly affect our condition and the very form and organic expression of our personality hereafter. Let men from early childhood to farthest age have this conviction ingrained into their minds, and by the laws of heredity coming generations must develop its beneficent effect.

What an illustration we have in the case of Shelley, the illustrious poet, of the struggle of the intuitional element in his nature against inherited conceptions of life and its issue! His father and grandfather were both bigoted atheists, rejecting all belief in deity and a future for man. Shelley had atheism in his blood, and it broke out before he had ended his collegiate career. And yet in his poetry and in some of his letters he at times throws off the Sadducean incubus, and cognizes his immortality as clearly as he ever did the sun at noonday. In a letter in the possession of Mr. C. W. Frederickson, of the city of New York, addressed by Shelley to his father-in-law, Godwin, are these words:

"With how many garlands we can beautify the tomb! . . . Surely if any spot in the world be sacred, it is that in which grief ceases, and from which, if the voice within our hearts mock us not with an everlasting lie, we spring upon the untiring wings of a pangless and seraphic life — those whom we love around us — our nature universal intelligence, — our atmosphere, eternal love." *

At another time, shortly before the storm in the Gulf of Lerici in which he lost his life, he said: "Another and a more extensive state of being, rather than the complete extinction of being, will follow that mysterious change which we call death." His poems are rich in passages in which the spiritual assumption flashes out through the folds of his inherited unbelief.

Indeed, poetry loses its quality of poetry the moment it becomes Sadducean. George Eliot (Mrs. Lewes-Cross) has to disguise her dismal unbelief in a gush of sham enthusiasm when she would pass off as poetry the embodiment of her conception of our posthumous influence on the world as the only real and desirable immortality. So artfully is the poor, thin, little conception disguised and padded out with swelling words that the passage is often quoted in religious collections as expressing the Christian idea of a future state. She sings, or affects to sing, thus:

* See a pamphlet by Charles Sotheran (New York, 1875), entitled "Shelley on the Immortality of the Soul."

> "O, may I join the choir invisible
> Of those immortal dead who live again
> In minds made better by their presence. . . .
> May I reach
> That purest heaven, . . .
> Be the sweet presence of a good diffused,
> And in diffusion ever more intense!
> So I shall join the choir invisible,
> Whose music is the gladness of the world!"

Upon all which Mr. Burchell's sufficient comment would have been, "Fudge!"

That there are persons even among Spiritualists who are temperamentally indifferent to a future life, and to whom the idea of utter extinction is not disagreeable, I have already shown. The assurances of immortality are based on something less fluctuating than the desires of the human race. The best men may be subject to moods when it may seem to them that they could "lie down like a tired child" and welcome an endless sleep. And so that state of mind which can regard annihilation as more desirable than continuous life, though a morbid and exceptional state, is not wholly out of the line of my sympathies. But the normal and healthy state is undoubtedly that of a full appreciation of life as life; that sense of the well-conditioned child to whom the mere act of living is joy enough.

An immortality of *post mortem* influence is (in the estimation of the English positivist, Frederic Harrison) the right, the sufficient, the manly aspiration. Continuation of life such as savages and little children imagine — such as the vulgar look forward to — such as Socrates and Christ believed in — is to this superfine philosopher a scandal and an offence, exciting only his disdain and his derision.

In commending to us his charming substitute for the immortality of the vulgar conception, he remarks: "Now we" (*i. e.* the positivists) "make the future hope, in the

truest sense, social, inasmuch as our future is simply *an
active existence prolonged by society.*"

And when the bereaved mother, mourning for her darling
child, demurs to this, and asks, " What is to me the good
of society, if my darlings and I are to be no better than
clods of the earth after a few short years?"—the sublime
Comtian affects to turn the tables on her by replying, in a
burst of scorn,—" This is the true materialism! Here is
the ' physical theory' of another life! This is the unspiritual denial of the soul, the binding it down to the clay of
the body!"

After these, his actual words, it will not surprise the
reader to learn that Mr. Harrison waxes exceeding wroth
over our facts, which, if true, convert his cheap thunder
into a theatrical sham; and so he denounces Spiritualism
as a "disgusting subject," charges men of science with
"dabbling" in its "filth," and describes the intelligent investigators in London, who satisfied themselves as to the
genuineness of the phenomena through Slade, as "grovelling before the trickery of a Yankee conjurer!"

There would seem to be something like consternation
mixed with all this wrath. The air of serious *hauteur* with
which Mr. Harrison affects to look down on the sordid aspi-
rants to immortal life, as if they were haggling for a miserable two-and-sixpence, would be comical did it not suggest
an eccentricity prompting an emotion of compassion.

Mr. Harrison has, as he believes, very exalted notions
of the soul, but he thinks that immortality, in the vulgar
sense, would detract from the soul's dignity instead of en-
hancing it. He rebukes materialism for "exaggerating the
importance of the physical facts and ignoring that of the
spiritual;" but the spiritual, in his new and independent
vocabulary, simply means our posthumous influence. In
his estimation, it is *much more spiritual to exert influence
as a dead man than as a living.* Since our posthumous in-

fluence, through our innocent errors of opinion, or our well-intended acts, is as likely to be bad as good, the comfort supplied in his teachings on this point is not very great to the ordinary conception, though he thinks it is " but a pessimistic view of life" which would contradict him. IIe tells us there will be a " providential control over all human actions by the great Power of Humanity!" As, apart from his esthetic misgivings, his great objection to the fact of immortality is, that he " can attach no meaning to a human life to be prolonged without a human frame and a human world," — the reply of a Spiritualist would be: There is both a frame and a world for man in the continued life which he enters upon when he leaves the physical frame and this world of the external senses.

Among the active iconoclasts of the day Mr. Leslie Stephen, of England, is one of the last to whom Spiritualists should address a word of discouragement. In pointing out the weak places in current religious beliefs, and showing how far short of the needs of the modern scientific mind are the common theological teachings in regard to the soul, he is unwittingly clearing the way for the advent of a psychological science which shall accept human immortality, not only as a postulate of the reason, but as an inference from demonstrable facts.

IIe is very far from entertaining any such view of the case himself. An appeal to Spiritualism disturbs his philosophical equanimity, and prompts him, as we have seen it does Mr. Harrison, to give way to expressions of anger and contempt, not weighty with conviction to judicial truth-seekers. IIe remarks of Spiritualists, that " they really show how belief in another life may be twisted into a most grovelling form of materialism ;" which simply means that Mr. Stephen dislikes what we claim to be, not theories, but facts ; facts quite irrespective of the question whether they may strike a fastidious person as " grovelling" or exalted.

In the next life, as in this, it may depend wholly on the character of the individual whether he " grovels " or aspires.

In a paper in a late number of the *Fortnightly Review*, Mr. Stephen informs us that " the so-called belief in a future life — whether in hell or in heaven — has always been in reality a dream, and not, strictly speaking, a belief at all." Repudiating as he does our facts, he may consistently entertain this theory, and regard it as a clever explanation of all religious phenomena, including the martyr's defiance of death, and other remarkable incidents in human history, significant of an overmastering faith in God and the unseen world.

That every man is the measure of every other man, in regard to the developments of his interior or abnormal faculties, is a fallacy into which the shrewdest thinkers not unfrequently fall through simple ignorance of certain supersensual, but not supernatural, facts, known in all ages of the world to observers under whose experience they have occurred. The argument of a class of minds of which Mr. Stephen is a type, is : " *I* cannot see without the use of my eyes ; why should another man be able to do so? *I* do not fall into trances, and see and hear unutterable things ; how can you expect me to believe that one Saul of Tarsus was any more favored than I am in this respect? If Slade or Watkins can get independent writing from some unseen, intelligent force, by holding out a slate, why should not *I* be the recipient of a like manifestation?"

In saying that the belief of men in a future life " has always been in reality a dream, and not, strictly speaking, a belief at all," Mr. Stephen shows simply that his prepossessions blind him to notorious facts. Pythagoras, Hesiod, Pindar, Socrates, Plato, Aristotle, Plutarch, and most of the great thinkers of antiquity, founded their belief in the immortality of the soul on actual phenomena, objective or subjective, as proved by Spiritualism, verified by observation and sanctioned by reason. To say that these men did not *believe*, but merely dreamed, is to utter a *sottise*, utterly destitute of truth.

Melancthon says: "I have myself seen spirits, and I know many trustworthy persons who affirm that they have not only seen them, but carried on conversations with them." Luther bears testimony equally strong to the existence of the departed in spiritual forms; so do Calvin, Richard Baxter, Knox, Oberlin, and hundreds equally eminent. Does Mr. Stephen suppose that the thousands of sincere men who countenanced the witchcraft persecutions had really no "belief" in the existence of spirits, — in the certainty of a future life? Does he suppose that men like Glanvil, Henry More, Baxter, and Wesley, were merely pottering over their foolish "dreams" when they asserted their solemn convictions, based on a knowledge of phenomena, that death does not kill a man, but simply leaves him a spirit in a spiritual world? There must be something lacking in the sympathetic capacities of one who can set down such men as either hypocrites or dupes.

Mr. Stephen offers this explanation for the belief in immortality among uncivilized tribes:

"The infantile intelligence is tolerant of contradictions; it is not surprised on discovering *that a body which was covered with earth and burned with fire is again appearing in its former state;* and the fact that death ends life is but slowly forced upon it by experience. If my dog saw something which recalled me after my death, he would accept the vision without the least shock of surprise; the childish mind certainly, and, we may presume, the savage mind, is in the same stage."

It is a dual body, and not the body that was "covered with earth," that the "infantile intelligence" believes in. Is it possible that Mr. Stephen did not know this? Mr. E. B. Tylor, who in his "Primitive Culture" has examined the question thoroughly and without bias, tells us, that in reply to the question, "Are there spirits?" he found all nations, even those in the lowest state of culture, answering Yes.   And as if to show how directly opposed to the truth is Mr. Stephen's wild assumption, Tylor adds the following conclusive testimony (vol. i. pp. 384, 387) :

"The belief in spiritual beings appears among all low races with whom we have attained to thoroughly intimate acquaintance. . . . The conception of a personal soul or spirit among the lower races may be defined as follows: It is a thin, unsubstantial, human image, in its nature a sort of vapor, film, or shadow — *the cause of life and thought in the individual it animates;* independently possessing the personal consciousness and volition of its corporeal owner, past or present; capable of leaving the body far behind, to flash swiftly from place to place; mostly impalpable and invisible, yet also manifesting physical power, and especially appearing to man waking or asleep as a phantasm separate from the body of which it bears the likeness; able to enter into, possess, and act in the bodies of other men, of animals, and even of things."

Mr. Stephen's notion, therefore, on which he bases so much of his abuse of Spiritualism and denial of immortality, is simply a blunder unbecoming in one who assumes to give scientific instruction on the subject of the foundations of human belief in a future state, and who would ascribe it all to *dreaming.*

In Mr. Tylor's account of the nature and genesis of the belief among the "low races," it is interesting to find how accurately their notions on the subject of the spiritual body correspond with those got from the well-established facts of Spiritualism.   We are surprised that so subtle a thinker as Mr. Stephen should not have seen at once that the stubborn realism of that "infantile intelligence" of which he scornfully speaks, would of itself have saved it from confounding the body "covered with earth and burned with fire" with the spiritual body assumed by the departed human being for the purpose of manifesting itself to mortals in the flesh. It is just because the "infantile intelligence" of the savage is *not* "tolerant of contradictions," that he believes death has not ended the individuality of the man who can manifest himself in a form and dress similar to those by which he was known in the earth-life.

Mr. Stephen's notion that a dog would not feel "a shock of surprise" at seeing the dead return, is a wholly gratuitous and unscientific assumption. The dog that had lain stretched for days beside the lifeless body of his master, and had marked the decay of the once familiar features, would in all probability have run away, howling with terror, if that master should suddenly have appeared to him in another but similar body, resuming the vigorous, life-like appearance, the absence of which was the cause of the poor brute's lamentation. The student of psychological phenomena among the lower animals will recall numerous facts to justify this conclusion. Dogs and horses have been known to show great agitation at occurrences which seemed to imply what a human being might call a spirit manifestation.

"There is not even a fragment or shadow of ostensible reason," says Mr. Stephen, "for confining immortality to man and excluding brutes." This is a too confident bit of dogmatism; but he should have known that Spiritualists very generally do not exclude the brute creation from immortality. Space must be cheap in a universe without bounds, and Omnipotence is a great word. There is room enough for all. Mr. Stephen should not have been silent on the fact that eminent philosophers like Leibnitz, eminent Christians like Bishop Butler, and eminent physicists like Agassiz, have believed in the immortality of the lower animals. "The common opinion which would consign to an eternal death all organized beings, man alone excepted, would impoverish the universe," says Charles Bonnet, the great Swiss physicist; and many Spiritualists agree with him. Nay, they go as far as Sir J. E. Smith, the eminent English botanist, who said, " I can no more explain the physiology of vegetables than of animals without the hypothesis of a living principle in both." If there is an illimitable spirit-world, and if life is a blessing, why should anything perish utterly in its spiritual part any more than in its physical?

Plutarch says : " The corruption or death of any creature is not its annihilation or reduction into a mere nothing, but rather a sending of the dissolved being into an invisible state." To the inquiry whether the soul is immortal, Apollonius, one of the great mediums of antiquity, replied, " Yes, immortal, but like everything." The essential life of all things is imperishable. In the present state of scientific discovery, he who believes only in the existence of what he can see and weigh is not so much skeptical as credulous, and this would seem to be the predicament of Mr. Stephen ; for the fact that the soul parts with its mortal body seems to him conclusive that it parts with every possible kind of organism through which it may still preserve its individuality ; and yet chemical and mechanical science admits that an electro-luminous organism, invisible to the external vision, is among the possibilities.

" Still less can any argument," he says, " be given for a future immortality which is not equally valid in favor of the past." What he would seem to mean here is that *post-mortem* existence implies eternal pre-existence, — a view which Plato entertained, which many modern Spiritualists, including nearly all those in France, who are disciples of Allan Kardec, adhere to, and which some commentators attribute to Christ himself. The attempt to use the hypothesis against the current belief in immortality merely betrays the shifts to which Mr. Stephen resorts in his special pleading. That all souls pre-existed potentially in God is good orthodox teaching.

"Dream-land" is the favorite phrase on which Mr. Stephen rings the changes to belittle the belief in immortality. This "dream-land," he tells us, "is the embodiment of our hopes and fears." "The plastic world of the imagination yields to every passionate longing that stirs our natures." "The whole process is poetical in substance." "Pure emotion knows of no limits."

That he sincerely regards this as a final solution of the whole mystery we do not doubt; for he has the convenient faculty of turning a deaf ear to facts which threaten to dislocate his nicely adjusted theory. He poses himself in an attitude of supercilious pity towards the fast multiplying host of witnesses who testify to certain phenomena justifying the spiritual hypothesis. Such men he regards either as mendacious or under an hallucination.

He distrusts the authority of the *emotions* as compared with the speculative faculty by which he arrives at his conclusions. The real appeal, he tells us, of those who believe in immortality, is " the appeal to the emotions." His own severe logic we, the simple ones, would supersede " by a simple appeal to emotion."

Now the belief in immortality, founded on the thoughtful observation of actual phenomena and on personal experience, is no more " emotional" than Franklin's belief in the electricity he drew from the clouds was emotional. The assertion that the conviction of immortality in the mind of man, whether savage or civilized, is not in reality a belief, but made of such stuff as dreams are, shows the audacity of inexperience rather than the sobriety born of knowledge. We have given Mr. Tylor's confutation of the statement. Any one conversant with the writings of the fathers of the Christian church, especially of Origen, Tertullian, and Augustine, will bear testimony to the fact that the objective phenomena, indicating the agency of spirits, with which they were personally familiar, seem to form the very foundation of their earnest belief in immortality. The records of the Catholic church show how largely the belief has been vivified and intensified by a knowledge of phenomena to which the church herself has borne witness, and which she never has repudiated, though imposture may have been often mingled with genuine marvels.

The emotions may be mistaken in their swift conclusions, and so may the speculative reason err in its careful judgments. Infallibility is predicated of One alone. But the emotion that rebels at injustice, or flames up at meanness, or wakens to a tender delight at recognition of the beautiful — whether in external nature or in human action — is it not as likely to point to the eternally true as the reason which leads Mr. Stephen into the blunders to which I have directed attention? He speaks of the " poetical process " as if it were necessarily at variance with the scientific — as if, amid all that is symbolic and metaphorical in poetry, the grandest truths of existence were not often intuitively uttered by the uneducated and inexperienced bard. What has given Shakspeare his immense reputation if not the truths for which he finds expressive utterance, the touches of nature by which he makes the whole world kin? The higher " poetical process " may often be that where the poet is possessed by a universal truth, and made to " wreak it on expression." The lower may be that where he controls instead of being controlled, and loses his high inspiration. Even Shelley, as I have clearly shown, while externally an atheist, was internally a " demoniac man," with a faith in immortality intense enough to be the equivalent of knowledge.

The mistake of reasoners like Mr. Stephen is in weighing in the scales of the speculative reason alone a subject which demands the co-operation of all the faculties and all the energies, latent and developed, of the whole man for its consideration. To rule out all emotional and psychical testimony, and say to the unaided Reason, "Now you alone shall decide this question of immortality," (as if observation had not contradicted reason in thousands of great historical instances!) is as unwise as it would be while sitting in a railroad car not yet in motion, as another train moves by, to say to the sense of sight, "Now you alone shall decide whether our train is moving."

Emotions that contradict the reason often reach to a higher truth than Reason ever dreamed of. John Maynard, who stood at the helm of a burning steamboat till he could run it ashore, and saved a hundred lives by risking and losing his own, — was it his hesitating reason, or his swift emotional nature, that impelled him to the heroic deed? Is the nobleness of such a self-sacrifice any the less true because born of the emotions?

The function of the meditative reason, seizing only upon the relations of things, is important, and Spiritualists, who base so much on its deductions, should be the last to dispute this; but there is a reason deeper than that which even argues and doubts; even the reason which feels and decides without any conscious ratiocination or balancing of arguments. Therefore is it fundamentally true that "Nearly all truth is temperamental to us, or given in the affections and intuitions, and discussion and inquiry do but little more than feed temperament."*

As men used formerly to build up their mundane systems irrespective of the facts of geology and astronomy, so would pseudo-scientists in our day build up or pull down psychological systems, irrespective of the facts of somnambulism, mesmerism, and modern spiritualism. Mr. Tylor, as if anticipating a recent extraordinary disquisition from the pen of Mr. Frederic Harrison, truly remarks that "there has arisen a psychology which no longer has anything to do with soul;" and yet the definition of the

* Dr. J. J. G. Wilkinson.

soul, he tells us, " has remained from the first that of an animating, separable, surviving entity, the vehicle of individual existence." If belief in a future life has been at any time " a dream, and not strictly speaking a belief," it is because subjective speculations have been substituted for objective facts. Among early Christians the conception of a soul-body involved, larva-like, in the earth-body — a conception simple, obvious, and aboriginal — was generally held up to the time of Gregory of Nyssa (331–394), and of Augustine (354–430).

" It is manifest," says Hallam, " to any one who has read the correspondence of Descartes (1640), that the tenet of the soul's immateriality, instead of being general, as we are apt to presume, was by no means in accordance with the common opinion of his age." And Descartes, let it be noted, taught that *there are no valid proofs of the soul's immortality except those founded on revelation.* In full sympathy with the negative part of this notion, the modern Atheistic and Sadducean school would repudiate the proofs which Spiritualism brings of supersensual powers in man.

It is not to be marvelled at that these philosophers should be so extreme in their denunciations. Just as a Sadducean science seemed to be having things its own way, — narrowing down the notion of a substantial soul till, small by degrees and beautifully less, it was lost in outright unbelief, — up starts this portentous, ill-favored, modern Spiritualism, with its grotesque, unaccountable phenomena, and threatens to undo the work that the Büchners and the Haeckels, the Stephens, Frederic Harrisons, and Cliffords have been so busily engaged in. Is it a wonder that they lose their temper?

Mr. Stephen stigmatizes as " mere greediness for life " the belief of some minds in immortality. Just before this, with a slight inconsistency, he told us there is no belief at all, " only a dream." But now " it may mean the intense dislike of a selfish nature to part from all chance of enjoyment." "It means so strong a regard for one's own wretched little individuality that the universe seems worthless unless it is preserved."

And may not conscious mind logically and rightfully regard the whole material universe as worthless in comparison with itself? What is a universe of mere dust, and fire, and gas, compared with "the wretched little individuality" of a Shakspeare or a Newton? The mind that can create the beautiful, or measure suns and systems and their movements, is it not something grander than the suns and systems themselves, if these are to be dissociated, as they are in the philosophy of Mr. Stephen, from all reference to a Divine Orderer?

If, in using the phrase "greediness for life," Mr. Stephen means anything, he means to stigmatize by a dishonoring word that intense longing for a better and nobler state of existence, which many of the most exalted minds, of which we have any record, have experienced. That this longing may sometimes be felt by a "selfish nature" is not denied, and so may the apathy or the dislike that rests in indifference, or craves annihilation, be either a selfish prompting or a morbid idiosyncrasy. But an appreciation of the possibilities of life in an inexhaustible universe, and an intense desire to live and to love and to learn, in view of all that there is to live for and to love and to learn, may be a sentiment of all the most grateful to the Giver of life, supposing that there is an intelligent Giver. If it be selfishness, it is a selfishness godlike, aspiring, and communicative as the sun — a selfishness which all loving souls would commend as higher and better than the absence of it.

Mr. Stephen cannot well ignore the nobility of that desire for immortality inspired by the pure affections. He condescends to refer to it with an air of patronizing sympathy. He says of that "plastic world of the imagination," by which he characterizes the future life, "A world thus framed may, at times, represent the strength of love. We cannot and we will not believe in the loss of those whose lives seemed to be part of our essence. A belief caused by (I cannot say based upon) this passionate yearning is so pathetic, and even sacred, that the unbeliever may well shrink from breathing his doubts in its presence."

And then our compassionate "unbeliever" wipes his eyes, and goes on to say what he can to persuade the world that there is no future life, that it is all a dreamland, and that the saints, seers, and devout thinkers of the ages have been no better than idle and imbecile visionaries, imagining that they believed when they were only dreaming. He entirely ignores the vital, momentous fact, that the belief of saints and sages may have culminated in actual knowledge through their acquaintance with our phenomena.

The mind so circumscribed in the limitations of a crass, dead materialism that it cannot even believe that other men really ever *believed* in immortality, is rather a hopeless subject for argument or for fact. I have no expectation of softening the wrath which Mr. Stephen has expressed towards Spiritualism, but I trust that before venturing to discourse again upon the genesis of the belief in immortality, he will look a little into the facts, and explain them if he can. His assertion that there is no element in the belief but dreams and emotions, is exploded by a crushing weight of evidence to the contrary.

From actual phenomena known to savages as well as to civilized men, issues the first serious belief in immortality. As far back as tradition can go we find the belief, and we find indications of the origin of the belief. All history, all mythology, all literature, all medical science, contribute concurrent evidence to the establishment of this fact. The studious Spiritualist finds the phenomena corroborated and explained by the occurrences of our own day. The Hebrew and Christian Scriptures are a rich repository of these facts, many of which have no significance without the key that an intelligent Spiritualism supplies. Their unequivocal resemblance to those of the present day shows that they all belong to the same group.

Shallow and superficial investigators would relegate all spiritual phenomena to "dream-land," or treat them as explicable by prepossession, hallucination, hypnotism, or some kind of imposture. But such explanations no longer carry weight. Careful observers are beginning to multiply, and they demand a solution that shall not wholly ignore the irrepressible facts. When many thousands of intelligent contemporaries can testify to the reality of direct writing in broad daylight, under conditions in which there is nothing at variance with the most complete scientific satisfaction, the stupendous phenomenon is not to be got rid of by a " pooh-pooh," or by any oracular talk of " dream-land " and the fallibility of the " emotions."

The time has come when men who claim to be scientific must look such facts squarely in the face. And the time has also come when such speculations as those of Mr. Stephen in regard to the question of the origin of the belief in immortality, will be of little value unaccompanied by an admission and explanation of the great phenomena of Spiritualism. These have been placed beyond the range of the sharpest sarcasm, the most elaborate antagonism of the clever writers and amateur philosophers; and the best plan now for such opponents is to frankly admit them, and then try, like Mr. Stuart-Glennie, to show that they have no spiritual significance. Perhaps they may be more successful than he has been in the attempt.

21

CHAPTER XI.

THE SENTIMENT OF IMMORTALITY NOT UNIVERSAL. — MISS MARTINEAU. — WM. HUMBOLDT.— BRADLAUGH.— STRAUSS. — FELIX ADLER. — EMERSON. — BAXTER. — R. G. INGERSOLL. — DEMONIAC MEN. — W. K. CLIFFORD. — THE EMOTIONS VERSUS THE INTELLECT.

IF we may credit human testimony, the desire for a continuation of life after the dissolution of the earthly body is very different in different minds. To some, and probably to the large majority, the idea of utter extinction is repulsive. To others, and among them are persons of high culture and a pure morality, the desire seems to be feeble or fluctuating.

Acquiescence in a false psychology, with the adoption of the Cartesian notion, extinguishing the old belief in a spiritual organism, has been influential, not only in bringing about the prevalent skepticism in regard to immortality, but in engendering the indifference which is sometimes felt. That this often springs from mere temperament is also true. But erroneous conceptions in regard to man's psychical nature must unquestionably lead to notions which have their effect in impairing the natural desire for life's continuance.

I was well acquainted with the late Harriet Martineau when she was residing in Washington in the winter of 1834. She was then, if we may judge from her writings, a Unitarian. Subsequently she lapsed into atheism; but this seems to have been rather sentimental or temperamental than rational. "How absurd and shocking it is," she writes in one of her letters, "to be talking every day about our own passing moods and paltry interests to a supposed author and guide of the universe." But if that author is at the same time believed to be the source of our own life and nature, where is the logical absurdity? Here, instead of a reason or an argument, she simply expresses the state of her own feelings, or her own unreasoned conclusions, as if those were authoritative in the case.

But the judgment of one without an ear for music in regard to the productions of Mozart or Beethoven is about as valuable as Miss Martineau's opinion on a question involving the exercise of the devotional, or even the poetical faculty. She could believe in clairvoyance — in the power of a mortal in the flesh to read the thoughts of another person at a distance; but the conception of a clairvoyant, omniscient God was to her mind "so irreverent" as to make her "*blush*, so misleading" as to make her "mourn."

I fear there was something morbid in that "blush" — something that confounded moral or spiritual nudity with physical. To the philosophic mind meditation on the proofs of a clairvoyant faculty in finite man renders more easy the conception of an infinitely clairvoyant intelligence. To Miss Martineau it was suggestive of no grand possibility, not even of a supersensual faculty in her own constitution, pointing to uses beyond the tomb. The obvious significance in the great facts adverse to her Sadducean theory she either blindly ignored or set aside as cancelled by her own individual feelings on the subject. She had passion and earnestness; she could hate better than she could love; but she had no grand enthusiasm. From music she was excluded by her deafness. In the poetical faculty, so nearly allied to the devotional, she was deficient. Not one of her attempts at versification is now remembered by the many. Of philosophy she knew little; plainly her gifts did not lie in that direction. Yet with all these defects and perversions, with an utter absence of that insight which penetrates beneath the surface of things to the latent beauty or significance, there were few subjects in regard to which she did not have full confidence that Harriet Martineau could speedily qualify herself to become a teacher. In this self-confidence lay the secret of much of her power and success. She was a ready, industrious writer, commanding a style clear, animated, and incisive; but as an original thinker she has left no memorable work.

William Humboldt, brother of Alexander, offers another instance of one in whom the desire for immortality seems to have lacked the force of a motive. "I must avow it frankly," he says, "that, right or wrong, I do not hold much to the hope of another life. I could not make for myself another existence out of my human ideas, *and yet it is impossible for me to make it out of any other.* I regard death with absolute calmness, but without desire or enthusiasm." If William Humboldt could have acquainted himself with our phenomena, he would have learned, perhaps, that his "human ideas" in regard to a future life were more in harmony with the actual facts than he had ever dared to hope.

Charles Bradlaugh, the English secular leader and member of Parliament, seems to have been made somewhat uneasy by the spread of Spiritualism. He tells us he has cast off all belief in a future life, and that he feels remarkably well after it. He is above the miserable weakness of ever wishing to see again the parents, children, brothers, sisters, or friends, who he believes have passed on to blank annihilation. Some years ago there was a public discussion on the subject of a future life between him and James Burns, the well-known publisher of Spiritual books and periodicals. It ended, like all such discussions, in an acknowledgment of defeat by neither party.

But one fact was made evident. The only way in which Bradlaugh could make a show of maintaining his Sudducean

doctrine was by ignoring our facts. Tell him of clairvoyance, direct writing, or spirit-hands, and all he could say in
reply was, *Not proven.* He claimed to pursue the deductive, *à priori* method (like Dr. Beard), and his facile logic
lay in discrediting well-known phenomena. Mr. Burns pur-
sued the inductive method, presenting an impregnable array
of facts. Mr. Bradlaugh opposed to these facts his own
"true inwardness," his deductive reasoning, and his purely
individual convictions. His excuse for this course was
that it was not his business to explain certain psychological
phenomena, or to bring forward any scientific facts in opposition. "My reason against your facts!" seemed to be
the sum and substance of his arguments.

Now it plainly *was* Mr. Bradlaugh's business to show,
either that psychological phenomena do not occur, or that
there are no grounds for the induction that they are solved
by the spiritual theory. This he failed to do, and this he
did not even attempt to do; and it was well remarked that
there was more logic in the lucid presentation of facts by
Mr. Burns than in all the artificial mechanism of abstruse
propositions by which Mr. Bradlaugh assumed to evade the
force of those facts.

He exhibits the bigotry of the extreme Churchman in the
following remark, from which it would seem that there is
an orthodoxy in secularism as well as in sectarian religion :

"Although at present it may be perfectly true that all men
who are secularists are not yet atheists, I put it to you as
perfectly true that in my opinion the logical consequence
of secularism must be, *that the man gets to atheism if he has
brains enough to comprehend.* . . . The whole basis of our
secular cause is in direct ignoring and denial of the possibility of any such state of existence " (*i. e.* of any future
state).

So it would seem that in order to satisfy the orthodoxy
of this secular Pope, a man must "ignore and deny the

very possibility of a future state of existence." " There is no God — and Charles Bradlaugh is his prophet!" Such would seem to be the temper of his fulminations against those "brainless" persons entertaining the theistic belief, and against the possibility of an hereafter for man.

The wonder is, if he is sincere, that he should give himself the slightest concern as to what other persons may think in regard to Spiritualism, Republicanism, or anything else. If thought springs from a mere accidental disposition of certain molecules of matter, how can there be any absolute standard of truth? If people will not think as he wants them to, why not blame the molecules, and there let the matter rest? If matter and chance are kings, what logic is there in his taking the trouble he does?

Belief in spirit, in God, or in gods, comes to the race, civilized or uncivilized, through evidences of certain super-sensual phenomena, as manifested by men in the flesh and by spirits out of the flesh. And this belief is what Mr. Bradlaugh is trying to extirpate. He does not experience such things. Why should he believe that any one else ever did? But he is no more an infallible representative of the human race than the horse who used to eat beefsteaks was a representative of the equine race. The *genus* horse is graminivorous notwithstanding. Bradlaugh's mistake is in making his own idiosyncrasies and his own limited faculties the measure of the universe. *He* knows nothing about spirits, therefore there can be no spirit-world, and seership is all a delusion! *He* has no longing for immortality, therefore nobody else ought to have!

There was not long ago an illiterate mental calculator in Scotland who was asked how many letters there would be in a year's file of a daily newspaper of eight pages, each page having seven columns, each column one hundred and ninety lines, and each line thirty-two letters. The true answer, 139,873,440, was given in *ten seconds*. Shall we deny the possibility of such a faculty because it may be undeveloped in our own mental structure?

In his last work, " The Old Faith and the New," David F. Strauss tells us that the prospect of " the eternal persistence of life" would fill him " with dismay." But in saying this he ignores facts and analogies which might perhaps make the prospect less intolerable. He ignores the possible existence of psychical powers in our own constitution, which may proportion our day to our strength, and adapt our future horizons to our future capacities and needs. Above all, he sets aside the possibility of the superintendence of an infinitely beneficent Power, who has not so made us that life, in our healthy moods and rightly used, would ever be other than a blessing.

If we disregard all those facts of discrete mental states and other phenomena, verified in the testimony I have presented, we may logically fall into that state of " dismay " by which Strauss was affected. Spiritualism would have showed him how like the cry of a child in the dark were his apprehensions. It would have forced him to realize that the nature of man is complex; that there is an outward and an inward consciousness, distinct though not inherently separate, and that the inward may smile at the " dismay " felt by the outward at a prospect to which the faculties of the superior organism may stretch forward with a joyful attraction.

Mr. Felix Adler, the well-known liberal preacher, objects to what he calls the " morbid craving for immortality; " and even R. W. Emerson frowns upon what he stigmatizes as this " lust " after a knowledge of our immortality. Mr. Adler would direct the attention of men to " the more urgent needs of the present, of the *here*." Surely if anything can do that it must be Spiritualism, since it regards the future as but a continuation of present individual life, colored and shaped by the character and the affections, developed or formed in the " *here*." The subject has now become a branch of the physiology of the species.

It is not the *too much* but the *too little* of a genuine aspiration (call it *craving* if you will) to immortality that makes human life so often to our eyes a failure. Not the craving for more life, but the lack of appreciation of life itself, its vast significance, its splendid opportunities, and the overwhelming proofs which we now have of its continuance into another stage of being, with our individuality unimpaired, our affections purified and enlarged, — this is the real defect to be deplored.

To maintain that a new era of moral earnestness could be brought about without the great factor of a trust in immortality, is an assumption wholly at variance with the facts of human nature, taken, not in their exceptional aspects, but in the general intuitions and experiences of the race.

A " rationalistic religion " with the element of immortality left out is a delusion. Mr. Adler would have us adorn life with all nobleness, all deep affection, and all strenuous effort, and at the same time to be so indifferent to life *per se*, that we shall cherish no intense wish for its continuance beyond the charnel-house; to love children, parents, friends, with profound affection, and yet to be quite indifferent to the question whether or no, after the agony of parting on this shore of time, we are likely to see them in another and a better world.

His assertion that " the common opinion about souls originated in an erroneous explanation of the phenomena of dreams," is a repetition of one of Strauss's arguments, and is an utter fallacy in the sense in which it is presented. The history of Spiritualism shows that the belief in immortality was inspired by actual objective phenomena, and by the medial powers of the soul itself, prompted often, perhaps, by the influence of independent spirits.

Utterly fallacious, too, is the notion that an assured knowledge of a future life, such as many Spiritualists now have, would be inconsistent with the activities of the present. All history shows that the most active men in their day and generation have been men who had what Goethe calls the " demoniac " nature ; men interiorly aware of their spiritual endowments, and often wiser than they knew in regard to a future life ; such men as Pythagoras, Socrates, Aristotle, Cicero, Plutarch, Mahomet, Shakspeare, Richard Baxter, Martin Luther, Henry More, John Wesley, Melancthon, Swedenborg, Robert Burns, Benjamin Franklin, George Washington, Thomas Paine, Napoleon Bonaparte, Louis Napoleon, Thiers, Guizot, Mazzini, Garibaldi, Bismarck, &c. Most of these men knew our phenomena and were avowed Spiritualists in the modern sense ; and all believed in the soul's immortality. Look at the amount of activity compressed into the earth-lives of these men. Mr. Adler must reverse his theory if he would have it in keeping with notorious facts.

The sentiment of immortality, as it relates to the pure affections, the love of kindred and friends, is a consideration which must not be left out of the account, though I have shown that the positive belief in immortality springs less from the emotional side of our nature than from the rational, when fortified by the actual phenomena which have made the belief so universal. " It is to that sense of immortality with which the affections inspire us," says Henry Thomas Buckle, " that I would appeal for the best proof of a future life." " It must be true because it is a necessity of the affections," said Hortense Bonaparte. The normal and natural feeling is well expressed by Richard Baxter (1615–1691), one of the most estimable of English theologians. He says :

" I must confess, as the experience of my own soul, that the expectation of loving my friends in heaven principally kindles my love to them on earth. If I thought I should never know them and consequently never love them after this life is ended, I should in reason number them with temporal things, and love them as such. But I now delight to converse with my friends, in a firm persuasion that I shall converse with them forever; and I take comfort in those that are dead or absent, as believing I shall shortly meet them in heaven, and love them with a heavenly love that shall there be perfected."

Few men probably have uttered more sarcasms in ridicule of the Bible and the grounds for a belief in immortality than Col. Robert G. Ingersoll, of Illinois, a man of great natural endowments and a ready eloquence. But at the funeral of his brother, E. C. Ingersoll, in Washington, D. C., June 2d, 1879, this accomplished scoffer, giving way to the emotional element in his nature, changed his tone somewhat while in the face of death, and said :

"Life is a narrow vale between the cold and barren peaks of two eternities; we strive in vain to look beyond the heights ; we cry aloud, and the only answer is the echo of our wailing cry ; from the voiceless lips of the unreplying dead there comes no word, *but in the night of death hope sees a star, and listening love can hear the rustle of a wing.* He who sleeps here, when dying, mistaking the approach of death for the return of health, whispered with his latest breath, ' I am better now.' Let us believe, in spite of doubts and dogmas, and tears and fears, that these dear words are true of all the countless dead."

"Stars and rustling wings ! " Truly it would seem that the emotional nature is more than a match for the intellectual, when some dread reality summons it to the rescue. It is when sorrow makes it a necessity of the heart that the certainty of our own immortality and that of our beloved flashes through the clouds of doubt and anguish to the heart in which love has really yet a place.

To the man at once strong in the affections, and knowing our spiritual facts, the " narrow vale between the cold and barren peaks of two eternities," is the vestibule to an ampler life; and death, instead of coming in his old skeleton form with a dart in his hand, comes as a gracious angel, beckoning us to a fairer shore, and to a reunion with the near and dear already there.

Professor W. K. Clifford, an English mathematician of rare promise, died in 1879, at the age of thirty-four. Up to the time of his taking his college degree he held " extreme High-Church notions." A rebound from one extreme to its opposite is apt to occur; and so it is not surprising that he became "an extreme and uncompromising rationalist," and made " many enemies by the relentless severity of his writing on topics that are conventionally handled with delicacy and caution." He drew his little diagram of the whole origin and scheme of the universe as dexterously as he would a geometrical figure on his blackboard. A little mind-stuff here and a little matter-stuff there, and the whole puzzle was solved. At least so thought Mr. Clifford at an age when most of our great men have just begun to realize faintly the depths of their own ignorance. One single proof of direct writing annihilates his whole Sadducean system.

We are told that among his " advanced" views was that of " the finality of conscious existence in this life; " that he " looked for no future, but saw and knew the inutility of wasting one's thoughts in vain expectations." His dogmatism, based on undemonstrated hypotheses, was singularly at variance with his mathematical training. Freed from his professional limitations, his imagination, unchecked by scientific certainties, seemed to revel in the wildest flights of mere speculation.

We are told by Mr. Pollock, his biographer, that " as never man loved life more, so never man feared death less; " to which it is added: " he fulfilled well and truly that great saying of Spinoza, often in his mind and on his lips: ' *Homo liber de nulla re minus quam de morte cogitat*' (the free man thinks of nothing less than of death)." But if the sentiment was " often in his mind and on his lips," then he must have thought of death a good deal; else why the frequent vaunt that he did not think of it? I see nothing especially admirable in an apathetic attitude towards death. It is often as much a proof of imbecility as of mental strength. The Chinese coolie has it in perfection.

One of Clifford's remarks was this: " We are going to establish ourselves in a godless world and cast our eyes up to a soulless sky." Of course the utterer of this absurdity was the bitter opponent of Spiritualism, which roused him as a red flag rouses the bull of the arena; and no wonder, since our preterhuman phenomena are the downfall and the disgrace of his crude speculations. These phenomena are more easily demonstrated now than many of the conclusions of orthodox science; more accessible than many admitted facts in pathology; as verifiable as those of analytic chemistry, or of physical astronomy.

Providence has thus given us something more than the testimony of the affections — unspeakably precious as that is — something more than the affirmations of the heart, on which to found our trust in immortality. When a new generation shall be trained up to accept it as a fact of science, the effect cannot fail to be conducive to the moral and religious advancement of civilized man.

To rise to the " height of that great argument," — the proofs of the soul's immortality, — we must realize that there is a soul, at once transcendent and immanent, in the macrocosm as well as in the microcosm; in the universe as well as in this fleeting apparition of flesh and bones forming man's physical organism. Without such a conviction there can be no earnest religious feeling, free from all superstition and disharmony. And without religious feeling a knowledge of our immortality lacks that element of vitality and aspiration which can make it a power for good, a reno-

vator, a purifier, and an uplifter. Unless there is a supreme
spiritual tribunal of absolute right, justice, and love in the
cosmos, immortality would be a doubtful boon; having
faith in such, and thus having faith in God, we see rifts of
light through all that is obscure; the significance and
grandeur of life begin to dawn upon our finite and fallible
minds, and the evils, perplexities, and sufferings of this
brief span of time are lost in the ineffable compensations of
eternity. Without the bias imparted by such a rational
and inspiring hope, a knowledge of the mere externals of
Spiritualism may carry with it no more of saving grace than
a knowledge of the tricks of a juggler or the feats of an
acrobat.

The greatest truths address themselves more to the feelings
and the will than to the intellect. A truth like immortality
must be felt before it can really become a truth to the individual. The frigid assent of the intellect alone cannot
make it an inspiration and a sanctifying force. The merely
phenomenal facts having been investigated and accepted as
true, a life-long task, nay, a never-ending task, lies before
us in studying the relations of the stupendous truth to
life, to science, to philosophy, morality, and religion. Surely if "God and immortality" was a creed sufficient for the
prophets, and for Christ, it is sufficient for the earnest
Spiritualist; for it includes all that there is of true and
essential in all the creeds and all the religions ever formu-
lated in the thoughts of the pure in heart. The fatherhood
of God, the confraternity of all intelligences partaking in
the divine life, the immortality of all souls, the supremacy
of the law of love, and of the law of right, — such are the
great realities which Christ came to teach; and such are
what Spiritualism reaffirms.

CHAPTER XII.

THEISM IN THE LIGHT OF SPIRITUALISM. — THE DIVINE PER-
SONALITY. — THE INSTINCT OF PRAYER. — THE GENERALI-
ZATION ENCIRCLING ALL OTHERS. — THE DOCTRINE OF
SPHERES. — PSYCHOMETRY. — ILLUSTRATIVE FACTS. — ORI-
GIN OF THE THEORY OF OBJECT-SOULS. — INCAUTIOUS IN-
VESTIGATORS. — CONCLUDING REFLECTIONS.

I HAVE said elsewhere that Spiritualism is not a form of
religion. So far as it is a realization of the great facts of
God and immortality, it is religion itself. It proves to us
the existence of ethereal beings, exercising a preterhuman
power over matter. Nay, it proves that our deceased
friends are still alive, and, inferentially, that there must be
a spirit-world, however impenetrable it may be to mortal
sense.

It would be a narrow conception not to suppose that
what is true of our planet may be possible for all others
throughout the universe; that they too may have their
human occupants, some perhaps with organizations and
powers superior to our own; that every planet may have
its spiritual sphere; that all created intelligences must,
either before or after the dissolution of the earth-body,
have, in some state, the privilege of intercommunication;
and that in the hierarchy of spirits there must be some
inconceivably superior to all that it is our present privilege to know of by direct experience.

All these are inferences fairly deducible from facts;
facts which have either been verified by actual scientific

demonstration, or which are analogous with such as have been so verified. But is there not still another, an all-comprehending inference, which follows inevitably from those named? The cosmos shows the supremacy of one Intelligence and one Will. Even the atheistic philosophy of Hartmann claims to prove this by a series of acute demonstrations drawn from the positive sciences. The theistic conception thus becomes corroborated by the practical proofs of the existence of finite and subordinate spirits; each one destined to realize at some period of his immortal life that he too is a child of the Infinite.

The Supreme Being, if he has Intelligence and Will, must be also conscious, since there can be no knowledge without a consciousness of it, active in some state or other. Using the word person in its large and ultra-etymological sense, He must be also personal, since consciousness involves personality. This does not depend, as Schelling, Hartmann, and even A. J. Davis, seem to think, on individualization through organism, nor on the relativity of a person, — on the distinction of a *me* from a *not me*. An eminent philosophical physicist, Hermann Lotze, remarks:

"Personality has its basis in pure selfhood — in self-consciousness — without reference to that which is not self. The personality of God, therefore, does not necessarily involve the distinction by God of himself from what is not himself, and so his limitation or finiteness; on the contrary, perfect personality is to be found only in God, while in all finite spirits there exists only a weak imitation of personality. The finiteness of the finite is not a productive condition of personality, but rather a bar to its perfect development."

The fact that there are finite spirits, conscious and clairvoyant, to whom we are in some way related, would justify the human instinct of prayer. Surrounded as we are by hosts of witnesses, not only of our acts but of our very thoughts, we may well believe that, as Christ dis-

tinctly teaches in what he says of little children, there may
be guardian spirits not inattentive to our wants, or impenetrable to our appeals. Should it be said that this belief
may lead to a kind of polytheism, the answer is, that, as we
can look only to good spirits for good, these must be such
as act, and would have us act, strictly in conformity with
divine law.

Many unconsidered cases of apparent spirit interposi-
tion — as where a man by a sudden premonition gives up
the idea of embarking in a certain steamer — may occur as
answers to interior prayers, of which the individual is not
normally conscious. A prayer for deliverance from physical danger may be answered without any violation of natural law. Spiritualism teaches us that prayer is no mere
shouting into a void, where there is no hearing and whence
comes no response. One claiming to be a freed spirit
says: "*We* pray for help whenever we want it, let the
object be what it may, except that it must not be an evil
object. Whatever is done must be done by the divine
sanction, and to Him your prayers should be addressed.
But he permits spirits to execute his decrees. You may
call on that spirit of God which dwells in the souls of
spirits to aid you. *We* do not pray to spirits, but to God."
All the great seers have been believers in the efficacy of
prayer.

Spiritualism being thus boundless in its diameter, and
embracing not only the visible universe but the unseen in
its indefinable circumference, — threatening to include and
absorb all minor forms of religion in its great generalization of God and immortality, — it is not surprising that
the organs of sects, not even omitting that little circle
labelled "Free Religionists," should be disturbed by the
prospect of a "scientific basis" for Spiritualism, and that
they should express their dissatisfaction, somewhat pre-
maturely, in no measured terms.

One thing taught me by my early experiences in mesmerism was the fact that there is a spheral emanation from all substances or objects, physical or spiritual. If I magnetized a handkerchief, or a tumbler of water, the somnambulic *sensitive* could always detect it. The test was repeated under so many varying conditions that the fact was conclusively proved. Are we not told, in Acts (xix. 12), that from Paul " were brought unto the sick handkerchiefs or aprons, and the diseases departed from them "?

From vegetables and trees we know there are physical emanations which we detect as odors. May there not be emanations from the psychical nature, as well as the physical — from that which thinks, as well as that which grows? How often my somnambule used to say of persons to whom she was introduced, " I like," or " I do not like, his sphere ! " In the activity of this faculty we may find an explanation of some of the phenomena of psychometry and trance-mediumship. It is not always necessary to hypothecate the agency of a freed spirit to account for these. The psychometrist touches a written paper or a fragment from an old building, and receives impressions which often turn out wonderfully accurate ; and the experiment has been repeated so often that no theory of chance will cover the facts.

May there not be spiritual *reliquiæ*, psychic auras, ethereal emanations, less transient than the physical, to which the medial subject is sensitive when brought within their sphere? He enters a room for the first time, and shudders at he knows not what. Gradually or swiftly an impression affects his consciousness, and he tells you that a murder or a suicide once occurred in that room. On inquiry you learn he is right. Whence came the impression? From some psychical aura left on the furniture or the walls, or from a communicating spirit?

The action of light will impress an image on the surface of

inorganic objects. A familiar experiment is to lay a key, or some other object, on a sheet of white paper and expose it for a few minutes to the action of sunlight, and then lay the paper away where it will not be disturbed. After several months, if the paper be carried into a dark place and laid on a piece of hot metal, the spectre of the key will appear.

Dr. J. W. Draper, Professor of Chemistry and Physiology in the University of New York, says: " I believe that a shadow never falls upon a wall without leaving there a permanent trace, — a trace which might be made visible by resorting to proper processes."

If a wafer be laid on a surface of polished metal, which is then breathed upon, and if, when the moisture of the breath has evaporated, the wafer be shaken off, we shall find that the whole polished surface is not as it was before, although our senses can detect no difference; for if we breathe again upon it the surface will be moist everywhere except on the spot previously sheltered by the wafer, which will now appear as a spectral image on the surface. Again and again we breathe, and the moisture evaporates, but still the spectral wafer reappears.

If such subtile effects may be produced by the agency of light, heat, or moisture, why may not thought be equally operative in leaving impressions recognizable by clairvoyant or spiritual senses? " The psychometrist," says Mrs. Maria M. King, " is impressed, in her or his sensitive organization, by ethers of the many grades that inhere in substance and forms, and attach themselves like symbolic characters to everything, and vaguely record unwritten histories of all times, all deeds, and all thoughts of men."

" Because," says Mr. G. H. Stebbins, " a person quotes from books he never saw, or tells of what he never knew in any external way, that is not final proof that he is under an external spirit-control. Psychometry and clairvoyance 'may sometimes solve it all; and sometimes we must accept the solution of direct spirit influence."

In his " Origin of Civilization " Sir John Lubbock says, " The so-called object-souls, souls of useful articles, — tools, implements, armor, houses, canoes, — have a place among the spirits of the inferior races ; " and he calls this " a pure-ly utilitarian conception of the soul." And yet the conception of the untutored savage may be an inference from actual phenomena, developed in his own psychometric experiences. That these may be mixed with delusions and false inferences is quite natural.

Why is it, we are asked, that our phenomena, even when admitted, make so little impression on many minds? It may be because they are so engrossed in thoughts foreign to the subject that they cannot afford to give it due consideration ; or it may be that they fail to recognize its vast significance, through the non-development of a faculty by which spiritual facts are recognized and appreciated.

A phenomenon that would excite even a dog's attention may be dismissed as meaningless by the unreceptive mind. One would think that a single positive experience in direct writing would give a man something to reflect on with interest for the rest of his life ; for it settles many questions in philosophy, theology, and positive science, which are still in dispute. It presents a fact utterly inexplicable by any theory consistent with the teachings of a Sadducean materialism.

After the putative spirits have demonstrated to us the essential fact that our deceased friends are still alive, — that spirits have a power over matter so great as to seem to us magical or miraculous, — are we not supplied with facts sufficient to challenge our best intellectual energy for their proper appreciation and study? Would we have the spirits go on and, saving us the trouble of further thought, enlighten us on subjects moral, religious, or scientific — subjects coming within the province of our own mental powers and duties?

How do we know that the very attempt to communicate with mortals does not place a spirit in a state of consciousness discrete from that which is habitual to him in the spirit-world — a state perhaps inferior to that, and one in which memory is clouded, or the power of thought is limited? The argument might be analogically pressed.

The mistake of incautious investigators is in not making enough of the clearly demonstrated and demonstrable phenomena which they already have. They would seek new wonders before they have begun to digest or appreciate the old. The natural consequence has been that they offer, as it were, a bounty for all sorts of fraud. The instances are notorious wherein persons with some little measure of medial power, but sadly impecunious financially, have given way to the temptation of getting up manifestations wholly or partly spurious. Hence the exposures which have created the impression that all medial phenomena are impostures or delusions. The fault is largely with immature Spiritualists themselves. They are too eager to witness and proclaim new and incredible phenomena. The demand naturally creates a supply and an over-supply. Some one medium, or medial pretender, tries to outdo his competitor in ministering to the blind, unhealthy appetite of over-hasty seekers, and hence come exaggerations and impositions. Such drawbacks are to be anticipated, but the course of Spiritualism must be none the less onward in the future, as it has been in the past, in spite of all rebuffs, misrepresentations, and assaults.

The injunction to "try the spirits" must be literally heeded, even when they come objectively to the observer. It is a *ruse* of a certain class of spirits to try to excite attention by assuming distinguished names. The credulity that accepts without question the report of spirits calling themselves Moses, Elijah, Plato, Aspasia,* John the Baptist, Judas Iscariot, Bacon, Swedenborg, &c., is quite as deplorable as the skepticism that rejects as baseless all these strange phenomenal manifestations.

That distinct human forms, suitably clad, are presented, and this where no theory of human fraud or hallucination is tenable, is a fact which science has got to accept and deal with. That in some instances these forms are fairly recognized and identified; that they can be seen, felt, and heard, " thus establishing their existence through the same three senses which take cognizance of the existence of our fellow-men ; " that they will prove by act or speech their relationship in the same way as persons do whom we do not scruple in our daily life to regard as bodily realities ; that they will manifest a preterhuman power over matter, and a wonderful clairvoyance in many surprising ways, far beyond the art of the conjurer, as the best conjurers themselves now admit, is also a fact that science will have to deal with ; since the facts are all the time multiplying, and the proofs becoming more cogent.

The circumstance that scientific persons have, as a general rule, kept aloof from the whole great subject, partly through a misgiving as to their ability to cope with it, and partly through their own *à priori* objections and rooted prejudices, has left it largely in the hands of those who, from defective training, or from a lack of the critical faculty, have supposed that all which may come from the unseen world must be authoritative and right. Messages that violate all the laws of logic and common sense have thus

---

* It is not denied that remarkable phenomena occur at times, which seem to favor the pretensions of these ancient spirits. Mr. A. L. Hatch, in a letter dated Astoria, L, I., Sept. 2, 1880, writes : " Your imagination cannot picture a form more perfect, more beautiful, than that of Aspasia standing before us. We asked if she could speak in Greek. She did so by giving us a Greek sentence, and what is more, quickly corrected me in the pronunciation of some of the words. I much doubt if there are living others who have been so corrected oy a spirit of twenty-four centuries past."

been accepted as *bona fide* communications from the world's great departed thinkers. Obvious *hoaxes* have been imposed as genuine representations or revelations, because they came apparently corroborated by proofs of preterhuman power. Stories of matches and marriages in the unseen world have been swallowed because the operating forces, whether of human or spirit origin, could impress the unwary victim by objective proofs of what seemed, and 'probably was, preterhuman action or knowledge.

These things only prove how important it is that science should change its attitude of haughty unconcern or abject fear towards our phenomena; that a new system of exhaustive investigation should be adopted; one uniting the method that allows the spirits to fix their own conditions with the method that accepts nothing as proved until it is presented under conditions sufficient for the most thorough and rigorous scientific verification. There is some truth in the following observation by Mr. William Oxley, of Manchester, England, a faithful investigator, who is one of those who would leave the operating spirits untrammelled by conditions; but it is only one side of the truth which he presents, and it must be supplemented by the other:

"A genuine lover of truth for its own sake, who enters this domain of occult science accepting the conditions which are allowed, though beset in the commencement with doubts and difficulties, will, by perseverance, soon receive ample proofs and tests of the genuineness of psychometrical manifestations and spiritual agency; while, on the other hand, the doubter who investigates for the purpose of discovering imposture and fraud, will discover what he or she thinks is sufficient to justify the pre-existing doubts, and sooner or later retires in disgust."

Let me illustrate the truth of this by an incident. A certain investigator objected strenuously to the condition of darkness under which the phenomenon of the floating guitar

was given. But he followed up the investigation nevertheless; and one evening, when a friendly burst of moonlight
lighted up the whole room through an accidental misplacing
of the curtain, he saw, what he had long wished to see, the
guitar high up by the ceiling, aloof from any visible support, and played on by some unknown force exercising intelligence.

It is the part of wisdom, then, to investigate without
prejudice under the conditions offered by the spirits, but to
admit nothing as proved until, by some unexpected en-
largement of the conditions, the proof wanting is clearly
obtained.

That psychometric impressions unverified are to be
trusted, would be a dangerous admission. Both psychometry and clairvoyance may be in fault, just as the man who
has jumped a ditch once may miss it at the second trial.
There is no such thing as finite infallibility. I must, therefore, wholly dissent from the notion of Dr. J. R. Buchanan,
that "We can attain a definite and accurate knowledge
to-day not only of Jesus, but of the Apostles and the
entire group of characters mentioned in the Bible" through
the psychometric or some related faculty. All biographical
history teaches us the fallacy of such pretensions; warns
us against their obvious incertitude and mischievous tendency. The seer of to-morrow may contradict the seer of
to-day. So it was in the past; so it will continue to be.
How many volumes have we had professing to give supplementary lives of Jesus and the apostles, through medial
impression or from the communications of spirits! And
each new volume contradicts its predecessors. I have
before me a work in French, dated as far back as 1866, and
sent me by the estimable author. It is in three large volumes, and is entitled "*Spiritisme Chrétien ou Révélation de
la Révélation;*" and further: "The Four Gospels, followed by the Commandments, explained in spirit and in

truth by the Evangelists, assisted by the Apostles and by Moses; received and arranged by J. B. Roustaing, advocate at the Imperial Court of Bordeaux." It is ably and clearly written, in the interest of the Kardec doctrine of reincarnation.

Reason cannot assent to such unverified pretensions. The moment we go one step beyond facts and their legitimate inferences, whether they come to us affirmed by spirit, seer, or medium, we are all adrift without a compass. There is enough of the wonderful in the demonstrable phenomena, without ingrafting on Spiritualism, proper and universal, the idiosyncrasies of individuals, whether in the unseen world or in this.

Spiritualism is simply the science of continuous life; of life in which the incident called *death* is a mere shedding of the outer envelope. The early Christians showed by their constant adoption of the butterfly as the emblem of their faith in immortality, that the old illustration of the chrysalis expressed their notion as well as it does that of modern Spiritualists: this, namely, that the psychical organism is involved in the physical. This science is based on facts that fully justify the spiritual hypothesis, and is warranted by a course of reasoning both inductive and deductive. Thus Spiritualism has a vital advantage over all those historical or traditional beliefs whose tendency it is to become weakened by time. Why is it that modern Christians who acquiesce in the facts related in the Bible, are unable to accept precisely similar facts when vouched for by some of the most eminent physicists of the present day? It is because all faith in the spiritual and the preterhuman has died out. On many minds the only hold which Christianity now has is in the excellence of its ethical teachings.

Mr. G. F. Green, one of the most careful writers on the subject, says he does not look to Spiritualism for any influence upon morality or religion from the revelation of any new and startling truths. He looks rather to the increased vitality of the belief in a future life; to the consequent widening and enlarging of our ideal of happiness, which he regards as the actual basis of all morality. The knowledge of our immortality must add an incentive for us to seek out for ourselves the true path. We must not look to advanced spirits for any infallible code. Religion is not a belief in certain dogmas. In the divine laws of our being we must find the moral law and the religious impulse. Thus science, and not dogma, must rule; since morality is the art of conforming our lives to the highest law expressed in our own nature, human and spiritual, mortal and immortal; while religion is the reverent sense of a power superior to our own, and able to affect our destiny.

The existence of beings in ethereal bodies, invisible to our imperfect senses, is an hypothesis which the latest discoveries in science make not only possible, but probable. It has been proved that all the great forces of nature are accompanied with vibrations of a form of matter so subtile that our purest atmosphere is dense matter compared with it. Only by their effects do these impalpable grades of matter become known to us; but these effects show that power is increased the less gross the matter becomes. Let the proof be given that intelligent beings, exerting a preterhuman power over matter, manifest their existence by their acts (as they have done), and there is no good reason why the man of real science should refuse to give the evidence its proper weight.

Even in dark circles the electric rapidity with which certain phenomena are produced is a sufficient proof of their preterhuman character. I have been present repeatedly at séances where a tambourine was moved from the table to the floor, and from the floor to the table, with such violence and inconceivable celerity, that no one could doubt that the force exerted was not that of a mortal. The conditions were perfect, as security against fraud; the movement, even in the light, would have been impossible; but occurring in utter darkness, and never causing the instrument to touch one of the dozen hands placed outstretched on the table, it showed that an abnormal power was at work, to which darkness was no obstacle, and which could effect the transfer with a velocity and precision wholly inconceivable unless done by faculties transcending the human.

The Pantheistic idea of the absorption of finite individualities in the life of the Infinite — even as brooks and rivers get their drops from the ocean, and return them to it — finds no analogy in the facts of Spiritualism, which teaches distinctly the imperishability of the individual and the continuation of the identical Ego. R. W. Emerson, in his pathetic poem on the decease of his little boy, expresses the Pantheistic conception in the following couplet:

> "The master, Death, with sovereign rite,
> Pours finite into infinite."

The theory is that the Infinite Mind keeps individualizing his exuberant life in organisms, but does his work so blindly that "the master, Death," keeps undoing what God has done, and reducing the life-process to an objectless pouring out and pouring back of the same essence. To which fantasy, Spiritualism replies: God, and not Death, is the master; and God has done his work with such unerring wisdom that a superior organism for man (and perhaps for the lower animals) is involved in the physical, and is always ready to take its place. God is not the absorber of human individualities, but the gracious, all-powerful One who eternally expands his own life in imparting it to subordinate beings; eternally enriches his own love by giving, and in seeing it reflected, as the sun is in the dewdrop, in the progressive happiness, wisdom, and love of his dependent creatures, and in the development of their as yet rudimental free will.

And yet Pantheism is true, though but a part of the truth. If man is the image of his Maker, if the finite is patterned after the Infinite, then the deductions from our facts justify the conception that the nature-element of Deity may in its consciousness be discrete from the omniscient consciousness of God in the Highest. Immanent in the universe, he may there differ in degree from what he is in that transcendent state in which he is above and beyond nature; — is the One and only Possibility by which all things have become possible and existent. Thus Pantheism is viewed as the inner circle of a grander Theism, and two ever-conflicting beliefs are found as harmonious as the convex and concave of the same crescent.

We may exist in the midst of a world of spirits just as we do in the midst of that world which was unknown to man till it was revealed by the microscope. Spiritualism assures us that this is not only a possibility but a reality. The universe penetrable to our senses may be but a fraction of that Infinite Whole patent to Omnipotence. Sir W. R. Grove, in his "Correlation of Physical Forces," remarks: "In very many of the forms which matter assumes, it is porous, and pervaded by more volatile essences, which may differ as much in kind as matter does." Sir Humphrey Davy hypothecates an "ethereal matter which can never be evident to the senses, and may bear the same relations to heat, light, and electricity that these refined forms or modes of existence of matter may bear to the gases."

I have but a word to say to that small class of would-be philosophers who, admitting our phenomena, would get rid of them by a "What of it? What do they prove?"

There are certain fundamental convictions of the human mind which are manifestly undemonstrable; and it is an easy matter for the extreme skeptic to question their truth. But such questioning, because of the lack of formal demonstration, is not always defensible on philosophical grounds. If the ultimate axioms, where reason compels us to make a stand, are rejected, it is useless to attempt to reason further.*

At every step in life we are obliged to recognize a power external to phenomena. Without this recognition we could not regard the world as external, for, strictly speaking, its phenomena are effects on us, and subjective. The recognition of what is outside us in space, and distant in time, depends, then, on the acceptance by reason of what transcends phenomena.

Reason may admit that her conceptions of such realities may be, must be, imperfect; but she will judge also that her conceptions, recognized as imperfect, are nearer the truth than the decision to reject all conceptions of the kind would be, since that would land us in extreme idealism.

Science has to transcend phenomena at every step; the whole fabric of human knowledge would collapse unless the testimony of consciousness was accepted to facts not found among phenomena, but inferred from them.

We all believe that the human beings around us are animated with conscious intelligence. Yet physical evidence of this there is none. Like our conviction of the past and of our own continued existence, it is an inference drawn from phenomena respecting what transcends phenomena; yet it commands the entire assent of reason, and hence takes rank among our fundamental beliefs.

All these considerations are ignored in the skeptical assumption that the reappearance of the form of a deceased friend, conversing intelligibly, manifesting recognizable traits both physical and mental, giving proofs of identity

---

* In carrying out this argument I am largely indebted to the late Thomas Martin Herbert's masterly work, " The Realistic Assumptions of Modern Science Examined." London: Macmillan & Co. 1879.

in a knowledge of the past, in affection for kindred, and in
other indescribable peculiarities appreciable only by the
spectator who has known and loved him, — that all this is
no evidence of the reappearance of that deceased person.

For such a phenomenon there is a cause, and reason
must obviously transcend phenomena in order to arrive at
that cause. The question whether the cause may not be
mundane rather than super-mundane is purely sophistical,
and has nothing to do with the vital fact of the trans-mortal
survival. The skeptic's position, if tenable, would be
equally fatal to all scientific progress by questioning the
ultimate grounds, the primary, undemonstrable convictions,
on which all science is based.

One of our evangelical assailants tells us that " it is the
mistake of the Spiritualist that he makes a religion of what
should be a science." Are we then to understand that *to
know* is less a warranty for religious feeling and hope than
to *believe*, or rather to try to believe?

It is for the very reason that Spiritualism has a Scientific
Basis in known and demonstrable facts, that it offers the
surest ground for religion. It shows us that the only
hurtful heresy is the wrong thinking that leads to wrong-
doing. It proves to us that as we sow we shall reap.

Some persons, in whom the religious or devotional instinct may be yet feeble or undeveloped, may long remain
untouched by the vast religious significance of a knowledge
of immortality; but in times of bereavement and great
affliction it may rush back to the heart with a divine,
awakening meaning and force; and sorrow may reveal to
us that the certainty of a reunion with our beloved has in
it, for the heart that is not petrified, the highest and purest
religious element, since it must give rise to the profoundest
gratitude to the Infinite Giver of life and love.

Concessions.

I GRANT that of the facts here affirmed to be real, many are very strange, uncouth, and improbable; and that we cannot understand them or reconcile them with the commonly received notions of spirits and the future state.

I allow that there are many over-credulous persons; and that frauds, impostures, and delusions have been mixed up and confounded with real facts in Spiritualism.

I grant that melancholy and imagination have very great force, and beget strange persuasions; and that many stories of apparitions have been but melancholy fancies.

I know and yield that there are many strange, natural diseases that have odd symptoms, and produce astonishing effects beyond the usual course of nature; and that these are sometimes quoted as explaining preternatural facts.

Postulata.

HAVING made these concessions, the postulata which I demand of my adversaries as my just right are:

That whether our phenomena occur or not is a question of fact, and not of *à priori* reasoning.

That matters of fact can only be proved by immediate sense, or by the testimony of others. To endeavor to demonstrate fact by abstract reasoning or speculation is as if a man should attempt to prove by algebra or metaphysics that Julius Cæsar founded the empire of Rome.

A certain amount and character of human testimony cannot be reasonably rejected as incredible, or as supporting facts contrary to nature, since all facts within the realm of nature must be natural.

That which is sufficiently and undeniably proved ought not to be denied because we know not how it can be; that is, because there are difficulties in the conceiving of it; otherwise sense and knowledge are gone as well as faith. For the *modus* of most things is unknown, and the most obvious in nature have inextricable difficulties in the conceiving of them.

Altered from REV. JOSEPH GLANVIL (1633–1680).

APPENDIX.

"A Scientific Basis of Belief."

The Rev. John Page Hopps, an English liberal preacher, is the author of a little pamphlet entitled " A Scientific Basis of Belief in a Future Life; or the Witness borne by Modern Science to the Reality and Pre-eminence of the Unseen Universe." As he pursues a somewhat different method from my own, but arrives at similar results, an outline or abridgment of his excellent *brochure* may be here appropriate. It should be premised that he has satisfied himself of the fact of direct writing and other spiritual phenomena, though he does not refer to them here.

If faith in God or Immortality depends on the conviction of the infallibility of the Bible, faith is already doomed. The marvellous spread of scientific knowledge has led to a totally new demand for evidence and demonstration as the antecedent to all belief.

The inquiry into a future life or an unseen universe is a strictly scientific one. But all the science we can attain to is relative to our limited capacities. The first thing to do is to take the whole subject out of the realm of mystery, unreality, fantasy, and awe, and make it the object of cool thought and, if possible, of scientific experiment. We have too long been accustomed to speak of the dead in a vague, dreamy, unreal way. A future life can only mean *the actual going on of the human being in spite of the incident called " death."*

The science of the present day, in hypothecating atoms as the ultimate constituents of matter, confesses that it does not know what an atom is. Even in relation to the world of *sense*, it is confessedly true that the ideal world, or world of consciousness, is immeasurably more vital than what is usually called the world of matter. Huxley himself affirms that the inner world of consciousness is the only one we know at first hand, — that the external world is only an inference from our sensations.

The illustration requires a little close thought. We hear the sound of a bell, but, in the exciting cause, there is nothing like the sound of a bell. Certain waves of air — in themselves only forms of motion — produce in us as sound, *something wholly different from what they themselves are.* We are not conscious of the waves of air, but only of the effect produced on us. This will show what science means when it says that we are more directly certain of states of consciousness than of states of matter. 351

In ordinary sleep, the fields through which you wander, the money you handle, the fruit you eat, the trees you see swayed by the wind, the people you meet; the ocean whose bright waves break on the shore, are all perfectly real to you in dreams; and you think they are real for the time: so true is it that consciousness, thought, and sensation are more immediately real to us than matter.

"Experience," says John Stuart Mill, "furnishes us with no example of any series of states of consciousness" without "a material brain; but it is as easy to imagine such a series of states without as with this accompaniment, and we know of no reason in the nature of things against the possibility of its being thus disjoined." He even says, "We may suppose that the same thoughts, emotions, volitions, and even sensations which we have here, may persist or recommence somewhere else under other conditions." This is all we ask, and this is perfectly scientific. Sensation, thought, and consciousness, are all in ourselves, and are absolutely unlike matter in all their peculiarities. In our present state they may be excited by certain conditions of matter, but this is no argument against the possibility of their existing independently of matter.

There is talk of the conveyance of mental consciousness by "brain-waves." What does it matter how it is conveyed? *The consciousness itself is not a wave.* Truly it begins to look as though an emancipation and not a destruction might come with the separation of our mental powers from fleshly control.

Our five senses do not measure the boundless reaches of being far, far beyond our ken. The greatest of all illusions is the common illusion that we see, hear, and touch all that might be visible, audible, and tangible. What we call the solid globe itself is an assemblage of atoms inconceivably small — so small that no eye can see, no instrument reveal them. What we call the vacant air is filled with light, and sound, and subtlest flashing forces, flooding every tiniest space with music and beauty, and ever flowing energy. It would only require a readjustment of our senses to make these a new heaven and a new earth to us.

Huxley says that "Astronomy demonstrates that what we call the peaceful heavens above us is but space, filled by an infinitely subtile matter whose particles are seething and surging, like the waves of an angry sea." And yet that "subtile matter" is so rare and delicate that the rarest known gas is as mud in comparison with it. The difference between a gas and a so-called solid substance is only the difference of atoms more or less close together, linked by some central unseen force.

Thus it is now a well-known fact of science that multitudes of so-called sounds, and objects of sight, and tangible objects, utterly elude us, simply because our senses are not fine enough to be receptive or explanatory as to them.

There is nothing corresponding to sound in what produces it. Tyndall tells us that though a whole park of artillery were discharged, the only result would be a disturbance of the atmosphere, and not sound at all unless an ear and a mind were present to catch the waves of motion and translate them into sound.

The microphone proves the presence about us of "innumerable

waves of sound, so slight as to be inaudible to us.   It reveals to the
ear a new world, even as the microscope has opened a new world to
the eye.   Thus our external senses are constructed to perceive only
an infinitesimal portion of the sights and sounds about us.   So it is
a mere *à priori* judgment, mere folly and presumption, to pronounce
of anything that it cannot be."

What Tyndall calls the " luminiferous ether " may be only what we
know as atmosphere in a more subtile state, but it is so attenuated
and elastic that it can convey the vibrations answering to light at a
rate of about 200,000 miles a second.   Compared with that, we, in
our ordinary atmosphere, may be said to be living in thick mud.
What a suggestion have we here as to an unseen universe, ay, and
as to exquisitely subtile beings living in it their refined and happy
lives!   Thus it is the admission of the most advanced science that
objects and even organized beings may exist in an unseen universe.

The other senses lead, in like manner, into the Unseen.   The
gases are as truly matter as the solid metals ; and hydrogen is as much
a substance as iron : and yet the one is solid to our touch, and the
other is as nothing to that sense : and the gas can readily pass
through the metal (just as a spirit may pass through a solid wall).
It is only habit and the limitation of our sense of touch that lead us
to think of matter in a certain subtile condition as less real than
denser substances.   A hand that could pass through granite is scientifically conceivable.   Thus there is nothing in a spirit-hand that violates a purely scientific conception.

So again with the sense of odor.   Odor does not exist, as such, till
the vibrating particles that produce it reach and affect the nerves
and brain.   " Sensations," says Huxley, " are, in the strictest sense,
immaterial entities."   Thus even now and here we belong to the
Unseen.

" We must resort to the unseen," say Stewart and Tait, " not only
for the origin of the *molecules* of the visible universe, but also for an
explanation of the *forces* which animate these mo.ecules.   So that
we are compelled to conclude that every motion of the visible universe is caused by the unseen, and that its energy is ultimately carried again into the unseen."   Is not this wonderfully suggestive?
What if the intelligence, the personality, that are here grown and
developed, pass into the unseen with their glorious gains?

Everywhere is the visible produced by the invisible.   All the glory
of leaf and flower, whence comes it? Every tint of color and essence
of odor existed first in the Unseen.   And what is true for us and our
tiny globe we may reasonably conclude is true in the vast universe
beyond.

Thus we arrive by the steps of admitted science at the stupendous
conclusion that the Unseen is at once the source, receptacle, and
laboratory of energy and vitality immeasurably surpassing anything
within the present experience of man.

But thought itself is a greater mystery than the existence of all
these finer forms.   The materialist has here a harder problem to
solve than any other connected with an unseen universe.   " We are
absolutely driven," say Stewart and Tait, " by scientific principles
to acknowledge the existence of an unseen universe, and to conclude

23

that it is full of life and intelligence — that it is in fact a spiritual universe and not a dead one."

With every advance in organization there is a corresponding advance in mind. The inference, the longer we ponder it, becomes the more inevitable, that Life and Thought, no less than Matter, though they may know vast changes and pass into higher or more subtile forms of being, are destined to find their home in the vast Unseen. Thus taking the universe as it is, and adopting the principle of continuity, the process leads us at once to the conception of an invisible universe, and to see that immortality is possible without a break of continuity.

We have then strictly scientific grounds (apart from the sufficient proofs given in Spiritualism) that even now the psychical part of man is developing powers that will enable it to survive the dissolution of the merely physical structure.

The great laws of evolution, continuity, and the conservation of force combine to justify the inference that if matter persists after its dissolution in one form, reappearing in another, so too will mind, which, though ending its connection with matter as we know it, may reappear under conditions immeasurably more favorable to its development and delight.

We have to follow matter into the ethereal regions of its more subtile modes of existence; and shall we not follow mind also into those unseen regions, especially when we see that matter everywhere seems to be manipulated and directed by mind?

Imagine the life-principle united to a spiritual body as subtile and exquisite as itself, and having its sphere of activity in a world perfectly adapted to its own sensitive, ethereal form of existence; — surely you would there have everything that could give the most thrilling realization of life, with all its possibilities of progress and of joy.

Ulrici describes the soul of man from a scientific point of view as a refined, continuous, subtile substance, permeating the whole material structure of the body, and attaining to the grade of spiritual being because it has attained to the grade of *conscious* and *intelligent* existence. It is then this spirit-body which goes out from the physical body at death; for death is an orderly stage in a natural process, and only dissolves that which is outermost, in order that the real man may take the next great step in the ceaseless march of progressive being.

The view here taken of the Future Life makes us largely the determiners of what that life shall be to us. It leaves us alone with personal character, and with that great law of all life, " Whatsoever a man soweth, that shall he also reap."

Over-hasty Charges of Fraud. — (See page 18.)

When Miss Wood, the well-known materializing medium of Newcastle, England, visited Macclesfield in 1877, she was denounced by one of the sitters as guilty of a fraud. The *Advertiser* of that place defended her position at that time, and it now states, in its issue of August 28 (1880), that the gentleman who made the attack called upon the editor a short time since and acknowledged that he was in error, saying he would make a confession to that effect to Miss Wood whenever he might have the pleasure of meeting her. Many other charges of fraud, brought without proper discrimination, have had a similar issue.

Direct Writing. — (See page 35.)

Almost daily, while revising this work for the press, new testimony has come to me, justifying my adoption of the two great facts of direct writing and clairvoyance as typical proofs of the fundamental truth of Spiritualism, and presenting a truly scientific basis.

Mr. G. B. Stebbins, of Detroit, Mich., author of "After Dogmatic Theology — What?" (1880,) and other much esteemed works, — a gentleman most favorably known to me personally, — was present at a new and interesting manifestation of pneumatography, or spirit-writing, at the camp-meeting at Cassadaga Lake, N. Y., August 21, 1880. The medium was Mr. R. W. Saur, of Titusville, Pa., a German some thirty years of age, and, according to Mr. Stebbins, "an intelligent, sincere, and devoted man." Mr. Stebbins's testimony is published in the *Religio-Philosophical Journal* of Sept. 4, 1880. He and Mr. O. P. Kellogg saw two clean slates tied together. The medium, apparently "under a strong influence," sat in a chair before an audience of two hundred persons. He held the slates on the outspread fingers of his extended hand, while Messrs. Stebbins, Kellogg, and several other witnesses stood by, "hearing distinctly the scratching of the bit of pencil inside, as it rapidly traced the letters, — the dotting and strokes being easily heard."

The slates were turned over by the medium's hand as one side seemed full, and then the pencil moved rapidly on, and he soon handed the slates to Mr. Kellogg, but took them back, saying (probably under influence of the communicating spirit), " I will write the name." Mr. Stebbins says : " We heard the pencil again a moment, and then opened the slates to find the following message clearly written. I copy it exactly, punctuation and all :

"FRIENDS OF PROGRESS: I am glad to be here, and much pleased to write this. I thought it was a good opportunity for this large assemblage to prove what has often been done, the immortality of the soul. Now I well know that some will dispute this *fact*, but what if they do? I know the world is still quite full of these, on this point, respectable ignoramuses. I will close by stating one fact. Friends, depend on my veracity. I tell you most emphatical, the Spirit-world is peopled from our world, and they cannot depend upon another man's light for their salvation. They must not only believe and know for themselves, but they must do *the work* for themselves. Do right, be true and good, that is what counts.   Truly yours,   H. H. ROUSE."

The rest of Mr. Stebbins's testimony is as follows :

"I at once read this to the audience, and Mr. Kellogg said to me, 'A Mr. Rouse, from Titusville, whom I knew well, the chief of police in that city and the brother of this H. H. Rouse, who left the

earth some few years ago, is here. I will find him.' He found him
near the door where he had been standing, showed him the slate-writing, and he at once said, with tears in his eyes, ' That is from my
brother,' and took from his pocket a letter, the last he had from that
brother, not long before his death, compared the writing, and found
that on the slates a good *fac-simile*, the signature being especially
perfect. He loaned us the letter, and on careful examination I call
the slate-writing an excellent *fac-simile*."

To this, Dr. A. B. Spinney adds, under date of August 22, 1880,
"I heartily indorse the above statement, as I have seen the slate-
writing and the letter, and they " (in their chirography) "are exactly
alike."

Mr. E. A. Chapman, of Lowell, Mich., writes (July 26, 1880):
"Henry Slade now gets the direct writing while the two slates hang
suspended from a gas-jet. He allows *any one to bring his or her
slates*, or to select from a pile of his own, *tie and suspend them
from the gas-jet, take them down, untie and read them — he never
touching the slate at all ;* or he will permit the slates to be held in the
hands of the sitters, the writing coming or being produced under
those conditions — *he not touching the slates* — the scratching of the
pencil inside invariably being heard, and corresponding to the
message."

Since there is nothing " so brutally conclusive as a fact," how long
do Messieurs the " scientists " expect to make a stand against facts
like these?

Guldenstubbé and Direct Writing. — (See page 46.)

In the Paris *Revue Spirite* for July, 1880, is an interesting account
from the pen of M. Leymarie of a visit to Versailles, made by Baron
Guldenstubbé, by order of the spirits. He was required to go with
certain lad.es named, whom he was to invite, and evidently for a
special purpose. While in the gallery at Versailles the Bishop of
Orleans, M. Dupanloup, passed on his way to celebrate Mass in the
chapel. Knowing the ladies referred to above he stopped and addressed them, and also the Baron, to whom he expressed his regrets
that he adhered to a strange faith and one hostile to the Church ; that
he was a follower in fact of Luther, who would suffer in purgatory
for the division he had caused in said church.

The Baron replied that he did not think that Luther was in purgatory or in hell, and that as a proof of it, if the Bishop would place
a blank piece of paper on Luther's portrait, there would come some
evidence of his (the Baron's) belief. The Bishop tore a piece of
paper from his register and placed it as suggested. After a few moments he took it down and found written upon it :

> " In vita pestis eram Papæ,
> In morte mors ero. — LUTHER."

(" Living I was a pest to the Pope ; dead, I will be his death.") They
were all greatly astonished. The Bishop extended his hand to the

Baron and his sisters (both mediums), asking permission to visit them in Paris. The permission was obtained, and he frequently availed himself of it subsequently.

Robert Dale Owen testified that he accompanied the Baron and his sister Julia to various chapels in Paris; that he (Owen) laid down sheets of his own paper, without pencil or writing-materials; that, retiring a few paces, but never losing sight of the paper, he found an intelligent message written upon it in every case.

Professor W. Stainton-Moses tells us that for five years up to the year 1878, he had been familiar with the phenomenon of direct writing. This had occurred both in the presence of recognized *psychics* known to the public, and of ladies and gentlemen in private, who possess the power and readily procure the result. "In the course of these observations," he says, "I have seen psychographs obtained in closed and locked boxes as in the case of Baron Guldenstubbé; on paper previously marked and placed in a special position, from which it was not moved; on paper marked and put under the table, so as to get the assistance of darkness; on paper on which my elbow rested, and on paper covered by my hand; on paper enclosed in a sealed envelope; and on slates securely tied together." See "Psychography, by M. A. Oxon." Boston: Colby & Rich.

Testimony of Dr. T. L. Nichols. — (See page 83.)

Among the most experienced students of Spiritualism is Dr. T. L. Nichols, now of 32 Fopstone Road, Earl's Court, London, S. W., the author of several physiological works of great value. More than two years ago I received from him the following letter (now for the first time published), dated London, June 26, 1878, and written in reply to some inquiries of mine:

"My mother was a Boston woman, my father came from Cohasset, and they went, during the war of 1812-14, to Orford, N. H., where I was born in 1815. I attended my first course of medical lectures at Dartmouth College, 1834, but drifted into journalism, and only completed my course and took my diploma at the New York University in 1850. Since then I have been rather a medical writer and sanitary reformer than a medical practitioner. I knew you by sight when you had your office in Fulton Street, New York. Coming to England in 1861, I was for ten years a correspondent of the *New York Times*, and also, to some extent, a contributor to English periodical literature. You will find my name in the list of contributors to Chambers's Encyclopædia. My most important works in England, if I may use such a term in regard to any of them, are my 'Forty Years of American Life,' and 'Human Physiology the Basis of Sanitary and Social Science.'

"I saw something of Spiritualism in America, and had in New York, and later in Ohio, the most positive and convincing evidence of the existence of spirits and the genuineness of what are called 'spiritual manifestations.'

"During the past year Mr. W. Eglinton, a young Englishman

about twenty years old, and a very powerful physical medium, has been a member of my family. He first came to Malvern as a patient, and has been with us. in Malvern and London, ever since. I have had, I think, about fifty séances with him, attended in most cases only by members of my own family, and sometimes intimate friends. I have applied many tests, and satisfied myself, beyond all doubt, of the individuality of the spirits whom we have seen and felt, and talked with for many hours.

" I have in my possession *direct writings and drawings done under absolute test conditions* by departed spirits with whose handwriting I am familiar as with my own. I have an endless cord — that is, one I carefully tied and sealed — which, while my hand rested on the seal, had five knots tied in it. I have had the observation of matter passing through matter, in a chair being 'threaded' upon the arm, while the hand firmly clasped another's hand, seven times — and tested the fact by tying the two wrists together with fine thread, and by myself holding the other hand.

" 'The last materializations I have seen were a few days ago at Malvern, in my own garden in the summer twilight, when every object was distinctly visible. There was no cabinet. The medium, Mr. Eglinton, lay on a garden bench in plain sight. We saw the bodies of our visitors form themselves from a cloud of white vapor, and then walk about, robed all in purest white, upon the lawn where no deception was possible. One of them walked quite around us, as we sat in our chairs on the grass, talking as familiarly as any friend. Arthur Hildreth, son of the late Richard Hildreth, the historian, and his wife, sat beside me, while Mrs. Nichols sat on a stone balcony some twenty yards distant. This was all our party.

" The 'sheeted ghost,' whose fine white drapery we had seen made from a white vapor before our eyes, came round behind me, took my hat from my head, put it on his own, and walked off with it to where the medium was lying; then he came and put it on my head again; then walked across the lawn and up a gravel walk to the foot of the balcony and talked with Mrs. Nichols. After a brief conversation he returned to the medium and gradually faded from sight.

" I have known this 'ghost' for more than a year, and can have no possible doubt that he is what he strongly asserts himself to be, as distinct an individuality as I am myself.

" I have to say, then, that, with some pretensions to science, with the training in accurate observation of a practised journalist, and an experience of spiritualistic phenomena running through some twenty-five years, I cannot see that any facts are established by stronger proof than the existence of individual human spirits, who have been separated from their earthly bodies, but who have, under certain conditions, the power of giving us evidence of their existence by signs, writings, speech, and the assumption of visible and tangible bodily forms.

" You are quite welcome to make any use of my testimony in this matter. I cannot make it too strong. The intelligence of the spirits with whom I have conversed *is not dependent upon, or limited by, that of the medium, or of any one in the circle.* They do things impossible to be done — they know things impossible to be known — by and to those to whom they come.

"The theories of those who wish to banish spirits from Spiritualism may be ever so ingenious, but they do not meet the facts. I do not doubt your existence though I cannot identify your handwriting; but I have several letters from a young lady who died in 1864, the handwriting of which I can prove by many witnesses.

"Wishing you every success in your good work, I remain,

Faithfully yours,

"T. L. NICHOLS, M.D."

"EPES SARGENT, ESQ."

The Witchcraft Excitement. — (See page 101.)

Dr. W. B. Carpenter, in his work against Spiritualism, tells us that "in 1658 a woman was hung at Chard Assizes for having bewitched a boy twelve years old, who was seen to rise in the air and pass some thirty yards over a garden wall; while at another time he was found in a room with his hands flat against a beam at the top, and his body two or three feet above the floor, — *nine people at a time seeing him in this position.*"

Is it not lamentable to see men of the present day, with scientific pretensions, trying to explain away a simple case of levitation, testified to by nine sane witnesses, by the theory that the witnesses were "prepossessed," hallucinated, and made imbecile by their failure to cultivate "scientific habits of thought"; that "they first surrendered themselves, without due inquiry, to a disposition to believe in occult agencies; and having so surrendered themselves, they interpreted everything in accordance with that belief."

And we are to accept this as explaining why nine persons in a case of life and death, testified to seeing what, according to the Carpenterian superstition, they did not see and could not have seen!

Mocking Spirits. — (See page 103.)

Among the fully authenticated spirit phenomena of the last thirty years, those which took place in the house of the Rev. Mr. Phelps, at Stratford, Conn., in 1851, were among the most remarkable. That some of them were by mocking or mischievous spirits is not improbable. Spirit-writing, without visible human agency, was among the early occurrences at Hydesville, Rochester, and Auburn; and it was a common phenomenon at Stratford. Sometimes these spirit-writings would be enclosed in a book and thrown down; sometimes wrapped about a key or nail, or anything that would give a momentum, and thrown into the room. Often they were seen to fall from above; this occurring frequently when the doors were closed, and it was not possible for any visible agent to have been the cause. Writing would appear on the wall at times, made, as it appeared, with a pencil. On one occasion Dr. Phelps was writing at his desk, and, turning his back for a few moments, without leaving his chair, turned again to his paper, where he found written in large letters, "Very nice paper and very nice ink for the devil." The ink was not yet dry, the desk was not two feet from the Doctor as he sat, and he was certain that he was entirely alone in the room. Many mocking messages were written; some of them bearing hard on Dr. Phelps's Calvinistic views. He wrote me confirming these facts.

Phantom Forms. — (See page 115.)

William Crookes, F.R.S., testifies that on one occasion, Mr. Home being the medium, "a phantom form came from the corner of the room, took an accordion in its hand, and then glided about the room, playing the instrument. The form was visible to all present for many minutes, Mr. Home also being seen at the same time. Coming rather close to a lady who was sitting apart from the rest of the company, she gave a slight cry, upon which it vanished."

Testimony of Professional Conjurers. — (See p. 130.)

Dr. W. B. Carpenter has often referred to professional conjurers as "trained experts;" but when they go against his prepossessions their testimony is worthless in his estimation. I have instanced the names of several of these. Mr. T. A. Trollope informs us that another celebrated conjurer, Bosco, "utterly scouted the idea of such phenomena as were produced by Mr. Home being performed by any of the resources of the juggling art;" and, lastly, Lord Rayleigh informed Mr. Wallace that he took a professional conjurer to Dr. Slade's, and that the phenomena happened with considerable perfection, while "the conjurer could not form the remotest idea as to how the effects were produced."

Jacobs, from whom I have quoted (p. 130), has written a letter to the Scientific Society for Psychological Studies at Paris, announcing his adhesion to the spiritual theory of the manifestations.

Clairvoyance. — (See page 133.)

"If ordinary vision were as rare as clairvoyance," says A. R. Wallace, "it would be just as difficult to prove its reality as it is now to establish the reality of this wonderful power. The evidence in its favor is absolutely conclusive to any one who will examine it, and who is not deluded by that most unphilosophical dogma that he knows *à priori* what is possible and what is impossible."

Wallace and Darwin. — (See page 143.)

Alfred R. Wallace, the distinguished naturalist, who shares with Darwin the honor of originating the theory of natural selection, gives this brief definition of Darwinism : " It is the theory of the origin of the countless species of plants and animals from ancestral forms by means of natural selection." In a communication to that indefatigable and eloquent proclaimer of the truths of Spiritualism, James M. Peebles, Mr. Wallace writes : " Darwinism may be true as far as it goes, but not be the *whole* truth. Darwin's laws of natural selection and variation are true laws, which will account for much — perhaps for all — the material organizations of plants and animals. He admits an influx of life from the Creator at first. I think an influx of a *higher life* occurred when man appeared. He does not *think* this necessary. This is the *real difference* between us." The italics are those of Mr. Wallace himself.

Identity of Spirits. — (See page 184.)

My friend, Professor Wm. Stainton-Moses, of London, who to medial sensitiveness both as regards mental and physical phenomena unites high intellectual gifts and thorough collegiate culture, has studied carefully the subject of " Spirit Identity," and written an excellent little work on the subject, which I commend to those who still doubt whether there have been evidences of spirit-identity. On page 50 he says : " For a long time I failed in getting the evidence I wanted ; and if I had done as most investigators do, I should have abandoned the quest in despair or disgust. My state of mind was too positive ; and I was forced, moreover, to take some personal pains before I obtained what I desired. Bit by bit, here a little and there a little, by steps which I do not detail here, that evidence came, and as my mind opened to receive it, ⸱⸱me six months were spent in persistent daily efforts to bring home t⸱ me proof of the perpetuated existence of human spirits, and of their power to communicate with me and give evidence of their unimpaired individuality, and of the unbroken continuity of their existence."

Formation of the Spirit-Hand.—(See page 197.)

Dr. J. Garth Wilkinson, of London, well known as an eminent physician and the erudite translator of some of Swedenborg's writings, once saw a spirit-hand at a circle of inquirers, and requested that it might be laid on his forehead. He thus describes the result :
" This was deliberately done, and I felt the thrilling impression as the palm was laid flat upon my brow, where it remained for several seconds. During the interval in which I felt it, I had abundant opportunity of examining most closely the arm and fore-arm. . . . . Bending over as I did to the vacant rim of the table, I saw how the arm terminated, — apparently in a graceful cascade of drapery ; much as though an arm was put through the peak of a snowy tent, the apex of which thus fell around the shoulder on every side. On leaving my forehead, the arm at once disappeared, and I watched it go. It was drawn into the same drapery, but so naively that I can only

liken it to a fountain falling down again, and ceasing into the bosom
of the water from which it rose."

Eugène Nus, author of "*Choses de l'autre Monde*" (Paris, 1880),
testifies to having seen a luminous hand lift a musical box from a
table, carry it about the room and up to the ceiling, and then place
it under a bed. The same thing happened with a bell, which was
agitated in the air, carried rapidly to the extremities of the room, and
then at his request brought and deposited in his own hand. The light
was so subdued as to make the luminosity of the phantom-hand apparent.

Spirit-Photography. — (See page 204.)

In reference to the possibility of photographing the forms presented by spirits, Mr. A. R. Wallace remarks: "We are in a position to state, not only that it has been frequently done, but that the
evidence is of such a nature as to satisfy any one who will take the
trouble carefully to examine it." After presenting this evidence, he
adds: "We find, then, that three amateur photographers, working
independently in different parts of England, separately confirm the
fact of spirit-photography — already demonstrated to the satisfaction
of many who had tested it through professional photographers. The
experiments of Mr. Beattie and Dr. Thomson are alone absolutely
conclusive; and, taken in connection with those of Mr. Slater and
Dr. Williams, and the test photographs, like those of Mrs. Guppy,
establish as a scientific fact the objective existence of invisible human forms, and definite, invisible, actinic images."

Referring to the series of other physical phenomena, Mr. Wallace
says: "They form a connected body of evidence, from the simplest
to the most complex and astounding, every single component fact
of which can be and has been repeatedly demonstrated by itself;
while each gives weight and confirmation to all the rest. They have
all, or nearly all, been before the world for twenty (thirty-three)
years; the theories and explanations of reviewers and critics do not
touch them, or in any way satisfy any sane man who has repeatedly
witnessed them."

"My position, therefore, is, that the phenomena of Spiritualism in
their entirety do *not* require further confirmation. *They are proved
quite as well as any facts are proved in other sciences;* and it is not
denial or quibbling that can disprove any of them, but only fresh
facts and accurate deductions from those facts." If all this was true
in 1874, what an amount of evidence in confirmation has accumu-
lated up to the year 1880!

Robert H. Collyer, M.D. — (See page 215.)

The Dr. Collyer here referred to published in London, in 1876, a
pamphlet entitled "Automatic Writing; the Slade Prosecution;
Vindication of the Truth;" in which he writes: "Mr. Slade has

presented to myself phenomena which are not susceptible of any explanation based on trickery or fraud. Being thoroughly convinced that the phenomena are genuine, I should be alike untrue to my own sense of independence, truth, and honor, if I did not vindicate his honesty of purpose." As Dr. Collyer was not a Spiritualist, this testimony may carry all the more weight with the skeptical.

Phenomena through Mrs. Mowatt. — (See page 224.)

In the account of the phenomena through Mrs. Mowatt, want of space compelled me to omit many facts of interest. Having, under her own prescriptions while somnambulic, been restored to a state of vigorous health, she went upon the stage to retrieve the pecuniary fortunes of her husband. The late Edward L. Davenport, the American actor, whom I had known from my youth up, became acquainted with her professionally, and when Mr. and Mrs. Mowatt were going to try their fortunes in England, he accompanied them. Before their departure I imparted to him, by the direction of Mrs. Mowatt in her somnambulic state, all the information that would enable him to induce somnambulism in her in case she should fall ill. He also had several interviews with the "gypsy," as she called her higher self, before they sailed. Early in my mesmeric experiences with her a puzzle arose which I thus expressed to her while somnambulic: "You always speak of your lower self in the third person, and you never speak of your present self in the first, and you object to being addressed by either your Christian or surname. How shall I call you?" "Call me *gypsy*," she replied. "Then I suppose we must give a corresponding name to your waking self. Since *she* does many things that you disapprove of, suppose we call her *simpleton?*" At this she clapped her hands in glee, and said, "Nothing could be more apt." So the distinctions were adopted, and the two names were ever afterward seriously used, though not when she was in her normal state.

In the Chicago *Inter-Ocean* for January, 1880, appears an account by an "interviewer" of the information imparted by the widow of my old friend Davenport in regard to the mesmerization of Mrs. Mowatt in London. Mr. Mowatt had been ordered to Jamaica by his physician, and had requested Mr. and Mrs. Davenport to go and occupy his rooms, that Mrs. Mowatt might have the benefit of their care. Mrs. Mowatt fell ill, and was made somnambulic that she might prescribe for herself. The following is Mrs. Davenport's account of what occurred : —

"Throughout she called herself 'Gypsy.' She referred to her former self as 'Simpleton,' or more frequently as 'Simpy,' and her voice acquired a peculiarly wide-awake tone. She never opened her eyes, but could write equally well, and, by placing a sealed letter on her forehead, would reveal the contents. Of course this event, in spite of our efforts, became noised about, and attracted much comment, especially from the medical profession.

" 'Did any eminent physicians visit her?'

" 'Yes; it happened that during this time my daughter Fanny was born, and the well-known Dr. Westmacott, a nephew of the famous sculptor, was in attendance upon me. One day he jokingly inquired, 'What is all this I hear about your clairvoyant patient?' I told him the truth, and, of course, as he believed in nothing of the kind, he pooh-poohed. A little out of patience, I asked him if he would see her, and he promised to on condition that I would not mention his name or possible call. A week or two afterward he came to vaccinate Fanny, and after it was over I asked him to go up stairs with me. When he reached the upper hall, I motioned him to wait, and advanced to the door of the room; but almost before I entered, Mrs. Mowatt called out, in her clear, bird-like voice, "Fanny dear, you can bring your doctor in with you." '

"I assure you we were both astonished. When he advanced to the bedside, she said, 'Oh, you do not believe; you doubt; but Gypsy will prove strange things to you.' Dr. Westmacott replied, pleasantly, 'No, you are right; I do not believe, but I am open to conviction; but,' he concluded, laughing, 'it would be a sorry truth for a physician to find his patients able to take care of and prescribe for themselves, as they say you do.'

"The doctor then seated himself, and began questioning her, when she interrupted him by crying out eagerly, as a child might, 'Ah, doctor, you have something in your coat-pocket for me; give it to me quickly. I want to see it.' The doctor looked disconcerted for a moment, but replied, 'You are quite right; I have a package for you, and if, without opening your eyes or the package, you can tell me what it contains, I will believe, at least, that you are not humbugging us all.'

"So saying, he drew from his coat-pocket a flat package, heavily wrapped in thick, brown paper, securely tied and scaled with wax. Without hesitating, Mrs. Mowatt, her fair face shining with intelligence, took hold of the package and placed it against her forehead. In a moment she exclaimed, 'O what a strange old man! he looks like a Jew, and leans heavily on his stick. He is very old; his hair and beard are white —'

"'That will do,' said Dr. Westmacott, who had actually changed color, and he tore open the package, disclosing a photograph of Rubens's famous painting of 'The Jew.' He then subjected her to a number of other tests, with the same result, and when he left said that while he could not propagate such a doctrine, he could never ridicule it in the future as he had in the past."

The Money Test. — (See page 232.)

I have before me a little pamphlet entitled "Spiritualism and Charlatanism. or the Tricks of the Media, embodying an Exposé of the Manifestations of Modern Spiritualism by a Committee of Business Men of New York." The committee do not add much to our stock of knowledge, but I find here a pithy an l interesting letter from Henry Slade, in reply to their proposition to donate five hundred dollars to any charitable institution if he would give them proofs of direct writing. Under date of New York, March 18, 1873, he remarks :

"Your proposition does not come within the province of anything I might claim in regard to the manifestation of writing that has repeatedly occurred in my presence. Therefore I have no warrant or authority for accepting it: for obvious reasons. You propose that *I shall write* a line across a slate, or cause a pencil to write a line, without myself touching either slate or pencil.

"My dear sirs, you would have been just as consistent to have made this proposition to your nearest neighbor as to me,— because I claim the writing that has so often occurred in my presence during a period of some years is a phenomenon over which I have no control whatever. Therefore I have no authority to say that it will occur again. . . .

"It is not uncommon for me to sit with persons for these manifestations-and fail to obtain any. This is no disappointment to me. But when they do take place, my surprise can hardly be less than that of those who witness it for the first time. And were they never to occur again, it would be no evidence against the genuineness of those witnessed by thousands of intelligent men and women whose testimony would be taken as evidence in any court of justice upon any other question.

"This, it seems, you are trying to overcome by declaring that you have failed to witness what others may have told you they have seen. If that is satisfactory to you it certainly is to me; for I am fully aware that an acceptance or denial by one man, or any number of men, will make no difference with the facts. . . . The conditions you propose under the circumstances in this case would create that anxiety of mind with me that I could not for a moment expect the manifestation to occur."

Swedenborgian Antagonism. — (See page 290.)

Why is it that the Rev. Mr. Mercer and other orthodox Swedenborgians are so opposed to the Spiritualism that is not adopted under their forms and restrictions? It is simply because our free Spiritualism conflicts with their own little barren system of ecclesiasticism; a system entirely outside of all of Swedenborg's teachings, and originated by one Robert Hindmarsh, printer in London (1759–1835), who wanted a priesthood and a church. To him the so-called "New Jerusalem Church" owed its being; and it is his influence and teachings and not Swedenborg's that now rule in all these illiberal attacks on a free, philosophical, scientifically-based Spiritualism.

Phenomena among Indians. — (See page 339.)

See a letter from Chief Justice Larrabee, of Wisconsin, to the late Senator Tallmadge, of New York, giving evidence of the prevalence of well-known spiritual phenomena among the North American Indians. Clairvoyance, independent movements, and other strange manifestations are clearly proved.

Seeing in *The Shaker*, a monthly publication issued at Shaker Village, N. H., a statement of phenomena among the Indians by Granville T. Sproat, who as far back as 1836 was a government agent under Gen. Cass among the Lake Superior Indians, I wrote Mr. Sproat and received from him (1876) a reply authenticating the facts. In the year 1836, Big Buffalo, the chief of the Ojibways on the south shore, lost his only son, and was terribly depressed thereby. But soon after he came to Mr. Sproat with form erect and a joyful aspect. "I have seen him," he exclaimed; "Onwi, my son, is still alive! Yesterday in the *me-ta-wa* (sacred dance) I saw him. We were in the great dancing-lodge; and there Onwi came and joined in the dance. He spoke to us; he said it was weakness for us to mourn for him. He had seen our departed braves, and been welcomed by them. His step was light as a fawn's; his face bright as the sky overhead. He smoked the pipe of peace with us. How did I know it was he? Did I not mark his form, his features, his every look? Was he not dressed in the very coat I gave him — a present from the great father at Washington? How could I be deceived? Ask the aged men and they will tell you."

"I *did* ask them," writes Mr. Sproat, "and heard from them the same report. It was the theme of conversation in every wigwam of the camp. The old men spoke of it in an undertone with their heads bowed as if in reverence; and one day I heard Wah-chus-co, the great seer of the tribe, — taking a piece of birch-bark and drawing on it two spheres touching each other, — explain to his listeners that there were whole bands of joyous spirits passing from one sphere to the other, thus bringing together the inhabitants of the seen and unseen worlds."

Fallibility of Spirits. — (See page 340.)

"For our own part," says John Page Hopps, "we believe that these sensitive beings (mediums) have been *en rapport* with the unseen world; and we further believe that this accounts for and explains nearly all the so-called 'revelations' from the Most High; but we also believe — and this is the point of urgent interest — that the spirit-influences that have made themselves felt have been as diverse in their character and influences as could possibly be, and that in many cases influences that might almost be called diabolical have been indorsed with a 'Thus saith the lord.'

"Of course this suggests a grave danger, and we admit it; but it throws a flood of light on some of the gravest problems of ancient and modern times, and it is our surest safeguard against a danger, pernicious and perilous. Incursions from the spirit world have been a great fact in the history of the world in all ages; and the delusion that every such incursion comes with a manifesto or revelation from the Almighty has been a curse in all ages."

Palpable Form-Manifestations. — (See page 341.)

These manifestations have taken place among non-professional mediums, whose circumstances placed them above the need of being paid. A notable instance is that of Charles M. Tay, of Charlestown, Mass. (b. 1853, d. 1876). Mrs. Emma Hardinge Britten, one of the most gifted of the expounders of Spiritualism, says of him : "Music, poetry, and art formed the themes of his pure life and sinless aims. At length the buds of mediumship burst forth into radiant blossom, and Charles became the minister through whom the invisible operators of another world were rendered palpable to their mortal friends, and messengers of the glad tidings of immortality. Raps, movements of furniture, writing, both inspirational and automatic, were freely given. At length faces were seen, forms were materialized, and spirits of those whose bodies 'lay mouldering in the grave,' came clothed in flesh and blood, walking, talking, and making merry with their earth-loves once again. Exquisite music was made by spirits on various instruments. Flowers were brought and letters written by the hands of these invisibles. Whole sentences of advice, counsel, and instruction were spelled out in letters on the sensitive flesh. Every form of demonstration of the most powerful and convincing character was given freely. without money and without price. Patient, gentle, resigned, true, and pure, Charles Tay passed from this sphere by rapid consumption; but moved about in the midst of his large and loving circle of friends to the last. In the closing hour of all, the initials of his departed father's name (Rufus L. Tay, the well-known purchaser in 1855 of the Webster Farm, at Franklin, N. H.) appeared on the young man's forehead, beneath the tender mother's hand, as she wiped away the dews of death " These stigmata are a common phenomenon in Spiritualism; I have repeatedly witnessed them.

Moses Dow, Esq., of Charlestown, Mass., the well-known proprietor of the *Waverley Magazine*, testified in the *Banner of Light*, of March 22, 1873, without giving names, to the remarkable character of young Tay's free mediumship. At his séances recognizable forms appeared; roses, fresh, moist and cool, as if just plucked, were produced; and spirit-voices, speaking intelligibly were distinctly heard. Mr. Dow, a man of large means, and of whose perfect probity and intelligence as an investigator no one can have a doubt, testifies most emphatically to the genuineness of the phenomena through young Tay, who readily submitted to the severest tests.

The Proofs Accumulate. — (See page 357.)

In the London *Spiritualist* I find further testimony from Dr. Nichols. He gives an account of remarkable pneumatographic phenomena that occurred in the light. Of the medium on the occasion he says (September, 1880) : "After a careful watch of three years I have never seen the slightest reason to doubt the absolute good faith and honesty of Mr. William Eglinton." A blank card was ex-

amined, a corner torn off, and the card placed with a bit of pencil in
a solid box, one owned by Dr. Nichols for many years. The box was
closed and the hands of all present placed on the cover. Mr. Eglinton said, "Ask for something to be written in any language you
choose." Dr. Nichols said, "We have had Greek, Latin, and French;
let it be German." In a few moments, at a signal by raps, the box
was opened, and on the card was found the following :

> " Komm ! wir wollen dir versprechen
> Rettung aus dem tiefsten Schwartz
> Pfeiler, Säulen kaun man brechen,
> Aber nicht ein festes Hertz." — GOETHE.

The next experiment was to throw all the blank cards into a corner
of the room, and after them the pencil, the lead of which was now
broken off within the wood. In a few minutes signal raps were
heard. Dr. Nichols passed to the cards, and picking up one of them
found written upon it, in an entirely different hand from those previously received :

"MONS. HARGRAVE :
   La bonne fortune, et la mauvaise, sont nécessaires á Phomme, pour le rendre
habile ; et eussi la patience est amère mais son fruit est doux."

Below this was the word "*renversez*," and on turning the card
over was found written on the other side a sentence of nine words,
thought by Dr. Nichols to be Hungarian, or one of the similar languages of the East of Europe.

Again, on a marked card placed with a pen between two slates, and
these held firmly together on the table in the light by Dr. Nichols,
Mrs. Nichols, and Mr. Eglinton, there appeared, written with ink, in
a most beautiful and delicate hand, like the finest plate-engraving,
the following :

"Lord, who shall dwell in thy Tabernacle, or who shall rest in thy holy hill ?
— *Qui ingreditur sine macula, et operatur justitium : Qui loquitur veritatem in
corde suo, qui non agit dolum in lingua sua : Nec fecit proximo suo malum, et
opprobrium non accepit adversus proximos suos*, etc., etc. — The Lord's Tabernacle is, at this present, in this room. Evil, corruption, vice, nor wickedness
cannot get entrance. Why ? Blessed are the pure in heart, for they shall inherit
the Kingdom of Heaven."

All this must have been written in about twenty seconds. Dr.
Nichols concludes : " In a good light everything was done exactly as
I have described. How a steel pen could write on a card between
two slates held firmly together on the table, with the inkstand on the
upper slate, I am not able to explain — I only know that it was done.
The pen put dry between the slates was wet with ink when I took it
out." Still the writing may have been done without the pen.

Channing, Kant, and Swedenborg.

I have spoken, in my account of Mrs. Mowatt (page 224), of her
discussions, while somnambulic with Channing, on the subject of
Swedenborg. The great Unitarian divine, while in accord with the

Swedish seer on many points, was disposed to question the too human and earth-like character of some of his descriptions of scenes and occupations in the spirit-world. Mrs. Mowatt defended Swedenborg with discrimination; she admitted that some of his visions were probably subjective and imaginary, but contended that much of his testimony was in accord with the general report which spirits give of the state of things in the next stage of being. She was far from regarding him as infallible. She thought he was in error in describing the Moravians and other Christian dissenters as in a bad state because of their doctrinal tenets. She maintained that the only real heresy was the wrong thinking which led to wrong-doing. So long as a man was sincere and pure in heart, his mistakes on doctrinal and historical points could have no very serious or permanent effect upon his future happiness.

Channing was much pleased and interested, for he found her giving back to him, in many instances, his own thoughts; but at the same time maintaining independent views on some points. That she was in a state quite distinct from her normal state he was fully satisfied. Her earnest but childlike manner, the tone of her voice, the character of her thoughts, her eyes with the lids hanging loose and the balls rolled up, were all peculiarities that did not fail to impress him. When she passed back into her normal state, and all her somnambulic experiences were a blank to her, it was sometimes desirable that she should recall some one of them.· This I could cause her to do by an act of volition, and placing my hand on her head, without uttering a word. Here was another unequivocal proof of the actual objective effect of will-power. Out of many incidents I could cause her to recall and announce unhesitatingly the particular one on which I fixed my thoughts; and she would remain ignorant of all the rest. The phenomenon was confirmed by hundreds of repetitions.

We were in the same house with Channing some two weeks. I had known him from my early youth. We all had an affectionate parting with him, little supposing that it was the last interview we were to have here below with this truly great and saintly man.

In a deeply interesting little volume entitled "Swedenborg and Channing: Showing the many and remarkable Agreements in the beliefs and teachings of these writers," Mr. B. F. Barrett, to whose parallel passages I am here indebted, makes out a strong case of coincidence in moral and religious thought. Channing told me emphatically he could not accept Swedenborg's topography of the spirit-world, or regard him as otherwise than deluded in some of his "memorable relations"; but it is interesting to see how fully in accord Channing was with all the facts and inferences of Spiritualism in regard to essentials. In answer to a letter of inquiry from Mr. Barrett, Dr. Channing's son wrote: "Mrs. Anna Cora Mowatt has reported a conversation with my father about Swedenborg, which took place at Lenox in the summer of 1842. This is a definite, authentic report, colored, of course, by Mrs. Mowatt's personality."

In Chapter IX. of Mrs. Mowatt's "Autobiography" (1854), will be found a record of my mesmeric experiences in her case. The whole was revised and enlarged by me before publication. In it I say, in a letter to her: "In times of extreme emaciation, when you could be lifted like a child, and when all who looked on you and heard your paroxysms of coughing would turn away with the persuasion that you could not last through the season, you had always, in your somnambulic state, some pleasantry with which to dispel the fears of the standers-by. Your views of death were so serenely assured, and such was the quiet satisfaction with which you seemed to look forward to 'the common road into the great darkness,' that, the nearer the prospect was brought, the more grateful it became. 'This King of Terrors was the Prince of Peace.' The separation of the waking from the somnambulic consciousness was most complete. Never, by any accident, could I discover that you brought into your waking state the slightest recollection of what occurred in your somnambulic; and this during a period of *three* years." (In the body of this work I erroneously set down the period as *two* years.) The curious reader will find in the Autobiography many further particulars of my experiences.

In her account of Channing she says: "He then told me that he had read a portion of Swedenborg's works with great attention, and he reverenced the author, although the doctrines had not as yet carried the same conviction to his mind as they had done to ours. In the subject of mesmerism he took the deepest interest. On two occasions he persuaded me to allow myself to be placed under the influence, that he might satisfy himself on several doubtful points. One was of the possibility of mind communicating with mind without the medium of language or any material sign. His experiment, I believe, convinced him that this could be the case." It has been well remarked that "the merest trifles are interesting that suggest to us *an action in man independent of his present material organization.*"

Swedenborg says: "After the dissolution of the body, a man's spirit appears in the spiritual world in the human form altogether as in the natural world." And Channing says (Memoirs, Vol. II. p. 22): "We shall be the same beings in heaven as on earth. . . . When Moses and Elijah conversed with Jesus on the Mount, they appeared in the human form, differing from ours only in its splendor."

Swedenborg says: "Instantaneous reformation and consequent salvation would be comparatively like the instantaneous conversion of an owl into a dove, and of a serpent into a sheep." Channing says: "I know but one salvation for a sick man, and that is to give him *health*. So I know but one salvation for a bad man, and that is to make him truly, thoroughly, conscientiously *good*, — to break the chains of evil habits, — to raise him to the dignity and peace of a truly religious life."

According to Swedenborg, heaven is a *state* and not a *place;* so likewise is hell. Both, he says, are within the soul. Pure, unselfish love makes the one; and a supreme self-love makes the other. Channing says (*Works*, Vol. IV. p. 52): "I learn more and more that the great springs of happiness and misery are in the mind, and that the efforts of men to secure peace by other processes than by inward purification, are vain strivings. Salvation, heaven and hell, have their seat in the soul."

Of faith in immortality Channing says: "This faith is lamentably weak in the multitude of men. To multitudes, Heaven is almost a world of fancy. It wants substance. The idea of a world in which beings exist as pure spirits, *or clothed with refined and spiritual frames*, strikes them as a fiction. What cannot be seen or touched appears unreal. This is mournful but not wonderful; for how can men who immerse themselves in the body and its interests, *and cultivate no acquaintance with their own souls and spiritual powers, comprehend a higher spiritual life?* . . . This skepticism as to things spiritual and celestial is as irrational and unphilosophical as it is degrading."

Channing urges it upon us to seek some clearer, more definite conception of the future state. He says: "That world seems less real for want of some distinctness in its features. *We should all believe it more firmly if we conceived of it more vividly.*"

Swedenborg says: When a man "enters the spiritual world, or the life after death, he is in a body, as he was in the natural world. He sees as before; he hears and speaks as before; and when he is touched, he feels as before. He also longs, desires, wishes, thinks, reflects, is affected, loves, and wills as before." Channing says (Memoirs, Vol. II. p. 212): "We shall be the same beings as on earth; we shall retain our present faculties, our present affections, our love of knowledge, love of beauty, love of action, love of approbation, our sympathy, gratitude, and pleasure in success. *We shall probably, too, have bodies not very different from what we now have.*"

Swedenborg says: "This I can positively affirm, that a spirit has more exquisite sight, and also more exquisite hearing, than a man in the body; and what will seem surprising, a more exquisite sense of smell, and especially of touch; for spirits see, hear, and touch each other." Channing says (*Works*, Vol. IV. p. 228): "A new sense, a new eye, might show the spiritual world compassing us on every side. . . . Is it at all inconsistent with our knowledge of nature to suppose that those in heaven, whatever be their abode, may have spiritual senses, — organs, by which they may discern the remote as clearly as we do the near?"

In his Memoirs (Vol. II. p. 20), Channing says: "We need not doubt the fact that *angels whose home is in heaven visit our earth and bear a part in our transactions.*" And he says of our departed friends: "To suppose them forgetful of the world where they began to live, is to make that life worthless, and to blot out a volume of invaluable experience. . . . Our friends who leave us for that world do not find themselves cast among strangers. . . . The closest attachments of this life are cold, distant, stranger-like, compared with theirs. . . . We are too apt to think of heaven as a solemn place. It ought to be viewed by us as a place of cheerful society. . . . Perfect social happiness is reserved for a higher stage of existence. . . . This happiness would be wholly lost, were men in heaven to lose their peculiar characters; were all to be cast into one mould; *were all, in becoming perfect, to become perfectly alike.*" All this corresponds with what Swedenborg has to say on the subject

Swedenborg says of heaven: "No idle person is tolerated there, no slothful vagabond, no indolent boaster of others' studies and labors; but every one must be industrious, skilful, attentive and diligent in his own office and employment." And Channing says: " The truth is, that all action on earth, even the intensest, is but the sport of childhood, compared with the energy and ,activity of that higher life. It must be so."

Swedenborg says: "There is no determinate period during a man's regeneration at which he may say, I am now perfect." Channing says: "In this life progression is the universal law. Nothing is brought into being in its most perfect state. . . . Is it not natural to expect that in a future life our nature will be progressive? . . . Let us not imagine that the usefulness of the good is finished·at death. Then rather does it begin. Death has expanded their powers. We should represent them to our minds as ascended to a higher rank of existence, and admitted to co-operate with far higher communities."

If there is one great lesson uniformly revealed in the deeper facts of Spiritualism, it is the confirmation of Christ's saying that as we sow we shall reap. On this point Channing says: "Let us not listen for a moment to a doctrine so irrational, as that our present characters do not follow us into a future world. If we are to live again, let us settle it as a sure fact that we shall carry with us our present minds, such as we now make them; that we shall reap good or ill according to their improvement or corruption; and, of consequence, that every act which affects character will reach in its influence beyond the grave, and have a bearing on our future weal or woe."

How perfectly all this corresponds with what we get in those communications (few and far between, I grant) which come to us with intrinsic evidences of their high spiritual authority! Thus we see that by the reverent study of his own intuitions, coupled with those which plainly actuated the life of Christ, and indicated, though perhaps not unerringly, the essentials of all religions, Channing arrived at convictions precisely similar to those prompted or justified by a study of the facts and inferences of Modern Spiritualism.

Kant, like Channing, was an intuitionalist as well as a profound philosopher. He satisfied himself as to the genuineness of Swedenborg's clairvoyant powers, and has left an interesting letter on the subject; but he too regarded many of the so-called visions of Swedenborg as purely subjective. Of the latter's clairvoyant description of the great Stockholm fire (July, 1759), Kant, who investigated the case thoroughly, writes, " What can be brought forward against the authenticity of the occurrence?" He admits that Swedenborg's system corresponds with the conclusions of his own philosophy, and that " *a wonderful agreement exists between his doctrines and the deepest results of reason.*" Accepting Swedenborg, as most Spiritualists do, as a medium and seer unsurpassed in authority, yet subject to error and inherited prejudices, in spite of his protest to the contrary, they receive such testimony as that of Kant as an added corroboration of their own ethical and religious inductions from facts which they have empirically verified.